ALTERNATIVE APPROACHES TO ECONOMIC PLANNING

ALTERNATIVE APPROACHES TO ECONOMIC PLANNING

MARTIN CAVE and PAUL HARE

First published 1981 by
THE MACMILLAN PRESS LTD
London and Basingstoke
Associated companies in Delhi Dublin
Hong Kong Johannesburg Lagos Melbourne
New York Singapore and Tokyo

ISBN 0 333 26689 7 (hard cover)
　　 0 333 26690 0 (paper cover)

Typeset in 10/12 IBM Press Roman by
STYLESET LIMITED
Salisbury · Wiltshire

Printed in Hong Kong

CONTENTS

PREFACE

The aim of this book is to try to relate the experience of economies with varying types of planning systems to recent theoretical or analytical work on economic planning. We have both been concerned for a number of years with research into the operation of centrally planned economies and have become aware of the gulf separating the predominantly descriptive and institutional literature on planned economies and the theoretical literature on economic planning. We have sought to bridge that gap in this book by identifying and analysing certain major aspects of any planning system, the study of which helps to illustrate the actual behaviour of particular planned economies. We do not delude ourselves that we have wholly succeeded in this aim, but we believe that we have gone some way towards bringing the two elements — experience and theory — closer together.

The introductory chapter of the book sets out the major problems encountered in any planned economy, and briefly discusses the principal ways of dealing with them. The next three chapters comprising Part I give an account of planning in practice in a traditional centrally planned socialist economy, in a reformed socialist economy and in France, the major Western country using an indicative planning system.

As we have chosen to illustrate our discussion of planning with three particular economies, it is worth outlining the reasons for our choice. Amongst the socialist economies of Europe, the U.S.S.R. and Hungary stand at opposite poles in terms of the nature of their planning system. In the U.S.S.R. the traditional planning system which grew up in the 1930s has survived virtually intact, whereas in Hungary a serious and well-conceived economic reform was implemented in 1968 and its main features have survived to this day. The reform provides for greatly enhanced enterprise independence and the much greater use of markets to allocate resources. The planners rely heavily (but by no means entirely) on the conventional instruments of macroeconomic policy and upon the guiding role of the projections they prepare for the economy as a whole and for its individual sectors. In this respect, of course, their role is closer to that of the French planning commission, and one might expect some convergence between the methods of planning used in the two countries. Thus in a sense the Hungarian case stands between the traditional centrally planned economy and a system of indicative planning in a private ownership economy. One of our aims is to evaluate the experience of the three countries in this light.

Part II deals with the theory of economic planning. An introductory chapter sets out some of the basic issues, and this is followed by successive chapters dealing with informationally decentralised planning procedures, the theory of indicative planning, methods of plan implementation and the problem of incentives.

The two concluding chapters return to the practical experience of planned economies. The first discusses the use of mathematical models for planning, and the impact which these models have had in the U.S.S.R., Hungary and France, while the final chapter summarises our views about the appropriate ways of analysing planned economies and the prospects for economic planning.

Our previous work on economic planning has been principally concerned with the Soviet Union and Hungary. However, we have considered it worth while to extend the coverage of this book to the theory of indicative planning and to France's experience of planning, in order to bring out the similarities and differences which exist between the methods and role of economic planning in countries with different ownership systems and different degrees of centralisation of decision-taking. This may have led us into areas where our knowledge and understanding is incomplete, but we hope none the less that our decision is justified by the wider experience of planning on which we have been able to draw.

As is apparent from the concluding chapter, both of us agree upon the desirability in principle of economic planning, and we also agree on the scope for improving, if not for perfecting, planning systems. We hope therefore that our book may encourage some readers to think about some of the many unsolved problems of planning and perhaps contribute their own solutions.

We are grateful to Sue Robertson and Philip Hanson for reading several chapters and providing helpful comments, and express our thanks to Mrs A. Cowie, Mrs C. McIntosh, Mrs C. Newnham and Mrs W. Sharp for efficient and accurate typing.

M. C.

P. H.

1 INTRODUCTION

1.1 The debate about the possibility of planning

Although the planned economies of Eastern Europe and elsewhere are not successful in all respects, their performance must nevertheless be judged very favourably if the same criteria that we often apply to Western economies are applied to them, for in the last two decades the planned economies have consistently maintained full employment, and quite rapid growth rates, while avoiding for the most part the problems of inflation and severe overseas deficits which would have been their concomitant in the West. It is true that the economic achievements of Eastern Europe have not always matched their ambitious plans, but the achievements themselves have been impressive enough. Even the much less comprehensive and ambitious forms of planning which have been adopted in France have gone along with rather better economic performance than in much of the rest of Western Europe, though the direction of causality remains unclear.

In this context it may well seem quite unnecessary to enter into debate about the possibility of planning; clearly it is possible, and equally clearly it works. But there are two reasons why we should consider the question more carefully.

First, the performance criteria mentioned above were entirely macroeconomic, saying nothing about the economic behaviour of individual enterprises or households. It may turn out that apparent macroeconomic success is bought at the cost of grave failures at the level of microeconomics — certainly the literature on the planned economies contains numerous references to enterprise inefficiency, production of the wrong products, poor quality of production, and so on, amounting to a dismal catalogue of shortcomings. Yet it is rarely obvious how seriously one should regard such references. Sometimes they may be isolated instances, in other cases they could be more widespread but still not be very significant from a social point of view. For example, persistent failure to meet certain planned output targets may be acceptable either if there are readily available substitutes, or if the planners deliberately set the target too high in the expectation of inducing the 'right' amount to be produced. By neglecting this possibility some of the planning literature casually assumes the planners to be surprisingly unintelligent. Nevertheless, some problems remain and it still seems worth while to examine the possibility of planning from the viewpoint of microeconomic performance.

Second, at the time when the debate first arose (the 1920s and 1930s) there was no concrete evidence that a planned economy *could* function successfully.

The Soviet Union was just embarking on its first five-year plans and no other socialist countries were then in existence. At the same time the West was entering the Great Depression, from which it suffered throughout the 1930s. The experience of this period no doubt produced an extremely defensive attitude on the part of Western economists. While a few supported the new socialist experiment in the Soviet Union, many others were hostile to it, and tailored their arguments about planning accordingly. The result was a debate which raised many important points about the nature of a planned economy, and some of these points are still the object of vigorous discussion in modern theoretical work on planning. Parts of the debate, set out below, can usefully serve as an introduction to this book.

The debate was largely cast in theoretical terms, taking the general-equilibrium model of perfect competition as its starting-point. This model is itself debatable, of course, as became apparent in the course of the argument about planning; however, it is convenient to begin by accepting it, then criticise it later on, since that corresponds to the historical course of the argument.

The simplest form of the perfect-competition model sees the economy as a collection of firms and households, with no economic role to be played by government. Each economic agent, whether a firm or a household, responds to prices given by the market. These prices determine costs of inputs and incomes from the sale of output for the firms, which then select the production plans (supply functions for output, derived demand functions for inputs) which maximise their profits. Similarly, the same prices determine household budget constraints, subject to which households choose the consumption plans (demand functions for goods and services, labour supply) which maximise their utilities. For an arbitrarily fixed set of prices these supplies and demands, when aggregated over all households and firms, will not (typically) be in balance: for some goods there will be excess demand, and for others there will be excess supply. However, under certain conditions (to be discussed below) it has been shown that there is a set of prices (possibly more than one set) at which the markets for all goods and services will be in equilibrium. Such a set of prices is called a *competitive equilibrium*. It is often convenient to interpret equilibrium to mean that supply and demand for each good are equal. More generally the concept allows the possibility that the equilibrium may be characterised by excess supply, the corresponding price being zero; this is the case of 'free goods'.

Market theorists claim that an economic system based on free markets should be able to find a competitive equilibrium set of prices. Moreover, these prices, apart from equilibrating demands and supplies for all goods and services in the economy, have several desirable properties — which has given the study of perfect competition considerable appeal to economic theorists. Once the right prices are established it turns out that they are surprisingly economical from an *informational* point of view, in the sense that an economic agent need not know anything other than these prices, apart from information which pertains only to himself (preferences for the household, production possibilities for the firm); second, the prices provide the correct *incentives* in the sense that if agents take them as given and maximise profits or utilities, as relevant, they will take decisions which together yield an equilibrium. These two properties together are often referred to as the *decentralisation* property of competitive equilibrium.

In addition, the allocation of resources generated by equilibrium prices turns out to be both *technically efficient and Pareto efficient*. The former means that it would be impossible to produce more of any good without either (i) producing less of another, or (ii) using more inputs. The latter refers to an allocation of resources at which no household could be made better off without some other household being made worse off.

If this is the view one has of the market system, then it is not really surprising that proponents of central planning have come under attack, especially when they have intended that their planning system should supersede the market altogether, for the planners' main task is considered to be that of computing the equilibrium prices of a competitive solution. Even if the planners do not propose to employ the prices to enforce their chosen allocation but intend to issue direct instructions to firms and households, in effect it is still necessary to calculate the competitive equilibrium.

This is why Hayek (1935) considered planning to be impossible. He visualised quite correctly the immense number of demand and supply functions which make up a general-equilibrium system, running into several millions, and saw no practical method by which the planners could find a solution. Indeed, so immense is the system that even the most modern computers are unable to calculate anything like a complete solution, though recent work by Scarf (1973) has led to the development of some useful solution algorithms which work well for small systems of demand and supply equations. (An algorithm is a computational procedure for solving a given problem, usually by repeating parts of the calculation in order to obtain successively better approximations to the solution. These repetitions are called *iterations*.) We have to accept, then, that Hayek had a point, but his important argument is far from the end of the matter.

Hayek started by assuming that the market system could, and did, find a solution to the general-equilibrium problem, but he did not really specify how this happened. And once raised the question is not one to be evaded easily. Suppose, for example, that the market system is not initially in equilibrium; then there will be excess demands in some markets and excess supplies in others. Two difficulties with standard theory arise from this situation. To begin with it seems that prices no longer provide agents with all relevant information, for away from competitive equilibrium some agents will find that they have planned to produce too much of certain commodities, while others will be unable to satisfy their demands. Thus the informational economy of perfect competition is lost as soon as equilibrium is disturbed — and so are its optimality properties, unless equilibrium is quickly restored.

Also, in the presence of market imbalances one expects prices to be changing, but all agents are supposedly price-takers in the model of perfect competition. Arrow (1959) found one way out of this problem by conceding that in practice all firms set their own prices, with reference to their own market experience and expectations about what the equilibrium price will turn out to be. In equilibrium all firms charge the same price, but elsewhere there can be a range of prices for each product coexisting as a result of imperfect information on the part of buyers. Individual firms can behave as quasi-monopolists until equilibrium is re-established, since they all believe themselves to be facing downward-sloping demand curves.

Arrow's approach is undoubtedly realistic, but its complexity has prevented others from adopting it. Instead, an earlier and much simpler approach is still employed to 'explain' price changes in the course of adjustment to equilibrium: this is the device of the so-called Walrasian 'auctioneer'. The auctioneer is an additional artificial agent whose sole function is to observe the balance of supply and demand, raising prices where there is excess demand and lowering them in the opposite case with the aim of restoring equilibrium. But once the need for such an agent was recognised it was an easy matter for Lange (1938) and Taylor (1938) to step into the fray and propose that the state could carry out the required price-adjustment functions. Thus in their view a planned economy would mimic the operation of a market system by instructing the state-owned enterprises to behave in a profit-maximising way in response to the announced prices; similarly, households would maximise their utilities. And the planners, acting on behalf of the state, would collect information about the proposed demands and supplies and adjust the prices as required. In principle, therefore, the planners are not required to engage in the impossibly complex calculations envisaged by Hayek, and their task should be well within the limits of feasibility.

By providing the 'auctioneer' to call out the prices the planners might even be able to find equilibrium more effectively than the standard market system. Not only that, but their control over the disposition of profits, resulting from state ownership of the means of production, should enable the planned economy to operate with a more equitable income distribution than is normally possible with a market system. True, the market allocation is Pareto efficient, but that is compatible with virtually any distribution of incomes; the planners' allocation will also be Pareto efficient, and will be an improvement over the alternative market allocation when judged in the light of social preferences. (For discussion of social preferences and equality, see Arrow (1963) and Sen (1973).)

So far we have presented Hayek's argument against the possibility of planning, together with counter arguments by Lange and Taylor. We now examine the assumptions underlying the competitive model around which the debate centred in order to identify a number of the model's shortcomings. In particular, we must discuss more fully than before the questions of information and incentives in the economy; these issues are taken up in this section, while a proper treatment of intertemporal aspects of the competitive model, as well as of the problems resulting from uncertainty, are reserved for section 1.3 and Chapter 7 below.

Apart from the contentious assumption that equilibrium will be reached by the operation of normal market forces, the perfectly competitive model rests on certain other assumptions which have implications for the operation of a planned economy. The first of these is *convexity*, usually taken to mean decreasing returns to scale in the sphere of production, and also implying that demand functions arising from the household sector are continuous. (For a discussion of these convexity conditions and their implications, see Koopmans (1957) and Lancaster (1968).)

Now if the decreasing-returns condition always holds, there is no problem either with the basic competitive model or with Lange's reinterpretation of it as a model of the operation of a planned economy. However, if some firm experiences increasing returns to scale, the situation is very different. According to the model, the firm has to behave as a price-taker, in which case its profit-maximising decision involves producing nothing, or an infinite amount, depending on the ruling prices: no finite level of output can be an equilibrium position for this firm. Consequently it does not make sense to regard such a firm as a price-taker; alternatively, we could either supply the firm with some additional market information, for example the level of demand, or availability of one or more of its inputs, and allow it to maximise profits subject to these restrictions; or we could control the firm in a different way all together, by simply giving it an output target and instructing it to minimise the costs of producing at the target level. Thus where some firms have decreasing and others increasing returns to scale, it seems that the economy would function very badly if all firms were expected to respond to the same sort of price signals. Even in a market economy there would be a case for treating some firms differently, for example by national-ising those subject to increasing reutrns. Likewise in a planned economy one should not expect to control all firms in exactly the same way, though much of the theoretical literature tacitly assumes that one would. Different types of firm require different information or different incentives or both if they are to function satisfactorily from a social point of view (see Portes, 1971).

A second standard assumption of market-equilibrium theory is the absence of externalities in production and consumption. These result in divergences between social and private costs and benefits of various activities but cause no difficulties as far as equilibrium is concerned; their drawback is that the resulting equilibrium may not be technically efficient and certainly will not be Pareto efficient. However, the standard remedy of introducing appropriate taxes and subsidies to bring private costs into line with social costs (similarly for benefits) is equally appropriate both for the market model and Lange's market-type planned economy. What is not so easy is calculation of the correct taxes and subsidies, for these require the centre to accumulate considerable volumes of information about technology and preferences which would not typically be revealed in the normal course of operation of a system of markets. In some cases, of course, if the external effects are restricted to a small group of producers, the appropriate solution is a merger to internalise the effects; this case is likely to be rather less demanding, informationally, than the general case.

Lastly, we need to look at the price-taking assumption itself. From a purely theoretical point of view we can merely announce that firms are price-takers and end the discussion there, since there is little reason to query the price-taking behaviour in the household sphere. That is not really good enough, however, if we wish to construct a satisfactory theory applicable to planned economies. A sufficiently large number of producers of any product makes price-taking behaviour quite plausible, but large numbers are not always assured. Small groups of firms might be expected to collude and engage in various forms of imperfectly competitive behaviour. The standard means of preventing this involves the postulate of free entry and exit; this requires that technical information is freely available to potential entrants, which is not always true in a market economy but is much more likely to be true in a planned one. It also requires that the fixed costs of establishing a new firm should be fairly small. In a market economy this is a matter for private calculation and judgement, whereas in a planned economy proposals from individuals would have to be approved by the planners; since the latter would be aware of the possible adverse effects of a new entrant on existing firms, they may well perceive higher entry costs than would arise in a market economy. The force of these points would obviously depend on the commodity under discussion, but it would be very surprising if the free-entry assumption turned out to be fully justified either in a market economy or in a planned economy. Hence the firms in at least some branches of the economy are unlikely to behave in a perfectly competitive fashion, which again means the failure of optimality conditions and the need for government intervention even in a market-type economy.

Thus even in a market economy there are many reasons for the government to intervene in some way to regulate the outcome of market processes. In a planned economy the same reasons hold good, with the further addition of Lange's point that the basic function of the market 'auctioneer' could itself be taken over by the state and operated by the planners. Even in a market economy the function of 'auctioneer' is provided by such bodies as trade associations, forecasting organisations, market-research consultants, and so on. It is not costless. Now after this rather abstract introductory section, it is time to begin discussion of the more concrete features of planning processes.

1.2 Plan construction and implementation

However planning is conducted, and some specific alternatives are discussed in the next section, it is inevitably a complex activity. In this section we survey rather sketchily some of the main aspects of economic activity which might be considered to fall within the scope of state control under some form of planning system. Many of the issues raised are developed further in later chapters, with particular reference to the experiences of the Soviet Union, Hungary and France.

As the title of this section suggests it is very useful to begin by distinguishing between *plan construction* (often called *plan formulation*) and *plan implementation*. Normally, plans are established to cover definite time periods, though at times an alternative basis is preferable: for example, a plan to develop a certain industry might be very specific about the projects which need to be completed but quite vague on details of timing. However, taking time as the basis, the activity of plan construction should be going on before the plan period (i.e. the period to which the plan refers), while plan implementation consists of all the government policies introduced to secure realisation of the plan. As such it is normally carried on during the plan period. In practice, there is not such a strict separation between the two kinds of activity, since one plan is being implemented while the next is under construction. However, it is important to note that plan construction has a deadline to meet, for it is not usually feasible or economically desirable to continue plan construction far beyond the start of the plan period to which the new plan refers. Sometimes it can be worth while to allow part of the plan period to elapse before fixing the plan, if sufficient improvement can be achieved by the delay; this case is discussed by Marschak and Radner (1972), and also in Chapter 6 of this book. For the moment we neglect the possibility.

Let us look at the plan-construction period first, and then outline the salient features of planning activity; interestingly, whatever kind of planning system we have in mind these features are very much the same, which is one reason why it is useful to discuss the plan-construction period separately. It turns out that the most significant differences between alternative planning systems can be recognised in the various arrangements made for plan implementation. These differences will become apparent later on when we come to individual countries.

It is convenient to consider plan construction in terms of three essential stages: namely, analysis of the past, projections of the outcome desired in the coming plan period, and selection of the policy measures which should achieve that outcome. It would be foolish to make plans for future development without allowing for constraints implied by past commitments, and analysis of the past is the means whereby these are identified.

Such analysis includes not only the development of production itself but also foreign trade, incomes and consumption of the population, investment, credit, prices and the balance of incomes to, and outlays from, the government's budget. Study of these areas will also reveal what went wrong with the previous plan, as well as the respects in which it was more successful than expected. Too much of the literature on planning forgets that, if taken seriously, planning becomes an ongoing social process in the course of which society learns what hopes it can place in planning, while at the same time the techniques and procedures used in the light of experience and changed circumstances of economic life can be modified. This is what makes analysis of the past so important.

The second stage of plan construction is the projection of various possible outcomes over the plan period and choice of the preferred outcome. Often, the time available for plan construction, combined with the general complexity of the task, prevent more than one variant from being considered; such has been the situation in Eastern Europe, until relatively recently, and in that case there is no explicit question of choice. Any choices which arise are made somehow in the course of preparing the single plan 'variant'.

The possible outcomes depend both on the legacy of the past and on certain tendencies which are largely outside the control of whatever country we are concerned with. For example, although demographic trends can be influenced in the long run by means of state policy on abortion, contraception, provision for child care, health care in general, and so on, it is nevertheless the case that all potential entrants to the labour force in, say, the coming fifteen to twenty years will already be born. Hence planners wishing to secure full employment have no alternative but to accept this situation as a constraint, ensuring that their plans will indeed provide the right number of jobs with a suitable mix of skill requirements.

Foreign trade provides another example worth mentioning here. The planners may wish to import various types of machinery or raw materials, and face the problem of exporting enough to pay for these imports. In the very short run they may be able to incur overseas debts, but eventually the debt has to be repaid unless investment by foreigners in the domestic economy is acceptable on a permanent basis. In any case the problem facing the planners is that revenues from exports are likely to depend on general world market conditions beyond their control, while import prices are also outside their control. This uncertainty about trade prospects should encourage the planners to prepare alternative plan variants based on different assumptions about the development of trade — even the UK government began to do this recently in its presentation of short-term forecasting exericses. To be fair to the planners, however, it is hard to see how they could have included such a large oil price rise in their plan variants for 1971–5, and this was the major cause of balance-of-payments disturbances during that period. Thus foreign trade both constrains the planners and offers opportunities but it is always subject to substantial residual uncertainty.

Bearing in mind all the constraints the outcomes which the planners go on to project are alternative possible futures for the economy over the next plan period. These outcomes are usually expressed in fairly aggregated terms, referring to growth rates of consumption, production, and so on, and each projection is consistent with the major constraints of which the planners are aware. The government then has to select the feasible variant which it prefers, though we defer to Chapter 5 discussion of some problems arising in specifying an objective function for government.

It may appear that we have reached the end of plan construction. We have allowed for past experience and the most important constraints, considered alternative outcomes in the plan period and selected the one most preferred by government. Surely we should now move on to implementation of this plan. The problem is that we do not yet have a plan, for a plan is not the same as a preferred outcome. No government is in a position to issue instructions that

GNP should grow by 5 per cent p.a., nor can they demand that the trade surplus should be so many million roubles. Instead, all governments have to introduce a wide variety of economic measures, often called *instruments*, which induce or compel the other economic agents — firms and households — to produce collectively something close to the outcome desired. The last stage of plan construction therefore consists of the selection of an appropriate government policy — a set of economic instruments — with the object of bringing about the realisation of the outcome chosen at the second stage.

The range of possible instruments is immense, including monetary and fiscal policy as they are carried on in the West, price and wage controls, controls operated through the credit system, instructions concerning enterprise outputs or their use of material and labour resources, and so on. It would be pointless to give examples of detailed combinations of instruments which might be employed to put some plan in operation, since much of the rest of the book does just that. A few general remarks about instruments, however, may clarify a few points.

First, to the extent that instruments are established before the relevant plan period they have to be based on some view of the way in which exogenous events will turn out, for example the trade balance already mentioned above, or the harvest. While it might be desirable from a theoretical point of view to set tax rates which varied automatically with the state of the harvest, that is not usually considered a practicable proposition. Instead, at least some instruments have to be set with a view to the possibility that changes will be required during the plan period itself.

This observation leads on to a second issue: namely, the question of plan flexibility — given that some instruments have to be changed from time to time, for example prices, the exchange rate and some components of government spending at the very least, one has to ask how often it is desirable to make such changes. Certainly some stability is very valuable, in that it facilitates comparisons between what was planned and what actually happened, and provides a stable economic environment for enterprises. On the other hand, changed conditions require adjustments to instruments, and it can be very harmful to delay the adjustments, especially if speculative anticipatory actions are likely on the part of households or firms. On balance, different countries exhibit very different practices in regard to flexibility, with countries such as the United Kingdom modifying parts of its economic policy every few months, in contrast to many of the socialist countries where some details of enterprise plans are changed quite often but producer and consumer prices are rarely adjusted more than once in a five-year plan period.

Finally, it should be emphasised that all economies have certain characteristics which impart an element of flexibility into their day-to-day operations. Thus in most countries small departures from the plan are unlikely to call for any significant revisions in economic policy. These characteristics are such items as stocks of materials and final commodities, foreign-exchange reserves, and spare capacities of various kinds. Different countries may well choose or need to hold different amounts of such 'reserves', depending on the way in which their respective planning systems operate and the level of optimism built into the initially constructed plans.

A brief examination of plan implementation concludes this section. As already noted, plan implementation comprises all the planning activities which go on during the plan period. If the plan goes well, that will involve little more than monitoring progress, different aspects of this being the responsibility of such diverse bodies as the national bank, departments concerned with foreign trade, prices, wages and employment, and various industry ministries. To a large extent such monitoring merges into the first stage of constructing the next plan. However, if all does not go according to the original plan, for example because certain industrial projects are not completed in time, then the situation no longer remains so straightforward.

The most important task of plan implementation is to ensure the smooth functioning of the economy by correcting or mitigating the effects of mistakes in the initial plan. It is not only pointless but totally impossible to construct a perfect plan, though improvements in technique can undoubtedly help to avoid some kinds of error. Rather than attempting the impossible, therefore, the planners should devise procedures for responding effectively to imbalances as they are revealed in the course of monitoring plan fulfilment. Without being very specific about the type of imbalance or disproportion under discussion, it is difficult to produce a very useful theory of plan implementation, though several aspects of it are discussed in later chapters. In contrast, economic theory has met with much greater success in formulating the plan-construction problem in quite a general and illuminating way. Some of the developments in this area are surveyed in Chapters 5 and 6 below.

1.3 Directive planning and indicative planning

Up to now, while introducing some general ideas, we have been deliberately vague about the details of the planning system under consideration. However, the remainder of this book is about the theory and practice of three quite distinct forms of planned economy: namely, the Soviet Union, Hungary and France. Indeed, many people would dispute our application of the term 'planned economy' to France. In order to justify our approach, therefore, we need to provide a certain amount of conceptual clarification, as well as a brief sketch of each of our case-study economies to indicate where they fit into the conceptual framework of the book. This is what we hope to accomplish in this section.

As the reader may well anticipate, the Soviet Union is taken as our example of a *directive* planning system, France our example of *indicative* planning, and Hungary is an intermediate case (though much closer to the Soviet end of the spectrum) which we sometimes refer to as a system of *indirect financial* planning. Despite the major differences between these systems there are two crucial similarities which, although not often dwelled on subsequently, should be borne in mind: namely, the operation of unrestricted household choice in determining purchases of consumer goods and supplies of labour to the sphere of productive activity. This is not to say that the markets for consumer goods and labour work in identical ways in each case, for the procedures for setting prices and determining the supply of consumer goods on to the market are not at all alike; likewise the systems of education and training and the regulation of the demand for labour, as well as the wage scales which may be offered to workers, show considerable variation. But the fact remains that in each case the individual is faced with a set of wage rates and possible jobs in the labour market, and a set of prices and potential purchases in the markets for consumer goods, among which he can freely choose. To simplify presentation of the argument we neglect the fact that at some time or another all three countries have experienced some form of labour direction and commodity rationing, which still persists to some extent in Hungary and more especially in the Soviet Union.

Another similarity worth mentioning is the agreement among all three countries of the appropriate period for medium-term planning; this is always taken as five years, and for operational purposes is normally broken down into a series of annual plans. Since economic conditions change and old assumptions are invalidated, it is not unusual for the last annual plan for a five-year plan period to bear only a distant relation to the original five-year plan. Moreover, in Eastern Europe and the Soviet Union it has happened in the past that severe economic difficulties (or sometimes a change of leadership) have led to complete abandonment of a five-year plan. The economies were then run by annual plans for a while, losing their usual temporal perspective. Interestingly, neither the Soviet Union nor Hungary abandoned their five-year plans for the period 1971–5 in the face of the oil price increases of 1973–4; the former, although a gainer, was still suffering from the effects of the very poor harvest of 1972, while the latter, a loser, was not obliged to begin its adjustment to the increases until 1975, when the Soviet Union raised the price of its oil part of the way towards world levels. France, however, soon had to make major changes to its five-year plan.

One of the major distinctions between our three types of planning system has to do with the instruments used to implement the plans. Table 1.1 summarises the position in respect of the most important policy variables. What we regard as the most fundamental or characteristic features of each system have been shown with asterisks. Thus in the Soviet case there is no doubt that direct instructions passed down the planning hierarchy to individual enterprises form the key element in understanding that country's economic-management system; most of the other policy instruments merely support or reinforce the allocation determined in this way, at least that is usually the intention. Since its introduction in the late 1920s, more than a decade after the 1917 revolution, the Soviet system of five-year and annual plans, with all its supporting organisations and procedures, has undergone numerous changes – some only of detail, some much more important. However, many of the basic features of the system are still quite similar to the forms they had assumed by the early 1930s. In any case, as it is not our object to provide an economic history of the Soviet Union in this book,

Table 1.1 Major features of economic policy

Policy object	System		
	Directive planning (Soviet Union)	Indirect financial planning (Hungary)	Indicative planning (France)
Enterprise activities	Inputs and outputs regulated by direct instructions from above *	Almost no direct regulation	Not regulated
Prices, taxes and subsidies	Mainly fixed centrally, wide variety of taxes and subsidies built into prices	Mixture of central and lower level price-fixing subject to regulations. Increasing tendency to enterprise-specific taxes and/or subsidies*	Only occasional price regulation, mainly in state sector. Taxes mainly general (like VAT) rather than highly differentiated
Profits	Abstracted to state budget after formation of enterprise funds	Taxation system, depending on enterprises' desired allocations to sharing and development funds	Standard tax on corporate profits; non-corporate profits taxed as personal income
Wages	Central wage scales, wage-fund controls at enterprise level. Income tax paid on highest wages	Some central wage-fixing; otherwise a tax on wage increases. Almost no income tax except on private incomes	Mainly fixed by collective bargaining between trade unions and employers. Sometimes government guidelines

Credit	Controls related to degree of plan fulfilment of each enterprise	Guidelines on branch allocation of credit; enterprises then compete for it to some extent	Monetary policy regulates total amount of credit; little detailed regulation
Investment	All but very small projects approved above enterprise level. Still often financed by non-repayable budget grants *	Major projects decided centrally, but enterprises also decide on many projects. Financed mainly by own resources or credits *	Branch requirements are in the plan. Firms have to make their own arrangements for implementation. Some major projects in state sector *
Budget (macroeconomic fiscal policy)	Always aims for balance	Normally balanced	Active instrument of policy; deficits financed by bond issue
Foreign trade	Wide variety of taxes, subsidies and direct controls. State monopoly	Taxes, subsidies and direct controls; some decentralisation	Some import duties, few other controls. Convertibility

* Indicates most fundamental or characteristic features of each system.

we shall confine attention to such aspects of its economic system that we believe to portray fairly accurately the way it functions in the early 1980s. (The more recent, and more interesting, reforms are mentioned in Chapter 3.)

In Hungary, since the introduction of the 'New Economic Mechanism' in 1968, there has been almost no administrative allocation of inputs or outputs at enterprise level. But the initially expressed intention to have firms responding relatively freely to market forces has not been realised, for a number of reasons referred to in Chapter 3. For a large proportion of firms in the Hungarian economy profitability has only a loose connection with performance in the market; much more immediate and increasingly pervasive is the system of special taxes and subsidies which largely controls what the financial state of each enterprise should be. Such taxes and subsidies are of course a central matter, which is why we describe the Hungarian model as one of indirect financial planning.

Turning now to France, a glance at Table 1.1 indicates that it does not engage in the activity of issuing instructions regarding the inputs and outputs of individual firms, nor does it employ distortionary taxation to a significant extent for regulating financial conditions of firms. In fact, the only means employed to control current economic activity is macroeconomic fiscal policy of the type applied in all Western countries. It is only when we come to investment that French planning has anything distinctive to offer, for here it goes beyond the usual approach of economists brought up with a very macro-orientated, highly aggregated view of the world. This standard approach typically confines itself to laments about the unduly low volume of investment, or more specifically about manufacturing investment, without mentioning any structural detail at all, whereas the French have sought to indicate not only the desired volume of investment but also its breakdown by major productive branches. The use of the word 'indicate' was deliberate here, since the plans are not translated into binding directives; rather, the plans are *indicative* in the sense that they provide firms and financial institutions with an indication of how the economy could develop, sometimes with tax reductions for those firms which move in the desired direction.

To define exactly what we understand by the concept 'planned economy' is no easy matter, though some idea of what it might include is implicit in the above discussion. We can, perhaps, agree that a *planned economy* is one in which the government is actively seeking to control the development of the economic structure. This fairly general definition presupposes that the government disposes of the means to make its control effective, which is reasonably clear for Hungary and the Soviet Union but less so for France. In practice, the French government probably could control developments much more precisely than it actually chooses to do. Essentially, the government regards its plans as information whose use should lead the market sector of the economy to develop more satisfactorily. Should we, therefore, regard this acceptance of market judgements as the negation of planning? We think not, though it is obviously a matter which could be debated at length. For some purposes a narrower definition of planned economy based on notions drawn from the property-rights literature can be useful by restricting the range of phenomena to be studied. However, we have avoided the legalistic complications of this literature by adopting a broad definition from the outset. (For a survey, see Furobotn and Pejovich (1972).)

Accepting this, a *planning system* can be defined as a set of institutions, procedures and economic instruments jointly specifying how a given planned economy is managed, as well as describing how it functions. Notice first of all that although Table 1.1 concentrated on economic instruments, these are certainly not enough to characterise a planning system. Second, one should not suppose that viable planning systems can be constructed at will merely by varying one or other of the basic constituents. Successful planning systems have a property which we can call *coherence*, implying that their component parts mesh together in a way which tends to be reinforcing rather than antagonistic. For example, there is not much point in struggling to improve methods of price formation if enterprises have no capacity to respond in an economically sensible way to the revised prices, or if they lack proper incentives to do so. This is just one of many possible examples suggesting that the attractions of piecemeal reform of a planning system are often illusory. And what emerges from subsequent chapters is that, despite their numerous problems, our three case studies are all examples of coherent planning systems. Without this characteristic they would be much less interesting economies to study.

1.4 A brief taxonomy

It may be useful to conclude this chapter by outlining a number of features of planning systems which are important in comparing different economies. Some of them have already been introduced in the discussion above, while others will be noted here for the first time and discussed more fully later on. For the sake of brevity we merely list the main points with occasional comments:

(1) *Periodisation of plans.* It is usual to distinguish between short-term plans (one year or less), medium-term plans (usually around five years), and long-term plans (fifteen to twenty years); the roles and relative importance of these plan periods vary considerably between countries.

(2) *Detail and scope of plans.* Plans for single enterprises, sector plans and economy-wide plans; aggregated macroeconomic plans, comprehensive and detailed plans.

(3) *Planning organisation.* Number of levels in the planning heirarchy and the main relationships between them; functional, branch and regional bodies involved in planning.

(4) *Information flows.* Vertical and horizontal flows; economic content of major information flows.

(5) *Policy instruments.* These were discussed in the last section; the most important distinction is between administrative (or quantitative, though this

term is not quite equivalent since it excludes prohibitions, for example instruments and price-type instruments. The latter may be determined by the central authorities or by the market. In the former case the term 'state' prices is sometimes used, in the latter the terms 'market' or 'parametric' prices are used.

(6) *Incentive systems*. These may be designed to elicit reliable information, to stimulate precise plan fulfilment, or to stimulate good over-all performance; incentives may be implicit in the price and tax system, or explicitly built into the system of plan indicators.

(7) *Preferences*. The functioning of planned economies is affected by the nature of the preferences to which most weight is attached; generally, we may distinguish planners' preferences and consumers' preferences.

(8) *Tautness*. Plans may be seen as mobilising society's under-utilised resources, in which case they are likely to be taut; or they may be regarded as statements of how the economy can actually develop under the prevailing conditions, in which case they will probably be more realistic.

Part I   Planning in Practice

2   THE OPERATION OF TRADITIONAL CENTRALLY PLANNED ECONOMIES

This chapter describes in outline how centrally planned economies allocate resources in their traditional mode of operation, before the reform movement of the past fifteen years. Essentially, we shall describe the economic system which began to operate in the Soviet Union in the late 1920s and early 1930s and which was transplanted to the other centrally planned economies of Eastern Europe in the late 1940s. The terminal date for this system is a matter of some controversy. Over the past fifteen years some centrally planned economies have moved decisively away from the traditional system, while others have clung to it with relatively small modifications. These changes are discussed in the next chapter, which focuses upon economic reforms. Our objective in this chapter is to describe an ideal type of traditional centrally planned economy. Although detailed institutional illustrations are often drawn from the contemporary Soviet economy, they are taken from those parts of it on which economic reforms have not substantially impinged. The use of the present tense throughout the chapter should not necessarily be taken as meaning that such an economy still exists in its pure state. (Few specific references will be given in this chapter. For a more detailed analysis, the reader is referred to the following: for the Soviet Union, Nove (1977), Gregory and Stuart (1974), Berliner (1976, chs 2–5); on Eastern Europe in general, Kaser and Zielinski (1970); on Poland, Montias (1962). Kornai (1959) gives a most penetrating account of the operation of the Hungarian economy under the traditional planning system, focusing particularly upon the relationship between the enterprise and its superior organisation. Berliner's study (1957) of the enterprise in the Soviet Union, principally based on experience in the 1930s, is extremely valuable, as is Andrle (1976).)

2.1 The organisational framework
Not surprisingly, the operation of a traditional centrally planned economy revolves around the process of plan construction and implementation, a task in which all economic organisations are involved to a greater or lesser extent. Within the production sector markets play no role in production decisions (except to the extent that the supply of labour and demand for consumer goods are determined by a market-type process – see section 2.4 below). Instead, the enterprise or basic management unit receives detailed instructions which lay

down what must be produced, what inputs are to be used, and where output, once produced, must be delivered.

In a market system organisations confront one another on what are (formally) equal terms; ignoring the internal operation of firms, communication is horizontal, between organisations operating at the same level; and exchanges take place on a voluntary basis. Within a centrally planned economy, on the other hand, organisations are located within a rigid hierarchy; (almost) all communication is vertical, between superior and subordinate, much of it having the character of a legally binding instruction; and finally, enterprises are both required to obey instructions and are debarred from taking actions not provided for in the plan — in other words, formally they have no residual discretionary powers (although they do exercise certain important informal powers, described below).

This state of affairs in centrally planned economies has advantages and disadvantages. Potentially a centrally planned economy can be controlled by the planners in a much more comprehensive way than can a market economy. The directors of the system have the power to arrange the productive capacity of the economy in any desired way, by amalgamating enterprises, for example, or choosing to adopt a regional rather than a ministerial system of grouping enterprises; they can prescribe any desired decision rules or procedures for the organisations thus created; and finally, within the framework of any organisational structure and any set of decision rules for subordinates, they can assign production targets or other targets as they choose. The disadvantages, of course, are the rigidity of the system, its tendency to stifle initiative from below, and the informational overload it places on the management system.

The option of revising the organisational structure of the economy is often taken up in centrally planned economies, though it is fair to say that the over-all framework has been fairly consistent. In the Soviet Union (which provides the basis of the description here) for all but eight of the last fifty years of central planning that framework has been a ministerial one, with the economy divided into sectors under the control of ministries, each of which is in charge of its appropriate enterprises. The exception to this practice occurred from 1957 to 1965, when the framework was a regional one, with each regional economic council or *sovnarkhoz* in charge of all production units within its area (with the exception of defence production, which continued to be controlled centrally). One of the reasons for the change was the desire to counter excessive departmental loyalties and to improve territorial planning, but the new system proved to have its own weaknesses: regional loyalties developed and specialisation of production was hampered. However, the post-1965 organisational structure does contain elements of the regional system. Some industries, generally the less important ones, are controlled at the regional level, with each of the thirteen republics of the Soviet Union having its own ministry; another group of ministries has both a regional and a national subordination (these are known as Union—republican ministries), while the major group of industries, including heavy industry in particular, is organised at the level of the Soviet Union as a whole.

The account of industrial planning below is based on this last group; but basically the same procedures are used to plan republican and Union-republican industry, and, more generally, other sectors of the economy, with the exception of agriculture, are planned in a similar way.

We now consider the organisational framework in more detail. At the top of the hierarchy stands the Soviet Council of Ministers (see Figure 2.1); this is the senior executive council of the Soviet government, though the major strategic decisions, in the economic as in other spheres, are in fact taken by the party leadership, and generally the party has its own hierarchy running in parallel with the government one described here. Attached to the Council of Ministers is the State Planning Commission, which is responsible for detailed planning work at the national level. The major industrial ministries (about thirty-five in 1977) are subordinate to the Soviet Council of Ministers and themselves comprise several departments which until 1973 were known as 'Chief Administrations' and which since 1973 have gradually been reorganised with slightly different powers and generally renamed 'Industrial Associations' (the earlier term will be used here; for a fuller discussion of associations, see Chapter 3). Some of these administrations are responsible for a part of the ministry's production, while others are responsible for specialised functions for the industry as a whole, such

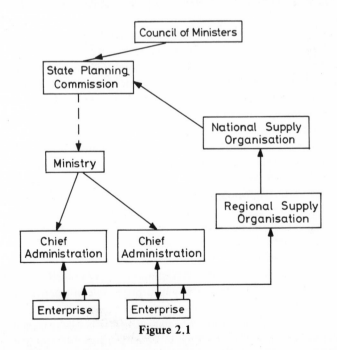

Figure 2.1

Note: The broken line linking the State Planning Commission and the ministry reflects the fact that the former lacks a direct executive authority over the latter.

as finance. Finally, the lowest unit in the hierarchy is the enterprise, which is subordinate to the ministry via a Chief Administration. Since 1973 enterprises in the Soviet Union have been progressively amalgamated into larger units known as 'production associations', and in many industries the latter are now the lowest independent organisation (although some production associations still accord some limited autonomy to the separate enterprises amalgamated into the associations). In 1977 there were about 44,000 basic units in Soviet industry.

What we have described above is the management hierarchy for planning production and controlling the implementation of the plan; this is the principal line of authority in a centrally planned economy. There remain, however, other important organisations whose functions are discussed in more detail in the following sections. The chief of these in the Soviet Union are as follows:

(1) The state committee for supply, attached to the Soviet Council of Ministers and responsible for planning and controlling the supply of inputs to enterprises.

(2) The state bank, which acts both as central bank and as a monopoly commercial bank for economic and other organisations; it also has a supervisory role as it only permits financial transactions which are authorised by the plan.

(3) The state committee on prices, attached to the Council of Ministers; this organisation is responsible for setting both wholesale and retail prices.

(4) The state committee on labour and wages, which is responsible for setting wage and salary levels.

(5) The state committee for science and technology, which is responsible for co-ordinating research and development.

Even this preliminary and simplified account of the organisational structure of a centrally planned economy shows how complex the hierarchy is. Evidently the problem of information flows within such a system will be a severe one — especially so since, as noted earlier, communication is normally required to be vertical, between superior and subordinate. This means that a message from one organisation to another must travel up the hierarchy until it reaches an organisation which is a common superior to both, and then travel down again. High-level organisations, which have a limited capacity for receiving and processing data, are thus overloaded; information is lost or distorted through aggregation. As the economy becomes larger and more complex the position deteriorates still further, and pressures for reform build up.

2.2 Plan construction

The chief instrument for resource allocation in the traditional centrally planned economy is the *plan*. The manner in which plans are constructed is therefore of vital importance. This section outlines that process.

Since the earliest period of their operation, centrally planned economies have attempted to compile an interlocking series of plans of different durations. The longest time period is the fifteen-to-twenty-year plan. Such a long time horizon presents serious problems of forecasting technological developments, and such plans can be little more than highly aggregated forecasts of possible future developments which set out priorities in broad terms. (The Soviet plan for 1976–90 presumably comes into this category, though it has not yet been published.) In 1979 it was decided to switch to a system of ten-year plans, prepared at five-year intervals and complemented by even longer-term programmes for major areas of technology.

Five-year plans are more important, and plans of this duration have now been compiled for fifty years in the Soviet Union and for thirty years in other centrally planned economies. The nature of the five-year plan and its manner of construction have changed substantially over this period. One of the major functions of the five-year plan is to establish an investment plan permitting a balanced development of the capacity and output levels of the economy in each of the five years, and an economic model which permits such co-ordination (the dynamic input–output model) is increasingly being applied (see Chapter 10 below). Five-year plans also have an important mobilising and propaganda role. They are normally approved at Party Congresses and hold out the prospect of substantial increases in output and living standards. Often, of course, the five-year plan needs revision in the course of its implementation – in the face of external shocks such as harvest failure, for example – and in any case it is compiled in fairly aggregative terms and does not identify in detail the executants of the targets which it contains.

The most important and detailed plan is the annual plan, often broken down into quarters. This plan sets out targets for all aspects of enterprise behaviour in great detail, and it is legally binding. Failure to implement the plan puts the enterprise director at risk of criminal sanction, though in practice such measures are taken only in extreme cases. The remainder of this section outlines the process of compiling the annual plan, and the next section focuses upon plan implementation at the enterprise level. The two aspects are closely interlinked, and this for the following reason: the performance of an enterprise director is evaluated and bonuses are paid to him on the basis of the performance of the enterprise compared with the plan. Hence much of the enterprise's effort is devoted to achieving a modest plan; in other words, the nature of the incentive system for plan implementation influences the process of plan construction as well.

Annual planning starts fairly early in the planning year, the year preceding that for which the plan is constructed (the planned year). The process takes place in a number of stages:

(1) The Council of Ministers, guided by the Party, sets target growth rates for the major sectors of the economy. These will not necessarily be the largest sectors, but will be those seen by the authorities as being of the greatest importance. The targets are often derived from the five-year plan, adjusted to take account of preliminary indications from the State Planning Commission about what is feasible.

(2) On receipt of these targets the State Planning Commission derives a set of output targets broken down by major product groups; these targets are set in the

light of the Commission's knowledge of, or estimates of, the output capacity of each industry, and the targets are passed on to the appropriate ministry.

(3) The ministry further disaggregates the output targets from the Planning Commission before passing them to its Chief Administrations for particular product groups; the latter then parcel the production targets out among the enterprises whose task it will be to implement the plan. This stage is completed by about April of the planning year.

(4) As soon as the enterprises receive their preliminary output targets, they calculate their input requirements, and pass this information on to the regional supply organisation. The latter aggregates all input requirements and passes the totals up the supply hierarchy to the state committee on supply, which communicates it to the Planning Commission. At the same time, enterprises negotiate with the ministry, and as a result of these exchanges production targets within the ministry may be reallocated. However, these changes will not normally be reflected in altered statements of input needs.

(5) The remainder of the planning year is occupied by attempts to ensure consistency between production levels and other sources of supply on the one hand and input requirements and other sources of demand on the other. The instrument which has been used for this purpose for more than fifty years in the Soviet Union is the *material balance*. A material balance consists of statements of categories of demand for a product group on one side and of sources of supply on the other (see Table 2.1). The organisation compiling the balance (the balancing agent) depends on the relative importance of the product group in question. In the Soviet Union the State Planning Commission compiles balances for the most important product groups (about 2,000 in number) and the allocations of the 300 most important of these have to be approved by the Council of Ministers. These 2,000 product groups account for almost 80 per cent of the value of goods produced. Less important groups, or sub-groups within a single balance approved by the Planning Commission, are distributed by the supply organisation, ministries or local organisations. But the State Planning Commission plays the central role in planning allocations.

By May of the planning year, therefore, the State Planning Commission is in a position to complete the entries in the material balances, and establish which

Table 2.1 **A simplified material balance**

	Supply side		Demand side
(1)	Current production	(4)	Intermediate inputs
(2)	Imports	(5)	Consumption
(3)	Stocks brought forward	(6)	Investment
		(7)	Exports
		(8)	Stocks required at year end
	Total available		**Total required**

goods are in deficit and which are in surplus. Historically there has been a tendency towards taut planning, with high output targets leading to excess demand. Many balances will therefore be in deficit, and the task of the planners is to achieve consistency. Within the framework of each balance the planners may overcome a deficit either by increasing supply or by reducing demand. We consider the latter possibility first.

One simple way of reducing total demand for a product is to reduce individual components of final demand — consumption, investment, or exports. Yet cutting investment or exports will endanger the growth or balance of payments of the economy. This leaves consumption, which has traditionally been considered a buffer or residual category, from which resources could be withdrawn in case of need. In recent years, however, the position has changed, and this category may make only a small contribution to eliminating the deficit. (See section 2.4 for an analysis of the determinants of the supply of consumption goods.)

This leaves the first category, input requirements or intermediate demand, as a possible means of cutting the imbalance. If there is a surplus in the balance of a substitute, then input requirements can be reduced by requiring some customers to accept an alternative. There may also be some scope for cutting down input requirements simply by forcing enterprises to produce more efficiently (indeed, to the extent that enterprises anticipate such a reduction, they may artificially inflate their input requirements and deliberately incorporate some slack in the balance which the planners can then eliminate). However, too sharp a reduction in input allocations will jeopardise the ability of the enterprises to fulfil their output plans.

The alternative means of eliminating a deficit is to increase supply. Of the items in the 'resource' side of the balance, increasing production is normally the only practicable means of increasing supply, as imports will be subject to a balance-of-payments constraint, and other sources are insubstantial or outside the planners' control. Increases in supply can be achieved either by switching productive capacity from surplus to deficit goods or by imposing additional output targets on enterprises. The latter carries with it the danger of requiring enterprises to produce beyond their production possibilities, but again to the extent that enterprises anticipate these extra targets in dealing with their superiors they will understate their true productive capacity.

Increased production targets, however, will create additional problems. Suppose planners eliminate a deficit in one balance by the method of increasing planned production. That will increase input requirements in other balances, the output of which is used to produce the good originally in deficit. Even if these balances were previously in equilibrium, they will now be forced into deficit. Eliminating these deficits by the method of increasing output will put yet other balances out of equilibrium. The basic problem is the interdependence of sectors in the economy, with outputs of one industry being inputs into another which produces inputs for a third, and so on. The material-balance system treats each commodity group in isolation rather than as part of an interdependent system.

Given enough time planners could successively take account of all the repercussions from one balance to another. In practice, however, they are short of time; they can consider only the most important input—output relationships between one sector and another, and eventually they are obliged to close the balances by artificially juggling with the figures. We shall see later how serious this problem is likely to be when we evaluate the planning process.

(6) The process of juggling with the balances usually takes until nearly the end of the planning year. After this date the plan goes for final approval to the Council of Ministers, and is then transmitted to enterprises via the ministries and Chief Administrations. At the same time, the supply organisation prepares the attachment plan, which assigns supplies of inputs to customers, and supplier and customer complete contracts laying down the final details. This is the first direct communication between the two enterprises.

In the description above we have not specified the units in which the plan is constructed. In principle it would be possible to construct a plan entirely in physical units. In practice, of course, this is out of the question in an advanced economy which (according to one Soviet estimate) produces as many as 20 million separate products. Extensive aggregation is clearly required to make the planning process feasible.

One obvious candidate for the role of aggregator is a system of prices. In traditional centrally planned economies the role of prices in resource allocation is limited. Allocations are made administratively, and prices remain constant for many years. Prices play a major role as aggregators, particularly at the upper levels in the planning hierarchy. However, planners also have an attachment to the use of physical units — measuring output in tons, or square metres, or simply in units of homogeneous output — and even at the highest level balances are sometimes denominated in these units. At enterprise level the output plan typically consists of a gross value of output target combined with more specific targets, often denominated in physical units, for principal products. This feature leads to distortions in plan implementation (discussed below).

We have explained how the production and supply components of the enterprise annual plan are constructed. In fact, the plan document the enterprise receives, in the Soviet Union called the technical, industrial and financial plan, lays down targets for other aspects of enterprise activity. The plan contains twelve divisions over all; these cover labour, investment, costs and profitability, a financial plan and an incentive scheme for the enterprise, as well as sections dealing with output and supply (see sections 2.4 and 2.5 below). Techniques based on the compilation of balances similar to those described above are used to allocate labour, investment and financial resources, and to prepare these divisions of the plan. In many cases the final plan document runs to several thousands of pages; and although many divisions of the plan are based on the output plan, there will not normally be time to eliminate inconsistencies, and the enterprise director must choose which part of the plan to give priority to.

* * *

We can view the process of output and supply planning described above in terms of an *input–output* model. Input–output is a way of representing the inter-relationships between the sectors of the economy either in an equation or in tabular form. (For a fuller account of the economic and mathematical properties of input–output models, see Dorfman (1958) or Leontief (1951).) We first consider the simplest case of a two-sector economy, using the following notation:

y_i = final (net) output of product i $(i = 1, 2)$

x_i = gross output of product i, including intermediate inputs $(i = 1, 2)$

a_{ij} = input of product i per unit of output of product j $(i, j = 1, 2)$

The relationship between the sectors in the economy can be represented as follows:

$$x_1 = a_{11}x_1 + a_{12}x_2 + y_1$$

$$x_2 = a_{21}x_1 + a_{22}x_2 + y_2$$

Gross output = Intermediate demand + Final demand

Solving these equations for x_1 and x_2 we derive:

$$x_1 = \frac{(1 - a_{22})y_1 + a_{12}y_2}{(1 - a_{11})(1 - a_{22}) - a_{12}a_{21}}$$

$$x_2 = \frac{a_{21}y_1 + (1 - a_{11})y_2}{(1 - a_{11})(1 - a_{22}) - a_{12}a_{21}}$$

In other words, starting from our knowledge of the a_{ij} (the technological input–output coefficients) we can calculate for any given level of final output the gross output necessary to sustain it.

For a multi-sector model matrix notation is more convenient. Let Y be a vector of final output, X be a vector of gross output, and A be a matrix of input coefficients a_{ij}. Then

$$X = AX + Y \tag{2.1}$$

Solving for X

$$X = [I - A]^{-1}Y \tag{2.2}$$

The elements of the inverse matrix $[I - A]^{-1}$ have a natural interpretation. If the elements of matrix $[A]$ are direct input coefficients (for example, the amount of coal required as a direct input to make one ton of steel), the elements of $[I - A]^{-1}$ are total input coefficients, both direct and indirect (i.e. the direct input of coal into steel, plus the input of coal required to make other inputs into steel, plus the input of coal required to make those inputs, and so on *ad infinitum*). Thus if $[A]$ is a matrix of direct input coefficients, $[I - A]^{-1}$ is a matrix of total input coefficients.

The matrix $[I - A]^{-1}$ can be computed either directly by inversion or by an iterative method which is instructive from a planning standpoint. We illustrate this first in a one-sector economy, where a_{11} is the direct input coefficient of the product into itself. For consistency,

$$x_1 = a_{11}x_1 + y_1$$

Total output can thus be computed directly:

$$x_1 = (1 - a_{11})^{-1}y_1$$

Alternatively, the total input coefficient $(1 - a_{11})^{-1}$ can be built up as follows. To product a net output of one unit, gross output must comprise the following: net output + direct input into that output + input into that direct input + input into that first-round indirect input + . . . ; i.e.

$$x_1 = (1 + a_{11} + a_{11}^2 + a_{11}^3 + \cdots)y_1$$

Assuming the sequence converges $(a_{11} < 1)$:

$$x_1 = (1 - a_{11})^{-1}y_1$$

In the multi-sector case, using matrix notation, $[I - A]^{-1}$ can be computed in a similar way (again assuming convergence):

$$[I - A]^{-1} = [I + A + A^2 + A^3 + \cdots]$$

Therefore

$$X = [I + A + A^2 + A^3 + \cdots]Y$$

What is the relationship between the material-balance scheme outlined earlier and the input–output model? Two points deserve particular attention. If the input–output model were used for planning purposes as we have described it, planning would start from a vector of net output targets; the centre would then calculate gross output requirements from equation (2.2), check these levels for feasibility, and make appropriate adjustments to initial targets, whereas the planning system above starts from gross output targets, and tries to achieve consistency between these on the one hand and their input requirements and the vector of final demand stipulated at the start of the process on the other. The material-balance system can therefore be interpreted in input–output terms as an attempt to compute a consistent set of gross output targets (X) by iteration on the basis of an initial estimate of those gross output targets (X^0) and a vector of net output targets (Y) which may be adjusted in the course of the planning process. The first iteration – calculation of direct input requirements – is made by communicating provisional output targets (X^0) to the production units, and collecting their input requirements (AX^0). Subsequent iterations are made within the planning office but on an *ad hoc* basis, balance by balance. In other words, planners are unable to calculate the full repercussions on all other sectors of altering the output targets in one sector. The best they can manage is to consider the first few rounds of consequential input changes. This can be represented as a substitution of matrix $[I - A]^{-1}$ by $[I + A + A^2 + A^3]$, allowing for three rounds of inputs to be taken into account.

The approximation is more accurate if the planners initially communicate X^0, an estimate of gross output, than if they simply communicate net output targets. Enterprises respond to X^0 with AX^0. The central planning board then computes successively:

$$X^1 = AX^0 + Y$$
$$X^2 = AX^1 + Y = [I + A]Y + A^2 X^0$$
$$X^n = AX^{n-1} + Y = [I + A + A^2 + \cdots + A^{n-1}]Y + A^n X^0$$

This will converge to $X^\infty = [I - A]^{-1}Y$. However, for a small number of iterations the estimate of X found by starting from X^0 is more accurate than that starting from Y the vector of net output targets (Montias, 1962, pp. 336–7).

Knowing matrix $[A]$ we can calculate the harmful consequences of approximations of this kind by computing the ratio of approximating matrix $[I + A + A^2 + A^3]$ to the full matrix $[I - A]^{-1}$. The smaller the ratio, the greater the inconsistency in the plan is likely to be. Such ratios have been calculated for the Soviet Union by Gillula (1977, pp. 76–7), who uses a reconstructed ninety-six-sector 1966 input–output table. The results show that direct inputs alone account on average for 50.6 per cent of total direct and indirect inputs (the values ranging from 29.6 to 72 per cent). Including first-round indirect inputs $(A + A^2)$ raises the proportion to 75.5 per cent on average (extreme values are 51.6 and 88.8 per cent). Adding one further round increases the average ratio to 87.8 per cent (values range from 67 to 94.7 per cent). The figures suggest that to truncate calculations showing the impact of one sector on others can lead to substantial planning errors.

There is one case, however, where such truncation can be avoided. In the special case where the matrix of direct input coefficients is triangular (i.e. all entries below the main diagonal are zero), the sector-by-sector approach of material balances can yield a consistent set of output targets immediately, provided that the central planning board deals with the material balances in the correct order. It must start with the sector which is an input only in its own production, and calculate its gross output level. The next sector to be balanced is the one whose output is only used as an input into itself and into the first sector (the gross output level of which is already known); the second sector can therefore be balanced independently. The process is repeated until a perfectly consistent set of gross output targets is found for all sectors in a single iteration. In the general case, however, this short cut is not possible.

Given, then, that errors of approximation are likely, how serious are their consequences? This question, too, can be answered within the input–output framework. If a sector provides inputs directly or indirectly into many other sectors, then an error in calculating that sector's balance will have ramifications throughout the economy. On the other hand, errors in the balance for a sector delivering its output principally to final demand will have fewer repercussions. Inspection of the inverse matrix will thus reveal those sectors where errors in the balance are particularly serious and cumulative (see Manove, 1973).

The discussion above *interprets* the material-balance system within the input—output framework. It does not imply that material balances should necessarily be *replaced* by input—output techniques. The growing role of input—output models in planning is discussed below in Chapter 10. Here, without describing properties, such as the assumption of a single constant returns to scale technique for each sector, which are common to both methods as represented here, we merely make a few preliminary observations which suggest that such a substitution has certain associated problems:

(1) The number of balances is often very large; input—output models would make computational demands which could not at present be met.

(2) The material-balance system has certain decentralisation properties lacking in input—output models, in which all information must be collected at the centre in the form of input—output coefficients. The material-balance system is potentially decentralised, in the sense that each sector need only collect information on total demand for its own output, and communicate its own input needs to the appropriate sector. This property is not fully exploited in the present system, except to the limited extent that the task of compiling balances is divided among several organisations.

(3) The material-balance system permits a more flexible system of aggregation than the input—output model. In the latter, direct input coefficients must be collected using the same sectoral breakdown of inputs for the whole economy (this is necessary to establish a consistent matrix for inversion); yet many of these coefficients will be zero. In the material-balance system, on the other hand, because each product is balanced independently, a different disaggregation of the economy can be made in each balance. Thus compilers of balances can concentrate on important users of each product (the identity of which will of course vary from balance to balance), and this will permit a more flexible use of information (see Hare, 1978).

2.3 Plan implementation

The execution of a plan which has been constructed in such detail could in principle be a fairly straightforward business. However, the reality of plan execution in centrally planned economies is quite different. The plan is not implementable as it stands, and this for two reasons. In the first place, the conditions assumed by the planners are not fulfilled. This is not only because the economy is subject to random and unpredictable influences, such as the weather for example: as the plan is constructed early on in the planning year it is based on information which is inevitably out of date. Second, even on its own assumptions the plan is inconsistent as a result of the way it is constructed; the balances for material inputs, labour, investment resources, etc., are finally closed in an artificial manner, and the resulting plan is often infeasible.

The consequences of asking enterprises to implement an infeasible plan are potentially serious. As noted above, in an interdependent economy a failure to execute the plan in one sector will jeopardise plan fulfilment in other sectors which use the output of that sector as an input. If these sectors are unable to fulfil their output plans, they will cause problems for some or all of the other sectors which they supply, and so on. Any shortfall will have potential repercussions throughout the entire economy. Enterprises will also suffer if their supplies arrive later than expected. Such late arrival of supplies is one of the factors responsible for the practice of 'storming', the concentration of production in the last part of any period (month, quarter). This practice has a harmful effect on quality, and to the extent that it is caused by supply delays it can become cumulative. These factors may seem to put in question the very workability of centrally planned economies. However, the problem is mitigated by several factors, some of which have a beneficial and some a harmful effect on the efficiency of resource allocation.

The systematic tendencies of enterprises to conceal production possibilities and exaggerate input requirements fall into the harmful category. Enterprise directors typically receive bonuses related to their performance *vis-à-vis* the plan in terms of certain major variables, such as gross value of output. Plan fulfilment earns the director a large bonus, over-fulfilment a small additional bonus. However, over-fulfilment in one year often leads to a higher plan in the next year, through a procedure known in the Soviet Union as planning 'from the achieved level' and in Western literature as the operation of the 'ratchet principle' (see Birman, 1978). In these circumstances enterprise directors will refrain from over-fulfilling the plan by a large margin, as explained in more detail in Chapter 9. Thus enterprises try to incorporate a 'safety factor' in their plans, in the form of reserves of excess capacity or surplus inputs accumulated against the possibility of a supply failure. This creates a buffer between one sector and another but at the cost of systematic under-utilisation of resources.

A second factor mitigating the consequences of inconsistencies in the plan is the enterprise's desire to have a potential ability to produce vital inputs on its own premises using resources under its own control. This potential is used when supply failures occur. The output thus produced allows the enterprise to fulfil its plan, but the quality is often low, and the system leads to weaknesses in plant specialisation, as shown by short and expensive production runs. Over the long term this defect may be very harmful.

A third factor enabling plans to be fulfilled is the unofficial system of exchange or supply which grows up in parallel with the official system. In a traditional centrally planned economy supplies of many goods may legally be despatched only in conformity with an allocation certificate from the central authority. In practice, enterprise directors find ways of circumventing these regulations, and continue to acquire or divert extra supplies when these are vitally necessary for plan fulfilment. This is often done by the exercise of influence within a group of enterprise directors who are willing to help one another out in emergencies. In the Soviet Union the person responsible for acquiring such extra supplies is known as a 'fixer' (*tol'kach*) (see Berliner, 1957, chs 11–12). The use of such unofficial sources carries certain risks for the director. If it is true that directors are only willing to take such risks to meet dire emergencies, then the unofficial system of supply may operate as an informal priority system, allocating resources when they are most needed. The fact that the planning authorities tolerate the unofficial system lends some support to the view that it does serve a useful function.

We have considered above only unofficial measures taken to make the implementation of the plan possible. The authorities themselves also intervene to change the plan of enterprises and to establish a system of priorities when the original plan cannot be implemented.

Superior organisations intervene in plan implementation in various ways. Ministries have the right to alter the enterprise plan at any stage of its execution and often do so, requiring one enterprise, for example, to increase its output to make up for a shortfall in another enterprise. Enterprise directors may seek the assistance of party officials in their search for scarce inputs. (For a graphic account of such a request, see Yanov (1977, pp. 22–7).) Finally, the planning organisations themselves establish priorities by instructing enterprises to supply particular customers first. As an example of the last form of intervention we can cite a telegram sent by a Deputy Chairman of the Soviet State Planning Commission in 1961: 'to prevent stoppages in its shops, I ask you to ship fully to *Rostelmash* (the Rostov agricultural machinery factory) ahead of other consumers, for orders of the second quarter' (quoted in R. Powell, 1977, p. 54).

The plan as executed therefore differs from the plan as constructed. R. Powell (1977, p. 52) has suggested that 'in the process of the plan's execution, mechanisms come into operation which have distinguishable efficiency properties, but of a particular sort. As the system's position is altered . . . towards outcomes which are increasingly dangerous in the eyes of the governing authorities, the odds rise and ultimately become high that these mechanisms will direct it away from the danger.' These mechanisms are partly unofficial and partly official. The result of their operation is to mitigate the worst consequences of the system of plan construction.

It should be noted, however, that the system of incentives at the enterprise level does promote serious microeconomic inefficiencies (on this see especially Kornai, 1959, ch. 2). Enterprises can often continue to produce unwanted and unsold goods and still count them towards plan fulfilment (production 'for the warehouse'). When a target for gross value of output is set, enterprises find it advantageous to produce material-intensive or unnecessarily expensive products. Setting targets in physical terms produces its own distortions. Products are designed to serve the interest of the producer rather than the user. Items measured by weight (cooking utensils, for example) are made unnecessarily heavy;

those measured by area (glass, for example) are made excessively thin. These distortions are widely recognised and discussed, but no method of overcoming them within the framework of the traditional centrally planned economy has come to light.

2.4 Consumption goods and the allocation of labour

So far this chapter has confined itself to the internal operations of the industrial sector, in which administrative control is pre-eminent. The relations of the production sector with the household sector are organised on different principles.

The *demand for labour* in a centrally planned economy is determined by the plan. Typically the State Planning Commission compiles a labour balance in the same way as it compiles material balances for products; for annual planning balances are broken down by region and skill category. The State Planning Commission attempts to correct imbalances by economising on certain types of labour and substituting others. The annual plan received by the enterprise will specify the number of workers it may employ and also a limit on the total wage fund of the enterprise. As in the case of other inputs, enterprises exaggerate their requirements and have little or no incentive to economise.

Wage rates are set by a central authority. Typically they are differentiated by the skill grade of the worker, the sector of the economy in which he or she is employed and (sometimes) the region of the country in which he or she works. However, many workers are on piece rates, and in the general atmosphere of labour shortage caused by taut planning there is some scope for wage drift (see, for example, Fearn, 1965).

The *supply of labour* depends on individual household responses to wage rates. Except for relatively brief periods there has been no attempt to allocate labour administratively, nor to oblige workers to remain employed at a particular enterprise. Indeed, one major feature of the labour market in centrally planned economies is the high turnover of labour. This is a result of the general tightness of the labour market. It is deplored by the authorities, who have, however, found difficulty in overcoming the problem (see D. Powell, 1977).

The *supply of consumer goods* is determined by the central planners, and consumer-goods factories receive output targets in the same way as other enterprises. The central authorities use market research and various other forecasting methods to try to meet the consumers' needs at a disaggregated level, but this is a recent development and, historically, centrally planned economies have not been entirely successful in this respect, as accumulations of unwanted consumer goods testify. We noted above a widely held view that output of consumer goods is a residual category which could be raided to meet shortages in other sectors of the economy receiving a higher priority. Portes and Winter (1977) have estimated supply functions for the consumer-goods sector in four Eastern European countries from about 1955 to about 1975. (The period varies from country to country.) Their procedure is to establish whether deviations of consumption from its time trend are proportionately stronger than deviations of total output from its trend. If true, this would suggest that consumption bears a disproportionate burden of shortfalls in total output. For Poland and the German Democratic Republic they did find some evidence of 'crowding out' of consumption by investment and defence spending. The evidence for Czechoslovakia and Hungary, however, suggested the reverse, i.e. that consumption was if anything protected in the period under consideration. Moreover, two other authors using different techniques found no evidence of crowding out of consumption in the Soviet Union in the period 1959–72 (see Green and Higgins 1977, p. 166).

The over-all retail price level of consumers' goods is planned in a way which should ensure consistency between the money value of demand and the money value of supply (this part of the planning process is known in the Soviet Union as 'the balance of income and expenditure of the population'). The money value of demand can be found from a knowledge of employment levels (L), average wages (w), income taxes net of transfers $(T$ – normally very low in centrally planned economies), and estimates of savings (S). The implied price level (p) and output level (C) of consumer goods should then satisfy the equation:

$$wL - T - S = pC$$

The central planners, controlling as they do all the variables in the equation (except S), should in principle be able to ensure a balance; whether they do so in practice we consider below.

The retail price of individual consumer goods is the sum of the wholesale price and turnover tax. Variations in rates of turnover tax for individual goods could in principle be used to ensure equilibrium in each market. However, this is not done in practice, and even if the over-all level of excess demand for consumer goods is zero (a controversial assumption in any case), there is certainly positive excess demand for individual products.

Over the past twenty-five years or more the general level of retail prices in centrally planned economies has remained stable. Some Western economists assert that this stability of the price index has to some extent been the result of statistical manipulation, and has in any case disguised a situation of repressed inflation. Such repressed inflation in the market for consumer goods would have spillover effects in other markets. Consumers unable to spend their incomes may add to their money balances and reduce their labour input. The latter effect would have the consequence of reducing supply still further and hence aggravating the repressed inflation (this cumulative process is known as the 'supply multiplier', by analogy with the conventional Keynesian demand multiplier – see Barro and Grossman, 1974, and Muellbauer and Portes, 1978).

The implication of the preceding paragraph is that a test for the presence of repressed inflation should be made on the basis of a properly specified and complete macroeconomic model. However, the formulation of such a model creates serious theoretical difficulties and practical applications have been sparse (see Howard, 1976, 1979; and Nissanke, 1979). Several writers analysing consumption behaviour in centrally planned economies on the assumption of equilibrium have produced plausible results. For example, Pickersgill (1976), using Soviet data for 1955–71, estimated the following equation:

$$S = -19.4912 + \underset{(0.0076)}{0.0585 Y_p} + \underset{(0.1451)}{0.3395 Y_{tr}}$$
$$\underset{(2.960)}{}$$

$$R^2 = 0.8911$$
$$DW = 1.1501$$

where S = savings, Y_p = permanent income (a two-year average of income), Y_{tr} = transitory income (the difference between current measured income and permanent income), the figures in brackets are standard errors, and DW is the Durbin–Watson statistic. Portes and Winter (1980) similarly estimate demand equations yielding a good fit for four Eastern European countries, and when they explicitly test for disequilibrium they find it generally to be absent.

These results, suggesting as they do a macroeconomic equilibrium in the consumer-goods market, are certainly at odds with anecdotal evidence and observations of queues and shortages. It is also noticeable that the build-up of cash balances in the Soviet Union has been substantial in recent years, deposits in savings banks increasing threefold from 1970 to 1978. However, Pryor (1977) finds that waiting-time in shops in centrally planned economies is fully explained by the low level of employment in retailing in those countries, and the build-up of household savings in the Soviet Union may be linked, for example, to the absence of consumer credit facilities and is not by itself evidence of disequilibrium (for an account of the issues at stake in this debate see Kornai, 1979).

2.5 Money and the financial system

As we have seen above, the allocation of resources within the production sector of a centrally planned economy is determined primarily by plan instructions which are to a considerable extent denominated in physical terms. In the planners' intentions the financial system in such an economy is subsidiary to or supportive of the output plan itself. However, the reality may be otherwise, and the behaviour of agents in the economic system may be modified by monetary variables.

The institutional framework of the monetary system in a centrally planned economy is fairly straightforward. The state bank plays the role of both a central bank (issuing notes, supervising foreign transactions) and of a monopoly commercial bank (performing conventional banking services for enterprises). The banking needs of households are catered for by savings banks which pay a low rate of interest on deposits.

In the above respects centrally planned economies have much in common with capitalist economies. The principal differences between the two banking systems lie in the fact that in centrally planned economies the bank has a controlling function.

This function is helped by the separation of the monetary system into two circuits, a cash-based system for the household sector and a bank-deposit system for enterprises. The link between the two circuits is made on the one hand by payment of wages to households by enterprises, and on the other by purchases by households in the state retail system. Hence currency normally returns to the production sector after only one transaction, exceptions occurring only when exchanges take place within the household sector, in the form of payments for private services, for example, or when households purchase goods on the private market for agricultural products. In the latter case the currency finds its way back to the state production sector when farmers purchase productive inputs or consumer goods. The simplicity of this system should aid the planners in maintaining macroeconomic balance, as described in the previous section, between aggregate consumer spending and the money value of consumer goods supplied. However, this balance is endangered by substantial accumulations of money balances by the household sector. Portes and Winter (1977, p. 360) found evidence in Eastern Europe that planners increase the supply of consumer goods when household financial assets are above trend.

In relationships between enterprises the use of currency is prohibited except for the most trivial transactions. (This observation applies to legal transactions. Currency for illegal transactions is sometimes accumulated by the employment of bogus workers, whose 'wages' are diverted for other purposes (see Berliner, 1957, p. 216).) Payments for goods are thus normally made by debiting and crediting accounts of the purchasing and supplying enterprise respectively. In addition, the bank will make a short-term loan to an enterprise with insufficient money to make an authorised transaction, but such credits are granted only for working capital, not for fixed capital (see Zwass, 1978, pp. 85–6). The importance of this is that the bank is able to exercise control over enterprises by refusing to authorise transactions not provided for in the plan. The same system prevents enterprises from exceeding the limit specified in their plan on their total wage bills (though the latter control has often been circumvented in some countries). The difficulty which enterprises experience in offering cash for above-plan shipments and the limited value of such payment to the supplying enterprise are among the factors encouraging the use of barter within the unofficial distribution system.

In the system described above enterprises have formal financial autonomy, subject to the provisions of the plan. However, in the traditional centrally planned economy enterprises have no discretion in the disposition of profits. Any profits made, after deduction of bonuses to which enterprise personnel are entitled, are transferred to the stage budget, where they are entered on the receipts side together with other revenue items. The expenditure side of the budget is made up of government disbursements on defence, social services and also on the economy (in particular, investment financed directly from the central budget). This arrangement means that the general level of prices within the industrial sector has little effect on the state budget, provided that it is insulated from retail prices. Consider the effect of an increase in wholesale prices, for example, matched by a reduction in rates of turnover tax. Enterprises as a whole will earn higher profits, and budget revenue will increase on this account. Revenue from turnover tax, however, will decrease by an equal amount and there will be no net change. Similarly, introducing or increasing a charge payable by enterprises to the state budget for the use of capital equipment will have no impact on enterprise behaviour if it merely institutes or increases interest charges (payable to the state budget) at the expense of profit (which is also residually payable to the state budget). Profits may, however, influence enterprise behaviour if they are a bonus-forming indicator.

The foregoing account treats the financial system in a centrally planned economy merely as a reflection of physical flows determined principally by a plan constructed at least in part in physical units and implemented by administrative controls. As far as the enterprise is concerned, this may well be a reasonable approximation to reality. Enterprises have no obvious motives for accumulating cash balances, as any legitimate purchases they intend to make will be automatically accommodated by a supply of credit from the bank. They have no incentive to hoard money in the expectation of being able to purchase inputs, because any such authorised purchase will automatically provide its own credit.

The position with the household sector is different, however. Households may wish to accumulate monetary assets; they will do so to space out consumption or in anticipation of price changes. The presence of repressed inflation in markets for consumer goods will have both an income and a substitution effect on demand for real balances, as it will both reduce real income and also encourage substitution towards demand for money in expectation of elimination of the excess demand for goods. For these reasons, even in a traditional centrally planned economy, monetary variables may impinge upon the operation of the real economy.

2.6 The problem of innovation

The system set out above has obvious weaknesses and obvious strengths. On the credit side it maintains an apparent high level of utilisation of resources, and it is particularly suited to mobilising these resources for the achievement of a few simply specified goals. On the debit side it leads to serious microeconomic inefficiencies and it becomes progressively harder to operate as the number of sectors in the economy grows, as the relationships between them become more complex, and as the structure of final demand becomes more varied.

Levine (1966) has suggested that many of the phenomena observed in traditional centrally planned economies are not inherent in the system itself but arise because the planners have attempted to operate it at such a high level of intensity, continuously raising the targets for enterprises by instituting a system of taut planning. (The possible role of taut plans in mobilising resources and generating enthusiasm is discussed in Hunter (1961).) In section 2.2 we noted the repercussions in an interdependent economy of the supply failures which inevitably accompany taut planning. The argument needs qualifying in the light of our subsequent observations about enterprises' wish to conceal reserves. Plans may not be taut in an absolute sense, in relation to the economy's theoretical production potential, but may still be taut compared with the capacity which enterprises in the given institutional framework are willing to reveal.

It is hard to say whether the argument thus qualified is well founded, as the propensity for central planners to set plans which are taut in the above sense is so widespread that it has not been empirically tested. However, if adopting slacker plans would solve some of the problems of centrally planned economies, it is by no means obvious that this would by itself solve a major and increasingly important problem — that of innovation. In many centrally planned economies the period of extensive growth when surplus labour can be employed in more productive sectors is now over. Increases in output must be achieved by means of intensive growth or productivity increases. Although there is no convincing econometric evidence, for the Soviet Union at least, that the rate of technical advance (i.e. growth of total factor productivity) is slowing down, labour shortages are occurring and returns to capital inputs seem to be rapidly diminishing. This leaves technical progress as the chief source of productivity increases and hence magnifies its importance.

The microeconomic disincentives to innovation in centrally planned economies are well known (Berliner, 1976; and Hanson, 1980). The lack of authority in the lower levels of the management system tends to rule out spontaneous innovation. Rather, enterprise directors regard new products or new processes as a threat to the orderly fulfilment of the output plan. Comparisons of technological levels between centrally planned economies and Western countries almost uniformly reveal that the former not only exhibit a lower level of best-practice techniques but are also slower in diffusing innovations throughout the economy (see Amann *et al.*, 1977).

Numerous attempts have been made in centrally planned economies to stimulate technological advance. Some of these are organisational in character: for example, research and development bodies may be brought under the same authority as production units, or a central body, such as the State Committee for Science and Technology in the Soviet Union, may be given expanded powers of co-ordination. Others involve changes in the incentive system for enterprises: for example, technologically advanced goods may have a higher price, or each enterprise may be required to produce 'new' products as a specified proportion of its output, a procedure which unfortunately encourages 'bogus' innovations. However, none of these measures has had the necessary galvanising effect on innovations at the enterprise level. The continuing failure to speed up the development and use of new technology has been one of the major factors behind economic reforms, which are the subject of the next chapter.

3 ECONOMIC REFORMS AND THEIR IMPACT ON PLANNING

In the previous chapter we discussed various features of what may be called the traditional planned economy, epitomised by the Soviet Union, but also characterising the Eastern European planned economies during the 1950s and early 1960s. (Of course, this system has never operated in France.)

Beginning in the late 1950s several of the socialist countries came to realise the need for, and considered the possibilities of, economic reform. In many cases the reformed systems involved rather minor adjustments to the traditional model, designed to secure improved economic performance while retaining much of the traditional and familiar institutional structure; the Soviet Union is the most important such case − a conservative reformer − and we outline the main elements of reforms in that country in section 3.1. A more comprehensive approach to reforms was taken by Hungary − a radical reformer − as we shall see in section 3.2.

In the course of examining and debating various types of reform ideas arose concerning the operation of systems of planned economic management which were often far too radical to have any hope of political acceptance. Nevertheless, the issues raised are not only important and interesting in their original Eastern European context, but also have some relevance for discussions of planning in market-type economies, notably France. In this connection we can only cover a limited set of issues in the space available; accordingly section 3.3 covers the development of horizontal links and its implications for macroeconomic planning, while section 3.4 introduces some discussion of incentives and plan implementation as a basis for the fuller treatment of these issues in Chapters 8 and 9.

3.1 The Soviet economic reforms

Several reasons have been adduced in explanation of the economic reform movement which spread through the socialist bloc in the early 1960s. The most obvious reason, first, was faltering economic performance. A second reason related to the gradual shift from so-called extensive to intensive growth processes. Third, the increasing complexity of economic activity became harder to regulate effectively by means of the traditional planning tools; in particular, there was increasing emphasis on the need to promote faster technological progress. Fourth, the inefficiencies of the traditional system itself became more apparent, especially in Eastern Europe where central planning was still rather young.

Finally, the smaller, more open economies experienced increasing difficulties in trading successfully and efficiently with the West, and sought reforms to improve matters in that sphere. It is worth expanding on some of these points now in order to provide some background to the Soviet economic reforms (see also Bornstein, 1977).

In the socialist countries the most widely used indicator of economic performance is the growth rate of net material product, often supplemented with indicators for particular sectors like industry and agriculture. While one may question the use of or reliance on such measures, it is undoubtedly the case that performance in these terms is what influences the political leadership in Eastern Europe to introduce policy changes from time to time. Accordingly, Table 3.1 reveals how these indicators have developed for the Soviet Union since 1965; in particular, the tendency for growth rates to fall is quite evident. It is not surprising, therefore, that there have been some moves towards economic reform in an attempt to check the prevailing tendencies.

However, it is not merely the growth rates of output which are changing but also the availability of factor inputs, especially labour. To a very large extent growth in the socialist countries has been facilitated by the transfer of enormous numbers of relatively under-employed agricultural workers into those branches of industry to which the five-year plans devoted most attention. As a result it proved possible for industry to develop in what has come to be called an 'extensive' fashion. This involved the use of increasing inputs of both labour (from agriculture) and capital (financed through the very high savings and investment ratios which characterise all the socialist countries). But by the early 1960s reserves of labour in particular were becoming exhausted; indeed, the planners in some countries were concerned that too many people had left agriculture, particularly in the younger and more highly skilled groups. Consequently, growth in the future could not be based on continuing increases in the labour input into industry but would have to depend much more on productivity gains brought about by more efficient investment. This change of emphasis was officially referred to as a switch from 'extensive' to 'intensive' growth. Table 3.2 shows the changes in the pattern of factor inputs in industry in the Soviet Union since 1965, reflected in the rising capital intensity of production.

While it may not have been too difficult to recognise the increasing labour shortage, it was rather less obvious what should be done about it. It was gradually accepted that plans would have to place much greater emphasis on technical progress and innovation, implying that new means might have to be found to stimulate this throughout the economy. Moreover, other forces besides the developing labour shortage were creating pressures in the same direction, for the Soviet economy had grown rapidly under its system of five-year plans, and despite all the well-known inefficiencies of this system it had succeeded in raising living standards substantially by the early 1960s. As a result consumers became increasingly 'choosy' and demanding, no longer accepting all the poor-quality goods which were purchased in times of poverty and shortage. They expected a

Table 3.1 Growth rates in the Soviet Union 1961–80

	Net material product (NMP)	Consumption	Fixed investment	Industrial output	Agricultural output
1961–5	6.5	6.3	6.2	8.6	2.4
1966–70	7.7	8.4	7.6	8.5	4.2
1971	5.6	7.7	7.3	7.7	1.1
1972	3.9	5.7	7.0	6.5	−4.1
1973	8.9	5.7	4.7	7.5	16.1
1974	5.4	7.0	7.1	8.0	−2.4
1975	4.5	6.5	8.6	7.5	−5.3
1976	5.9	3.0	4.5	4.8	6.5
1977	4.5	5.2	3.7	5.7	4.0
1978	4.8	4.1	6.0	4.8	3.0
1979*	2.0	3.3	1.0	3.4	−4.0
1980 (Plan)	4.0	4.5	2.7	4.5	8.1

* Provisional.

Sources: *Naradnoe Khozyaistvo SSSR; SSSR v tsifrakh; Ekonomicheskaya gazeta* (various issues).

Table 3.2 Capital intensity in Soviet industry 1965—78

	1965	1970	1972	1974	1976	1978
Capital intensity (index, 1965 = 100)*	100	134	155	178	204	229

* The index measures capital per worker in industry.
Source: Narodnoe Khozyaistvo SSSR, various issues.

wider range of goods to be available, incorporating more imaginative design, and including many of the recent technologically advanced products based on the new industries — electronics, plastics, and so on. Such demands had repercussions throughout the economy, gradually enforcing higher standards of engineering and more carefully controlled production in general. This naturally reinforced any already existing pressures to improve technology and accelerate the pace of innovation.

In addition, the rapidly widening range of products, together with their increasingly complex technical level and the sheer volume of output, is causing immense difficulties for the traditional planning system. The old system is rather effective in directing resources to meet certain clearly specified priorities but seems to become less and less effective as the complexity of the planning task increases. This increasing complexity, allied with the problem of accelerating technical progress, gives rise to a number of fundamental questions about the planning system which the various attempts at reform — both in the Soviet Union and in Eastern Europe — have sought to answer. These questions concern the desirability of organisational change, the possibilities for improving the incentive system, the problem of plan information and the improvement of planning techniques, and possibilities for some degree of decentralisation. Of course, in any particular proposal one cannot assume that these issues will be carefully separated, but it is useful to keep the distinctions in mind when assessing particular reforms.

Since the mid-1960s the Soviet Union has introduced a number of different measures of economic reform. These reforms began in 1965 with some major organisational changes introduced by Brezhnev and Kosygin, immediately following the fall from power of Khruschev. Under Khruschev the traditional organisational structure based on branch ministries had been replaced by a structure based on regional economic councils, the so-called '*sovnarkhozy*'. While intended to avoid some of the shortcomings of the branch structure — for example, the poor communication between branches and uneconomically long-distance deliveries — the regional structure was soon seen to have problems of its own. The regions developed undesirable tendencies towards autarky, and it became increasingly difficult to tackle problems which concerned an entire branch. As a result various state committees emerged in Moscow with responsibility for these very real problems; not surprisingly, these gradually assumed some of the powers previously devolved to the *sovnarkhozy*. Consequently, few were surprised when the leadership abolished the *sovnarkhozy* and reinstated the branch ministries in 1965. Parts of the material supply system continued to be based on a regional organisation, but apart from this the system of economic organisation reverted to something very like that in force before 1957.

This organisational reform was accompanied by the announcement of impending change in the enterprise-level incentive system. In 1962 Professor Liberman had opened up a period of debate about enterprise incentives by publishing some proposals favouring the use of profit indicators instead of the more traditional gross output indicators. He also favoured a general reduction in the number of compulsory plan indicators which enterprises should receive, as well as some widening of their autonomy. Although it was widely recognised that the traditional system of indicators had many defects (as we discuss in the last section of this chapter and in Chapter 9), Liberman's suggestions were initially received without enthusiasm. However, similar ideas were emerging elsewhere in Eastern Europe, and it was increasingly clear that something would have to be done to improve the incentives for plan fulfilment at enterprise level. Accordingly, reforms in the incentive system were also announced in 1965. (See Sharpe (1966) for various articles on Liberman's proposals.)

The 1965 reforms accepted some of the points made by Liberman and numerous other participants in the debate but adopted a fairly cautious and conservative approach. Thus the number of compulsory plan indicators was drastically reduced, leaving nine(!) in all. These are listed later, but for the moment we need only note that the gross output plan was no longer to be the main bonus-forming indicator. Indeed, the gross output target was formally abolished. The new bonus-forming indicators were to be the increase in the value of sales, and one of two possible profit-based indicators: the percentage increase in profits; or profitability, expressing profits as a percentage of the value of capital employed. Different branches used slightly different combinations of indicators without departing from the main principle of the reform.

The sales indicator was intended to encourage enterprises to take an interest in sales rather than output, countering the widely criticised tendency to produce unsaleable produce. But in the prevalent conditions of excess demand for many products the change can only have been formal. More fundamental change would probably have required rather looser plans based on somewhat less ambitious growth targets. The profit indicators were seen as synthetic indicators which combined the effects of sales efforts and cost reductions into a single indicator which could be compared between enterprises. Naturally, the effects of these new indicators on enterprise behaviour depend on the manner in which they affect enterprise incomes and the extent to which enterprises are permitted to respond flexibly to them.

Depending on the indicator values which an enterprise achieved in relation to its plan, payments were made into three newly established enterprise funds: namely,

(1) material incentive fund (for payment of bonuses to managers);

(2) social and cultural fund (which provides such services as housing for workers); and

(3) production development fund (to finance decentralised investment)

All the funds receive allocations from profits, based on rather complex rules and formulae which it would be tedious to repeat; in addition, the development fund receives part of the enterprise's normal depreciation allowance for the year. The remaining depreciation, and any profit not formally transferred to one of the three funds (whose sizes are subject to rather strict upper limits), are remitted to the state budget. This has the effect that for the most successful enterprises the effective marginal rate of profits tax is 100 per cent. It is hard to believe that this can be conducive to economic efficiency, but it is no doubt comforting to the central planners to leave enterprises with such small financial resources over which they can exercise independent control. To date there seems to be little evidence that the reform of incentives has had any important effect, and the Soviet press continues to be filled with articles on the well-worn themes of distortions resulting from the incentive system, lack of plan discipline, and the failure to seek high plans. However, we examine some of the more theoretical properties of this reform of incentives in Chapter 9.

Now incentive systems to which enterprises are subject may give rise to economic distortions, and this for at least two reasons. First, the systems themselves may be badly designed in that they simply invite enterprises to maximise a completely inappropriate – from an economic point of view – objective function; such might be said of the gross output indicator used as the basic for bonus payments before 1965. Second, sensible success indicators can yield unsatisfactory results if other features of the enterprises' economic environment are poorly arranged. A particularly important such feature is the system of producer prices.

Producer prices are those paid on transactions between firms; it is widely recognised that Soviet producer prices, while convenient for some purposes, suffer from a number of important defects. Any particular type of price may fulfil several different roles in the economy, which may be grouped together into the following categories: control and evaluation, allocation (information and incentives), and distribution. In the Soviet Union producer prices have characteristics which make them relatively satisfactory from the point of view of the control and evaluation function, and highly unstaisfactory as far as other functions are concerned.

Because of aggregation problems, which are quite inescapable, plans are usually expressed in terms of prices; similarly, performance by individual enterprises is reported and assessed in terms of prices. If control over production is to be effective, one might expect it to be helpful if the plans are formulated in the same prices which are subsequently used to evaluate the results. This condition is approximately fulfilled in the Soviet Union, where both plans and outcomes are measured in terms of producer prices which rarely change. Thus for most products prices at the start of a plan period will be the same as the prices in force at the end; even so the planners' task in assessing enterprise performance is somewhat complicated by the introduction of new products for which there was no price at the beginning of the plan period, the withdrawal from production of other products, and planned price adjustments for yet others. But these problems are comparatively trivial compared with the severe shortcomings of Soviet producer prices when we consider their possible role in guiding the allocation of resources.

It would be possible to present here an extensive account of the drawbacks of Soviet prices, but for reasons of space only the major issues are listed below, with some brief additional comments:

(1) the prices are based on average costs, in principle at branch level, but frequently at the level of an individual enterprise;

(2) they are not changed sufficiently frequently to remain in line with costs as productivity changes at different rates in different branches of the economy;

(3) the treatment of overheads and depreciation in multi-product firms is unsatisfactory;

(4) the treatment of the capital input was wrong before 1967, and only a little better thereafter;

(5) the connection between foreign and domestic prices is not conducive to efficient trade; and

(6) the general pricing rules are implemented with such serious administrative lags that, most of the time, much of the price system is not consistent with any coherent system of rules — it just happens!

Given the preference shown in much of Western economic theory for prices to be based on marginal costs, it is not surprising to find that point (1) above is frequently singled out for particular criticism. However, under conditions of constant returns to scale, and taking a fairly long-term view, average and marginal costs are much the same and the point loses a lot of its force. Admittedly, these conditions do not always hold good, but despite all the theoretical argument to the contrary we rather doubt whether the issue of marginal- versus average-cost pricing should be considered fundamental. In addition, point (3) is also a problem in Western pricing practices, and it is far from clear that Soviet solutions based on the application of fairly arbitrary rules for allocating costs between products are inferior to Western ones.

Of the remaining points (5) is relatively much more important in the case of the smaller, trade-dependent Eastern European countries and will be discussed in the next section in connection with Hungary. Points (2) and (6) concern the administration of the price system, and make clear why, even if the underlying rules were considered satisfactory from an economic point of view, the actual producer prices would bear so little relation to the prevailing levels and patterns of costs that they would be almost meaningless as guides to decisions about resource allocation. Finally, point (4) returns us to the Soviet economic reforms which are the theme of this section, for Eastern Europe and the Soviet Union have passed through a period of extensive debate about the proper way of measuring the costs which enter into price-formation calculations. This debate is still not finally settled, but some degree of agreement has been secured on the treatment of the capital input.

In considering the measurement of costs there was never any doubt about the treatment of material costs and direct labour inputs; most of the argument has concentrated on the mark-up, or surplus, to be built into the price system. For example, the traditional Soviet-type model tended to form prices by adding a mark-up calculated as a few per cent of direct costs plus overheads and depreciation. In a situation where enterprises are not expected — or permitted — to take important decisions about resource allocation such prices may be defensible. But one intention expressed in the Soviet economic reforms in the mid-1960s was that enterprises should have more independence than before, both in the sphere of current production and in the investment sphere. One may doubt the practical importance of such intentions, but it is certainly the case that they are not compatible with the traditional prices. In particular, aside from an element of depreciation, the traditional prices include no 'cost of capital', so that enterprises making decisions on the basis of these prices would be quite justified in regarding capital as costless. Following lengthy ideological arguments about the appropriateness of incorporating 'profits' into socialist prices, it was eventually recognised throughout most of Eastern Europe that capital charges had to be introduced. Such charges were introduced into Soviet prices with the price reform of 1967. From the point of view of efficiency this was a definite advance, though the resulting price system was not without its remaining defects. For example, although capital now had a price, this price was not the same in all branches of the economy: different rates of profit were built into the prices in different branches, presumably at least partly to ensure that investments previously undertaken would be able to show a profit.

The next reform requiring comment in this section is the major organisational change which was announced and which began to be implemented in 1973. This is the movement to form associations (referred to in Chapter 2). From the planners' point of view the advantages of associations are obvious — they allow the planners to control the economy by dealing with a much smaller number of economic units, which may well make such control more effective. In addition, it was hoped that the formation of larger units might allow greater benefits from economies of scale, though this must be regarded as somewhat doubtful since even before the reform the typical Soviet enterprise was already several times larger than the average Western firm (Nove, 1968, p. 202). However, there are two areas in which the development of associations may achieve more tangible benefits: these concern transport costs, and research and development. (For analysis of the associations, see Gorlin (1974 and 1976), as well as Berliner (1976).)

As already observed in our earlier discussion of the *sovnarkhozy*, enterprises in the Soviet Union frequently engage in uneconomically long hauls of materials and outputs. But if the enterprises involved could be combined into an association, then these transport costs could be internalised and there is a likelihood that more rational transport arrangements might be worked out. One way of doing this would involve some specialisation between the enterprises in the association, so that each produces a narrower range of products than before, presumably with greater efficiency. Thus the formation of associations can be regarded as another attempt to solve the problems which gave rise to the earlier reforms associated with Khruschev. Research and development can also be made more effective by creating a special kind of association (a science–production association) combining production facilities and research institutes. The latter had formerly been rather isolated from the production processes to which they were supposedly contributing new ideas. Since many research institutes are established to study the problems of an entire branch of production, links to a form of association make much more sense economically than links to an individual enterprise.

The process of transferring all enterprises into some form of association has proceeded more slowly than originally planned and there is some evidence that the reform has been impeded within the ministries by officials reluctant to lose powers. However, the process should be completed by 1981 or 1982. There are two main types of association. The smaller is the so-called 'production association', which often combines as few as four enterprises in some branch; the other type, the 'industrial association', is really a successor to the chief production administration or department within an industrial ministry responsible for an entire branch. Accordingly, the industrial associations are often nation-wide in scope. From an economic point of view the main significance in their separation from the ministry is that they cease to be carried by the budget, and operate on an independent accounting basis with extended powers. The Russian word *khozraschet*, which literally means 'economic accounting', is often used to describe their basis of operation, and enterprises using *khozraschet* are expected to cover their costs from their own revenues. The reform thus embodies a concentration of power within the middle level of the economic system, with ministries surrendering some autonomy and enterprises losing their separate existence.

The 1973 management changes were extended by a decree of the Central Committee of the Communist Party and the Soviet Council of Ministers which was adopted in July 1979 (see 'Ob ulushchenii', 1979). Its provisions are complex, and many of them are directed towards speeding technical advance and improving procedures for capital investment. But they also significantly increase the role of the five-year plan, by seeking to establish a system of targets or norms for each enterprise or association for a full five-year period. The annual plan, it is proposed, will be constructed within the framework of the five-year plan on the basis of a counterplan submitted 'from below' by production units.

The decree contains provisions for a new index of net ('normed') output (i.e. a measure of value added) for production associations, to replace gross value of sales, though the latter will be retained to assess the enterprise's performance in the delivery plan. It is also intended that contract discipline will be tightened. In addition, ministries as a whole are to be put on *khozraschet* and given full responsibility for making specified payments to the state budget, irrespective of their performance; this extends a provision of the 1973 changes to ministries themselves.

It is clear that many of the provisions of the decree are a natural extension of the 1973 management changes and of other earlier measures, particularly those intended to accelerate technical advance. In some respects, then, the decree builds on foundations created by a series of earlier experiments, the results of which must be considered satisfactory. The two principal novelties in the planning of output are the strengthening of the role of the five-year plan and the substitution of the net output indicator for one of sales. One of the major aims of these two changes is evidently to overcome the distorting effects of the incentive system on enterprise performance, especially from the operation of the 'ratchet principle'. It will be some time before the changes contained in the decree come into operation and take full effect, but it is worth noting that the problem of success indicators for production units has a long history of intractability.

In this outline of reforms in the Soviet Union we have seen that several directions of change have been pursued, including some quite major organisational adjustments, reforms to the incentive system and the system of producer prices. However, despite all the efforts, it seems that one has to characterise the Soviet reforms as piecemeal rather than radical and comprehensive, as will soon become apparent when they are contrasted with the much more thoroughgoing Hungarian reforms in the next section. This is not to say that more radical proposals have been lacking in the Soviet Union, far from it! The mathematical economists in particular have produced some extremely interesting proposals, but their ideas have not won much support in official circles; the only areas in which their views have been accepted are to do with the computerisation of parts of the process of collecting plan data and carrying out some of the required plan calculations, but we shall defer any discussion of these issues until Chapter 10.

3.2 Reforms in Hungary

Hungary is one of the smaller Eastern European countries, with a population only a little over ten million. By the early 1950s, in common with the rest of Eastern Europe, the country had adopted the Soviet-type economic model with its five-year plans and pressure for rapid growth based on the development of heavy industry. Unfortunately, Hungary's poor raw-material base and dependence on foreign trade made this model distinctly inappropriate, as soon became evident both to the population in general — as real wages fell for a while — and to the political leadership — when over-ambitious plans could not be fulfilled. Following the debacle of 1956 when a popular revolt against the regime was decisively crushed by the intervention of Soviet troops, Kadar was installed as the head of a new government; despite his inauspicious introduction to this position he remains there to this day and has succeeded much more than any other Eastern European leader in winning a remarkable degree of support from his people. In large measure this success must be attributed to Hungary's impressive economic achievements since the mid-1950s.

The most striking aspect of Hungary's performance is the degree of stability which has been attained over more than twenty years, in comparison with other Eastern European countries and most Western countries. Some of the more significant performance indicators are shown in Table 3.3, which sets the scene for the discussion to follow.

Table 3.3 **Performance indicators for Hungary, 1958—80**

Period	Annual growth rate of net material product (NMP) (%)	Annual growth rate in industry (%)	Annual growth in real wages (in industry) (%)
Three-year plan (1958—60)	7.1	11.6	1.9
Second five-year plan (1961—5)	4.4	8.0	1.3
Third five-year plan (1966—70)	6.9	6.6	2.7
Fourth five-year plan (1971—5)	6.5	6.4	3.3
Fifth five-year plan (1976—80) (first two years)	5.4	6.2	2.7

Sources: UN Monthly Bulletin of Statistics, various issues; *Statisztikai Havi Közlemények*, various issues.

Since the late 1950s the Hungarian economy has undergone a series of different economic reforms, the most radical being the series introduced at the beginning of 1968 under the name of the 'New Economic Mechanism'. (Detailed accounts of economic development and reform in Hungary are given in Balassa (1959), Friss (1969), Gadó (1972 and 1976), Portes (1972), Hare (1976 and 1977).) However, before discussing these particular reforms, and subsequent modifications to them, in any detail, it would be useful to comment on some of their somewhat less comprehensive antecedents. Given that the over-all perform-ance of the economy has been rather good, according to the summary statistics presented in Table 3.3, we should also explain briefly what has motivated the Hungarians to seek economic reform at all.

Many of the reasons for reform already mentioned at the start of the last section would certainly apply to Hungary, with a much greater emphasis on the need to improve the efficiency of Hungary's participation in international trade. Many of the most staunch supporters of the traditional Soviet model were purged from the Party hierarchy during or immediately after 1956, leaving a leadership with much more pragmatic views about economic policy. This leadership was ready to recognise the inefficiencies of the Soviet model and to consider proposals for change, though it did not initially go beyond a number of fairly cautious reforms intended to improve the way in which the traditional system functioned. Thus, although economic performance never declined sharply, nor faltered to the extent of precipitating an economic crisis as happened in Poland and Czecho-slovakia, for example, the Hungarian government was able to observe events elsewhere and anticipate developments at home sufficiently clearly to see the need for reform. Its ability to introduce reforms – even the early relatively minor ones – in a situation of continuing good economic performance, and with careful preparation, must have contributed substantially to their general accep-tance by, and support from, the population.

The first reform came in 1957, with a substantial reduction in the number of compulsory indicators built into the individual enterprise plans, and a thorough revision of the system of industrial producers' prices. The latter did not funda-mentally change the way in which these prices were to be calculated but was merely an attempt to make them correspond more closely to costs of production after a number of years without much adjustment in prices. The reduction in compulsory plan indicators was not an unqualified success: within a very short time the number of indicators was on the increase again. It seems that the standard response of the traditional Soviet model of a planned economy when it meets with difficulties in fulfilling plans is to add yet more indicators to the list already prescribed for enterprises; a similar sort of response can also be observed whenever the combination of plans and enterprise incentives led to enterprise responses which the planners considered to be undesirable. All this was predicted by Kornai (1959), among others, in work examining the behaviour and function-ing of the traditional Soviet model in Hungary in the early 1950s. Particularly in relation to light industry, this work was extremely critical about the inefficiencies of the Soviet system, leading to persistent failures to respond to the needs of the consumers, reductions in product quality, and so on. Merely reducing the number of plan indicators did not, in this context, make a great deal of difference, and the unsatisfactory experience of the late 1950s and early 1960s convinced many Hungarian economists that more fundamental change was needed in order to prevent the reversion to more centralised forms which appeared to be a characteristic of the Soviet model.

Before any more fundamental change came about, however, there was some further experimentation with partial reforms, as well as the completion of some reforms in agriculture which had been started at the beginning of the 1950s. Taking agriculture, we should note first of all that Hungary participated in the general drive towards a collectivised agriculture which swept through Eastern Europe at that time. The campaign was by no means a complete success, and met with considerable resistance from the peasantry, largely because the change was being imposed by an unpopular government and was supported by totally inadequate resources in the way of modern equipment, fertilisers, and so on, which would have been required to make the newly formed co-operatives economically attractive for their members. Consequently few people can have been surprised when many of the co-operatives simply collapsed altogether in the wake of the events of 1956. But a few years later the economic situation in the country was much more settled, and satisfactory growth rates were being achieved, and it was possible to devote more resources to agriculture without the planners being able to argue any more that industry was being 'starved'; moreover, food products were among Hungary's more important exports, especially to the West. As a result a second collectivisation campaign was launched in 1961 which met with substantially greater success; since the completion of this campaign there have only been very minor changes to the way in which agriculture is organised, and we shall make no further comment about it.

In state industry the main reforms in the early 1960s were rather similar to some of the developments in the Soviet economy several years later which we have already outlined in the last section. For example, this period saw both the introduction of capital charges as well as some organisational changes which involved an enormous increase in the concentration of Hungarian industry. The latter was an attempt by the central planners to gain a firmer degree of control over the economy's productive activity by drastically reducing the number of units over which they had to exercise such control. Enterprises and industrial co-operatives were amalgamated to form larger bodies, often referred to as trusts, though conceptually they are exactly analogous to what are now called associations elsewhere. Table 3.4 may help to illustrate the nature of the organisational changes that were taking place in the early 1960s; the table also reveals that the process of concentration has continued into the 1970s, albeit at a much slower rate. We shall see later on that such a high degree of concentration has been a source of serious difficulties in implementing Hungary's more recent and more radical reforms, and we shall have to consider quite carefully the factors

Table 3.4 Number of producing units in Hungarian industry

	1960	1970	1975
Number of state enterprises	1,368	812	779
Number of co-operatives	1,251	821	793
Total	2,619	1,633	1,572

Sources: Statisztikai Évkönyv and *Magyar Statisztikai Zsebkönyv*, various issues.

that have led to a continuation of the trend instead of a reversal.

There is one important area in which the Hungarian approach differed markedly from the Soviet, even before 1968: this is the whole field of foreign trade, which has always been relatively marginal for the Soviet Union but absolutely central to Hungary. Thus, while the former only exports about 6 per cent of its national product, Hungary was already exporting almost one-third in 1965, and by 1975 this figure had risen to 50 per cent. A little under two-thirds of Hungary's trade is conducted with her partners in Comecon, often under medium- or long-term contracts related to the five-year plans, and the remaining third is with the developed capitalist countries and with the developing countries. Because of this huge scale of trade in relation to national product, Hungary (together with Poland) was among the first Eastern European countries to begin thinking seriously about the question of efficiency in relation to international trade. Already by the late 1960s export efficiency indexes were being proposed which may well have helped to eliminate some of the more unproductive transactions. In addition, the question of the relationship which should obtain between domestic and world market prices in order best to stimulate the efficiency of domestic production was widely discussed; and there was some progress towards incorporating world-price considerations into the officially prescribed investment-efficiency indexes. All this entailed very few concrete measures, but nevertheless served to create a climate of opinion in which any serious reforms proposed for the Hungarian economy had to take full account of the need to stimulate greater efficiency in international trade.

After this sketch of the earlier, partial reforms, let us now turn to the more interesting ones for which Hungary has justifiably become renowned. The 'New Economic Mechanism' was introduced at the beginning of 1968 following three years of careful preparation. During the preparatory phase of the reform there was a wide-ranging debate on a number of the key issues, most notably the following:

(1) How radical the reform should be: there was a choice, essentially, between

further attempts to improve the traditional model and something more fundamental.

(2) Whether a whole series of co-ordinated measures should be introduced
simultaneously or in stages.

(3) Whether there should be changes in the instruments and methods of
economic policy alone, or whether these should be accompanied by major
institutional reforms.

Without entering into a discussion of the fascinating details of the debate we
may simply note the conclusions. On question (1) it was agreed that the reform
should be a radical one, and on (2) it was accepted that all the key elements of
the reform package should be introduced simultaneously. However, question (3)
was answered in a less radical way when it became clear that there would not be
any major institutional innovations associated with the reform. Although not
apparent initially, it soon turned out that the lack of such innovations was a
definite weakness of the reforms, and to some extent undermined their effectiveness right from the start.

For the sake of clarity it is probably best to list the main features of the 'New
Economic Mechanism', comment on them individually, and then conclude the
section by outlining some of the most significant modifications to the original
reforms which have been made during the 1970s, with the reasons for them.

Undoubtedly the most significant component of the Hungarian reforms was
the decision to abandon altogether the standard socialist practice of assigning
compulsory targets to each enterprise in each planning period; since 1968 enterprises have formulated their own plans in the light of their market situation and
the various economic regulators which determine the economic environment.
These regulators comprise the following major tools of economic policy:

(1) Price policy. The 1968 reform involved a complete recalculation of
producer prices on a new basis, and with new rules for their adjustment after
1968.

(2) Rules for the taxation of enterprise income. The 'New Economic Mechanism' allowed enterprises to keep much more income than before, both for investment and for payment of bonuses.

(3) Foreign exchange rate, and the system of taxes and subsidies on imports
and exports.

(4) Special taxes and subsidies on production.

(5) Credit policy.

While the regulators are certainly of great importance in helping to understand the day-to-day operation of the Hungarian economy, it is necessary to
note from the outset that certain residual powers and possibilities of intervention
by the central authorities also have to be taken into account to appreciate the
kinds of response which have been made to the problems arising over a longer
period.

In abandoning the traditional centralised procedure for formulating annual
plans and breaking them down to enterprise level the Hungarians were trying to

achieve two things. First, it was widely accepted that the central planners were simply unable to accumulate all the information that would be needed in order to calculate an annual plan that could form an adequate basis for enterprise production activity: the economy was just too complicated! Hence the attempt to do the impossible was bound to lead to inefficiency — with planners cutting corners in the calculations and imposing allocations which might be feasible, but which could be improved upon by the enterprises themselves. Second, since a substantial part of enterprise production activity is much the same year after year — this relates to Kornai's concept of 'autonomous reproduction' (for which see section 8.2) — and since we have already argued that the planners were not very successful in changing the part that had to be changed, it began to seem more important for the planners to pay more attention to longer-run trends and developments in the economy. Thus the end of detailed short-term planning was supposed to lead to great improvements in five-year and longer-term planning; despite the technical improvements which we discuss in Chapter 10, it cannot yet be said that this aim of the reforms has progressed very far.

Now if enterprises no longer receive detailed instructions from the central planners, and have to rely predominantly on the market signals as mediated by the regulators, then clearly the market must provide economically sensible signals, and the regulators relating to enterprise incentives should stimulate appropriate responses. It was in order to achieve such consistency within the economic mechanism that the Hungarians decided to reform several components simultaneously. Beginning with the signals the reform of producer prices was designed to provide enterprises with 'correct' information about the prevailing relative costs in the economy; the details of the reform are fairly complex, but in outline it was implemented as follows.

As in the standard Soviet approach, prices were to be based on costs, but the concept of 'cost' was changed, and some deviations of prices from the corresponding costs were to be permitted to allow for market demand and social preferences. The cost concept has acquired the label 'two-channel' because in addition to materials and labour costs, together with overheads and depreciation, the mark-up is related both to capital and to labour inputs. Thus there was initially built into the prices a 25 per cent mark-up on the enterprise wage bill; this is the so-called 'wage tax', which included social-security contributions. Then capital charges amounting to 5 per cent of the gross value of productive assets held by each enterprise had to be met, and a further 6.5 per cent return on capital was incorporated into the price calculations. This rate of return was differentiated by branch, and actually turned out to be higher than planned in 1968, being about 9 per cent, reflecting the inherent difficulty of properly estimating the costs of production which formed a major part of the pricing calculations. Subsequent experience with price revisions confirms that enterprises usually succeed in overestimating their costs, and hence have higher than the planned level of income in the year following a revision.

In principle price calculations should be based on products rather than enterprises, but in the Hungarian case there was rarely any conflict between the two since production is so highly concentrated; when the same product was produced by more than one enterprise a single price would be agreed, and special taxes and subsidies would be charged to ensure that low-cost producers could not make excessive profits, or high-cost producers losses. This is one reason for item (4) in the list of regulators above, on which we shall have more to say in a moment.

Given Hungary's desire to improve its trading efficiency, the prices of imports and exports also had to be allowed for in the price calculations. Many of the country's economists and planners believed that a substantial part of the existing trade was uneconomic, and that over time the pattern and direction of trade should be changed quite drastically; indeed, this was one object of the reform. However, it was accepted that such a change would take a long time to implement, and initially, therefore, the existing trade flows were taken as a basis for the reform calculations. As far as the price calculations were concerned, this meant that actual imports of materials and other inputs were simply assumed to continue, and were priced using the prevailing foreign currency prices and the new exchange rates established as part of the reform package.

Of course, it was not enough just to fix a new set of prices, because conditions would soon change – import prices would vary, productivity would change, new products would be developed, and so on – and adjustments would be required. Accordingly, the reform also included a set of rules for making such adjustments which were much less restrictive than the very centralised Soviet approach to price-fixing. These rules represented a compromise between the understandable desire of the planners to restrain inflationary pressures, while introducing the kind of flexibility into the price system required for efficient resource allocation. Products were divided into three categories, with free, limited and fixed prices respectively. Prices for products in the last category could only be changed by the price office, while free prices could be revised by the enterprises themselves subject only to some general guidelines; limited prices formed an intermediate category. A similar division of prices was also introduced for consumer prices, though these were not substantially changed, except to the small extent required to allow some simplification in the system of turnover tax. Typically, raw materials and basic intermediate products used by many other sectors (for example, electricity) tended to have fixed prices, as did essential consumer goods like bread; but prices involved in over a third of transactions were officially free in 1968, a proportion expected to rise over time. In the event the proportion did not rise much, and in the 1970s price control once more became more restrictive.

Let us now turn to consider the taxation of enterprise income, in many ways among the more fundamental parts of the reform. Aside from the wage tax and capital charges already mentioned, profits remaining after these payments have been made are subject to further taxation, the amount payable depending on the contributions made to the main enterprise funds. There is a small reserve fund held by each enterprise, but the two most important funds are the sharing fund — corresponding to the incentive fund in the Soviet Union — and the development fund. The former is the source of finance both for wage increases and bonus payments, while the latter is one of the sources of finance for enterprise investment, the others being various forms of credit and grant. The tax system introduced in 1968 specified exactly how profits should be apportioned into contributions to the two funds — perhaps because the managers were not initially trusted to make acceptable decisions — and then provided for a proportional tax at a rate of 70 per cent on the development-fund part of profits, and a steeply progressive tax on contributions to the sharing fund. Part of the enterprise's depreciation allowance was also added to its development fund. Since 1976 the arrangements have been somewhat simpler, with a general rate of taxation on total profits and virtually no restrictions on the division into the two funds.

The formation of the sharing fund gives enterprise managers an incentive to seek increases in the profits earned by their enterprise, since this gives them the possibility of higher incomes. Unlike the traditional centralised model there are no upper limits to the fund, nor is there the old problem that good performance one year will be rewarded by a much more demanding plan the next — the so-called 'ratchet' principle of planning. But there are still some countervailing factors which make the new incentive system rather less powerful in its effects than one might have expected.

First, there is a sharply progressive tax on wage increases which is designed to implement the central government's wage policy at enterprise level. Each year part of the national plan formulated by the government is a target for wage increases for the year. This is built into the tax system in such a way that enterprises may grant increases to that level, but if they wish to grant bigger rises than the approved percentage then they must pay the tax on wage increases; the tax is payable from the sharing fund and reaches rates of tax of up to 400 per cent! Clearly, therefore, an enterprise needs extremely high profits before it can seriously contemplate offering wage increases to its workers which are far above the central guidelines.

Second, although the payment of bonuses, unlike wage increases, does not involve any commitment to making the same payments in future years, and this is why the use of the sharing fund to pay bonuses is not subject to any further taxation, there are nevertheless some restrictions on the bonuses payable to any particular individual. Workers are not normally permitted to receive more than about 10 per cent of their basic annual wage in the form of bonuses, whereas managers can get up to about 30 per cent, the precise limit depending on the category of the enterprise (i.e. how important it is considered to be in the national economy). Managers can also receive additional bonuses from ministry funds which are not so closely related to current performance of their enterprises, but these, too, are limited; managerial salaries may even be reduced by up to 25 per cent if an enterprise performs badly. Overall, then, there are restrictions on the bonuses payable to any individual — presumably justifiable in terms of income-distributional considerations, important in a society where incomes earned in the socialist sector are not subject to income tax — which must inhibit to some extent the incentive effects of the sharing fund. (Hungary does tax incomes earned in the private sector, and some socialist countries, e.g. Bulgaria, tax all incomes. In the latter, however, the tax is proportional.)

Finally, the link between profits earned by an enterprise and the earnings of its employees has become much weaker since the introduction of the reform. It was originally intended that the less successful enterprises should gradually contract, and that this process should be encouraged by their inability to raise wages — they would therefore lose workers to other firms. However, diverging wage trends between different enterprises turned out to be politically unacceptable, and the whole process of structural change turned out to be much more intractable than had been supposed. When it became clear that enterprises which were not really economic were going to survive for an extended period, something had to be done about the wages they could pay; gradually a system of so-called 'wage preferences' developed which enabled many of the less successful firms to pay at least the wage increases specified in the annual plan.

Another element of the reform with a similar effect was the system of special taxes and subsidies which sought to ensure that enterprises did not make excessive profits or losses; this, too, implies that the profits measured in the enterprise accounts, and affecting wages and bonuses, are not a good measure of profits from a social point of view. The system prevents successful enterprises from gaining much reward for their efforts, though it would be hard to assess the real significance of this.

The foreign-exchange rate established by the reform was determined — roughly — as the average cost of earning a unit of foreign exchange, following lengthy theoretical arguments about the relative merits of alternative methods of calculation. In fact, it was necessary to establish two separate exchange rates because the *forint* — the Hungarian currency — is not convertible; effectively, therefore, Hungary operates with two more or less independent foreign-exchange balances, with convertible currency countries and with the Eastern bloc, respectively. The basic exchange rates in the new system were with the dollar and the rouble, and the reform replaced an extremely complex set of foreign-exchange multipliers, often differentiated by product group, by something more coherent and rational. However, the new system was not without its anomalies, since many trade transactions were either taxed or subsidised; but it should be emphasised that the reform made such distortions explicit instead of hiding them behind an incomprehensible welter of multipliers, and undertook to remove them as time went on. Regrettably, little more has been heard of this praiseworthy objective!

On the special taxes and subsidies on production, we have already made some passing comment, and little needs to be added. We should, however, note that just as for the foreign-trade activities just mentioned many of the initial distortions were introduced in order to leave various production activities with satisfactory levels of profit, the intention being to eliminate the distortions in a phased programme. Such a programme would either force enterprises to reduce costs or oblige them to drop certain lines of production altogether; in the case of taxes reducing them would stimulate the enterprises concerned to expand production.

And the reform did indeed provide for this kind of response by enlarging the sphere of enterprise investment. Several aspects of the 'New Economic Mechanism' contributed to the fairly substantial degree of decentralisation which took place in the area of investment, including the price reform and enterprise fund formation already discussed, but also including the credit system. The reform distinguished between two categories of investment – namely, state investment and enterprise investment; the latter refers to that part of investment on which enterprises are empowered to take decisions about individual projects, and amounts to about half of total investment, or nearer two-thirds of investment in industry. Development funds provide one source of funds for such projects, and so do credits. It was originally intended that enterprise investment proposals would compete for credits, and that the allocation would depend on the profitability promised by the various projects. But this soon gave way to a system whereby credits tended to be pre-allocated to branches and/or ministries on the basis of centrally determined preferences related to the national plan. In addition, it became possible to secure certain forms of subsidy for carrying out the types of investment favoured in the plan, with the result that firms increasingly linked their investment proposals to the plan and became less concerned to produce efficiently for the market. Without going into details it is probably fair to comment that investment is an area in which the reform effected the least amount of long-term change. Consequently, the same inefficiencies and strong tendencies to over-investment which characterise the traditional system still prevail in Hungary.

From the above discussion it is clear that the Hungarian reforms, with all their imperfections, marked an extremely important break with the traditional Soviet model of a planned economy. Since their introduction in 1968 the reforms have undergone a number of changes, mainly in the direction of a partial recentralisation of economic management. A significant early modification of this kind was the decision in 1972 that 'closer supervision' should be exercised over the fifty largest enterprises; it is hard to see exactly what this measure entails or involves, but a rationale for it might be found in the central authorities' fear that they were losing control over the economy. Similarly, and more understandably, the regulations on price control were tightened substantially in 1973. The new mechanism failed to eliminate the tendencies to generate the shortages which plague all the planned economies, and tougher price controls were regarded quite simply as one way of avoiding their inflationary consequences, though without pretending to solve the underlying problem. Indeed, even the nature of the latter is in dispute, with some recent analysis suggesting that shortage is a structural problem rather than a general economy-wide problem (Portes and Winter, 1980).

There is another reason for the trend towards greater centralisation of price control: namely, the increasingly unstable situation on world markets following OPEC's massive increases in the price of oil in late 1973. The impact of this particular increase was somewhat delayed for Hungary, since most Hungarian oil comes from the Soviet Union, and the Soviet oil price did not begin to move up towards the levels ruling in Western markets until January 1975. But other raw-material prices were also rising, and at a much faster rate than the prices of Hungary's exports were going up; over-all the effect was a sharp fall of about 20 per cent in Hungary's terms of trade with the West. These dramatic developments were initially simply absorbed in the state budget; imports were subsidised heavily to protect domestic production. However, such an expensive policy could not go on, so from 1975 a series of major price revisions was organised by means of which the new material costs were gradually incorporated into the system of producer prices. The consumer, unlike in the West, to a large extent continued to be shielded from these developments in world markets. During the period of adjustment to the new world market conditions import restrictions became more severe; these restrictions have continued through the 1970s as Western depression or sluggish growth has presented Hungarian exporters with increasing difficulties.

While the rather half-hearted and partial reforms introduced in the Soviet Union have hardly had any effect at all on the way in which planning is conducted, we might expect to find some more significant effects in Hungary. One such effect has already been emphasised, of course, namely the abandonment of the traditional instrument of annual planning − quantitative instructions directed to each individual enterprise. Perhaps surprisingly, planning at national level was not greatly affected by this; central balances and plan calculations went on much as before, though arrangements for plan implementation had to be revised. Consequently, the plans, particularly the annual plans, comprised the following elements:

(1) Central economic balances.

(2) Information on progress to be achieved with various types of state investment project; a list of major projects to be completed or started.

(3) Revisions to the economic regulators, required to fulfil the plan.

Item (3) is the new one, and replaces the earlier instructions. It was originally intended that the reform should develop towards regulators of general applicability − for example, uniform tax schedules for enterprises, and an increasingly competitive allocation of credit − and gradually abandon the differentiation of regulators, for example the various special taxes and subsidies, introduced at the start. But the trend has been exactly the reverse of this, with an increasing tendency to provide each enterprise with its own individual financial conditions through further differentiation of the regulators. Regulation is still indirect, but it would be hard to describe it as parametric: enterprises no longer take their decisions on the basis of given and fairly stable regulators but frequently enter into negotiations about what the regulators should be. Such developments have been widely discussed and criticised in Hungary, and may even be reversed to some extent if the next five-year plan reasserts some of the original reform principles. In the meantime we may conclude by emphasising once more that the Hungarian reforms have given enterprises an extremely valuable degree of flexibility in their production decisions, the benefits of which much outweigh many of the specific inefficiencies which are still so easy to point out.

3.3 The development of horizontal links

While the details of the two approaches to economic reform which have just been surveyed are very different, there are some similarities — at least in intentions, if not so markedly in actual achievements — which are sufficiently important to warrant separate treatment. The first of these, the development of horizontal links, is the subject of this section, while the second, concerned with incentives, is examined in section 3.4.

It is possible to consider economic reform as a means of modifying the information flows which are involved in the process of economic management. To put the matter simply to begin with we may suggest, for example, that reforms of the Hungarian type essentially replace information flows which are predominantly vertical (within the planning hierarchy) with horizontal flows (within markets, between customers and suppliers). While not totally misleading, such a view ignores some important aspects of the role played by information flows in the economy, including:

(1) All economies contain both vertical and horizontal information flows.

(2) The content of information flows as well as their direction is important.

(3) There are serious problems of aggregation, approximation and estimation.

(4) Certain types of information may simply be impossible to transmit in any meaningful form at all.

(5) Information flows are never independent of the incentive system.

Let us begin by commenting on the traditional Soviet model of a planned economy from an informational point of view. Most descriptions of the functioning of this system, including our own in the previous chapter, tend to emphasise the vertical flows of information within the planning hierarchy: control figures are prepared by the central planning office, broken down into targets for individual ministries and thence disaggregated further to targets for individual enterprises. The enterprises then respond by making alternative proposals, suggesting alterations to the initial plan, which are passed up the planning hierarchy and eventually result in the plan for the coming period; this, too has to be broken down to enterprise level before it can be implemented. Moreover, the control figures which initiated the whole process would themselves result from enterprise reports on plan fulfilment in the previous period, in addition to various characteristics of the macroeconomic environment not reflected in these reports —

for example, demographic trends, or developments in the balance between income and expenditure in the state budget, and so on.

But it would be a mistake to deduce from all this that information flows are all vertical — for although they specify many details of enterprise activity, plans are unable to specify (or even identify) the individual transactions in which any particular enterprise will be involved in the course of a plan period. Such transactions are constrained to be consistent with the plan in aggregate, but considered separately they are only constrained by the general procedures and legal arrangements to do with contracts between buyer and seller. Establishing these contracts involves considerable horizontal communication between the agents concerned and is absolutely crucial for plan implementation. Perhaps we can make this point more concretely if we list the plan indicators which a typical Soviet firm would receive in its annual plan, and then consider how the plan might be realised.

After the simplifications introduced by the 1965 reforms the following nine indicators were compulsory for each enterprise: value of sales, output composition (the assortment plan), total profits, profitability (i.e. the rate of return on capital), wages fund, contributions and receipts from the state budget, centralised part of investment, plan for innovations, plan for material supplies. Typically, the payment of bonuses was to be contingent on fulfilling the plan targets in all these areas, with the actual amount of bonus depending only on sales and profits (or profitability) — but we shall discuss bonuses in somewhat more detail in the next section. For present purposes the point to note is that this list of indicators, although quite extensive, does not actually constrain enterprise activities to the extent that one might expect.

This is for two principal reasons: namely, errors in plan formulation, and the aggregate nature of plan targets. From the discussion in the last chapter it is apparent that the process of plan formulation is extremely complex, involving substantial communication between the interested parties and a series of successive adjustments to the initial plan in order to secure the satisfaction of the various economic balances. Because of time constraints, among other things, the adjustments are inevitably imperfect and incomplete, and the process of breaking down the plan to enterprise level is very likely to introduce further errors. In addition, enterprises are frequently asked to undertake additional tasks, or accept other changes in their plan, in the course of the plan year, and such changes are unlikely to be reflected fully in the plans of all the other enterprises which will be affected. The result is that enterprise plans are often infeasible right from the start, or become so as a consequence of the subsequent amendments. This means that it is simply impossible to demand that enterprises fulfil their plans in respect of all the indicators specified in them, and the central planners often have to accept partial fulfilment. Enterprises themselves are well aware of the situation, which gives them a degree of latitude in deciding which indicators they will choose to fulfil.

The compulsory plan indicators seem to cover all important aspects of enterprise activity, yet even if the plan as a whole is feasible the enterprise retains considerable flexibility because of the aggregate nature of most targets. For example, the output-composition indicator is most unlikely to specify the output of each product of the enterprise; indeed, it would be very unusual for the central planners to have a complete list of the products which any given enterprise could produce. Instead, the indicators relating to output composition would give targets for a few of the major products, or certain product groups within the enterprise's production profile; thus for a clothing enterprise output values of children's clothing, ladies' clothing and men's clothing might be specified, with few if any details within these broad categories. Similarly, the material supply plan may indicate that an engineering works is to provide some steel castings to another firm making washing-machines; the quantity of such castings may well be given in tonnes, but the precise details would hardly ever be specified in the plan.

In the traditional Soviet-type economy, therefore, the role of horizontal links between enterprises is to fill in the details left open when the plan was formulated, and often to accommodate or correct errors in the original plan. The clothing enterprise mentioned above would conclude contracts with various retail outlets, or with sales departments within its own ministry, in which designs, types, sizes, delivery dates, and so on, would be agreed; of course, under conditions of shortage the buyers may not have as much say in these matters as they would wish. The engineering firm would enter into a contract with the washing-machine firm to supply castings of a particular quality, design and size, and at specified delivery dates. In principle customers can always refuse to accept defective or poor-quality goods, but with the initial plan being fairly taut, as seems to be the usual situation in the Soviet Union, shortages may not be uncommon and the customers may have little choice but to take what is offered. Moreover, the customer may not be permitted to shop around and seek alternative suppliers. Thus formal contracts can turn out to be relatively worthless under such conditions. In addition, any particular contract can be superseded at the whim of the administrative authorities to which the enterprise happens to be subject: for example, they can demand additional plan tasks which have priority over any contracts which the enterprise might already have made; or they can simply order the enterprise to supply its output to another customer. Generally speaking, Soviet law does not provide for much compensation to be paid to enterprises treated in this way, and there seem to be no formal constraints on what must appear to the enterprises concerned to be fairly arbitrary administrative interventions. Thus horizontal links are essential to plan fulfilment in the Soviet Union, but enterprises are never permitted to forget that their vertical relationships within the planning hierarchy almost always take priority in cases of conflict. It is against this background that more radical reform proposals have favoured a substantial extension of the role of horizontal links in economic management, both in the Soviet Union and in Hungary.

Thus the development of horizontal links is considered to bring two kinds of benefit: namely, a better use of the information available at enterprise level, and in principle a clarification of the enterprise's legal status. As already noted, much of the information passing up the planning hierarchy is subject to a considerable degree of aggregation and approximation before it becomes part of one of the material balances worked out at the centre. Errors inevitably creep into the central calculations, and the information is in any case unlikely to be complete; it is extremely hard to see how an enterprise can inform the centre about anything except its current activities, or some variants close to that pattern of production. Yet the enterprise itself may be aware of a much wider range of possibilities open to it, if only it had the opportunity to make an independent choice. These possibilities may involve the production of new goods, improvements in the organisation of existing production processes, more efficient uses of transport or storage space, and so on. Yet under the traditional Soviet approach to planning they may not come to the notice of the planners because the information which would have to be transmitted up the hierarchy would be so complex, and in any case the amendments required to the central plans would be more than usually difficult to compute. Thus even rather efficient reorganisations of enterprise production profiles and input requirements are likely to be introduced into the centralised system only after some considerable lag.

Let us now turn to the legal position of the enterprise. (Interesting comments on this question are provided by Höhmann *et al.* (1975, ch. 10) and in Eörsi and Harmathy (1971).) We can approach this by considering how a greater role for horizontal links affects the way in which enterprises operate. The most obvious point is that under such conditions enterprises would base their production decisions to a much greater extent on their own knowledge of their production possibilities and information obtained through links with other firms rather than on information passed down the planning hierarchy. Naturally, the nature of the information used by any particular firm would also be different: for example, it would include market-type information — estimates of demand, orders received, the market situation for substitutes and complements, and so on. Moreover, it is increasingly accepted that firms themselves are in much the best position to make effective use of all this detailed information, while central planners could scarcely use it all. But when firms do use such information their decisions about production would be implemented through a series of contracts with suppliers and customers — presumably the firms are free to choose who their partners would be, perhaps including the right to seek export sales when prices are favourable, or to import certain materials.

Clearly, therefore, firms whould have the right to make all these contracts, which implies some restrictions on the rights of central authorities to intervene in enterprise activity. Logically, the centre should give up all its powers of intervention, for the attempt to encourage the development of horizontal links implies acceptance of the centre's inability to control satisfactorily the details of each enterprise's production activity. And if enterprises are to make good use of alternative kinds of information, they should have a secure legal basis for doing so, with an assurance that arbitrary central interventions would not be permitted.

This does not amount to a complete ban on central interventions, but would entail, for example, that any such intervention which proved unprofitable for the enterprises concerned would be fully compensated, as provided by the Hungarian enterprise statute introduced with the 1968 reforms.

The promotion of horizontal links can now be seen to be quite a radical policy. In the Soviet Union, however, it has been interpreted somewhat more restrictively, implying only that enterprises gain more freedom to engage in wholesale trade. This means that the material supply system is being partially decentralised, and undoubtedly does give many enterprises a welcome flexibility in securing their own supplies without using the bureaucratic supply system for everything. But the central plan broken down to enterprise level still remains the dominant fact of enterprise life, and the centre shows no sign of abrogating any of its rights to intervene; accordingly, the new flexibility is likely to bring fairly limited benefits, since it is really just another attempt to 'patch up' the centralised system and avoid more fundamental change.

In its more radical interpretation the Hungarian type of approach to horizontal links has some important implications for the conduct of economic policy by the central authorities. We have already noted that they should abstain from the interventions which characterise the centralised model; instead, their economic policy should become much more macroeconomic in character. By this we mean that the centre should see its role as having two major dimensions. In the first the centre's task is to determine the environment within which enterprises operate — in the Hungarian terminology this involves fixing the economic regulators, the various tax rates, and so on, which affect enterprise opportunities and choices. The second part of the centre's role requires it to maintain macroeconomic equilibrium — that is, over-all balance in the labour market, goods markets, balance of payments, and so on. Of course, this was always seen as among the tasks of the central authorities, but the means employed would no longer be central instructions to each individual enterprise. Instead, the manipulation of prices, wages, taxes and subsidies would have to suffice, perhaps with the retention of central control over much of investment, as in Hungary.

To summarise this section, then, we may note that the development of so-called 'horizontal' links has been favoured by reformers both in Hungary and in the Soviet Union. But while the former has adopted a radical interpretation of the concept, involving a significant reduction in central interventions in the day-to-day conduct of enterprise affairs, the latter has taken an extremely cautious view. Even Hungary, however, with its increasingly differentiated economic regulators, has tended to restore some of the powers which allow the central authorities to intervene in production to a greater extent than was originally intended in 1968 — although it is possible that the earlier decentralising tendencies will be reinforced by revisions to the regulator system introduced in 1980. In any case it is always necessary, if the various economic agents are to use, develop and expand on the possibilities offered by horizontal links, for the links to be supplemented by an appropriate incentive system. To this we now turn, in the concluding section of the chapter.

3.4 The problem of incentives in planning

In all the economic systems discussed in this book incentives play an important role; the object of this section is to introduce some basic ideas about these incentives, leaving more detailed analysis to Chapter 9. Now, when students first begin to read about, say, the Soviet economy, they frequently find an extremely negative view of incentives. For example, there might be some discussion of bonuses for workers and managers, immediately followed by a long list of the 'distortions' which supposedly result from their application – poor-quality output, lack of interest in new products and innovation, inefficient use of inputs, lack of interest in the consumer, and so on. Aside from these microeconomic problems there are also the supposed effects of the bonus system on planning – the practice of 'storming', seeking a low plan, and the ratchet principle (also called planning from the achieved level). One wonders how the Soviet economy could continue to function reasonably effectively in the face of all these defects, and also why the planners tolerate them all if they could be put right merely by some modification of the incentive system; but the situation is more complex than that, as we shall see.

An incentive system is basically a set of rules which specify how the rewards received by certain economic agents are to be related to some measures of performance. Such a general definition implies that different systems may be distinguished in terms of several distinct characteristics, notably the following (see Zielinski, 1973; chs 5 and 6):

(1) Which agents receive the rewards.
(2) How large the rewards may be.
(3) How the rewards are related to the performance indicators.
(4) What measures of performance are used.

While there has been little debate on (1) in Eastern Europe, with a fairly general acceptance that all the employees of productive enterprises should get something, the issues raised by (2) have proved to be more contentious. Thus in recent years there has been widespread discussion both of the relative size of the bonus payments which should be paid to different employees in an enterprise, and of the maximum which any particular manager should be permitted to receive. In addition, points (3) and (4) have attracted considerable attention in connection with discussions of economic reform, both in the Soviet Union and Hungary (and elsewhere, of course, but we restrict attention to these two countries in this section).

In the traditional Soviet model the main performance indicator which affected bonuses (such indicators are often called 'success' indicators) was usually some measure of gross output, though the payment of bonuses was also supposed to be contingent on plan fulfilment in respect of all the other 'compulsory' indicators.

The measurement of gross output is not straightforward; in a typical multi-product enterprise it requires, first of all, the use of prices to aggregate outputs of different products. Moreover, since the production period in many enterprises can be quite lengthy, accounting rules have to be specified to include work-in-progress in the gross output total arrived at. Finally, special rules may be needed to cover such things as sub-contracting, the introduction of new products and control over quality. These measurement problems are not peculiar to this particular indicator, and are, indeed, considerably more serious for the more synthetic indicators such as profit, which may be preferable on theoretical grounds.

Once gross output was measured the amount of bonus actually paid out depended on the relation between achievement and plan. If the plan was under-fulfilled, even by a tiny percentage, no bonuses would be paid; plan fulfilment then secured a substantial bonus — sometimes referred to as the thirteenth month's wages, though it would often be much lower than a month's wages for production workers — and overfulfilment gave rise to additional bonuses. The principle was the same in all industries, though the amounts payable varied quite a lot, with the highest bonuses usually going to managers in the high-priority industries — i.e. heavy industry.

Operating with such a bonus function it is not too surprising that enterprises should practise 'storming'; this involves peaks in production activity towards the end of a plan or bonus payment period, usually a quarter or a year. These peaks arise because 99.9 per cent plan fulfilment secures no bonus at all, while 100 per cent fulfilment earns substantial rewards. Thus, if plan fulfilment is not already assured a few weeks from the end of the relevant period, the marginal value of additional effort rises sharply. However, other factors also contribute to the phenomenon of storming, in particular the position in regard to material supplies, and the tautness of the initial plan, so that modifying the bonus functions alone may not effect much change. Some properties of alternative bonus functions are examined in the fuller discussion of chapter 9.

The specification of a bonus function really amounts to a decision on point (3) mentioned at the start of this section. However, economic reforms have also been associated with changes in the success indicators themselves, which is point (4). Thus the Soviet reforms brought about a shift from exclusive reliance on the gross output indicator, which was widely criticised for its failure to make enterprises cost-conscious or interested in sales, to a combination of sales and profit-ability indicators intended to remedy both these deficiencies, and the 1979 decree mentioned above went further by providing for a net output indicator. The Hungarian reforms of 1968 had already been preceded by moves away from the gross output indicator, and the reforms merely confirmed the trend by establishing a measure of profits as the only success indicator. But while the Soviet scheme retained a bonus function in which payments depended on performance in relation to the plan, the Hungarian one went a step further in making payments dependent only on actual performance.

This distinction between the Soviet and Hungarian systems has some important economic effects. First, Soviet enterprises still have some incentive to understate their true capacities in the process of plan formulation, in order to secure an 'easy' plan. Over a period this tendency is no doubt constrained by the planners' response to overfulfilment, namely to demand a higher plan in the next period; this is the so-called 'ratchet' principle of planning, and it is a natural result of the planners' inability to estimate reliably the true capacities of the enterprises they are trying to control. Under such circumstances achieved performance is probably the best available measure of capacity.

Second, it is not clear that the use of the sales indicator has had important economic effects. In principle it should make enterprises concerned about their markets, and perhaps more interested in new products, but there are some countervailing factors. Thus a significant part of output is bought by selling agencies of the same ministry as the enterprise producing it; since ministry bonuses depend on the success of their enterprises, they have an obvious interest in buying the output whether or not the economy still requires it. Also, there is the same problem of treating work-in-progress as arose with the output indicator. Moreover, plans continue to be fairly taut at national level, and this point applies to Hungary as well to some extent, so that many enterprises are trying to sell under conditions of continuing excess demand and experience little difficulty in selling more or less whatever they produce.

Third, the Hungarian bonuses based on actual performance involve an important shift in the locus of responsibility as compared with the Soviet system, for in the latter if some enterprise fails to fulfil its plan the managers may be criticised, but they in turn would be quite likely to blame the central planners for their problems — for giving them an 'unrealistic' plan, for failing to ensure the proper deliveries of materials, and for sundry other reasons. Such criticism is unlikely to be completely unfounded, but it does have the unfortunate effect of diverting attention away from the enterprise itself. In contrast, the Hungarian approach makes it much harder for managers to blame the system, for if they object to any particular tax rate the centre can easily point to other enterprises which are managing much better under the same conditions. Hence managers are virtually forced to examine their own enterprise's production profile and cost structure in an attempt to improve its performance and to secure higher bonuses. While undoubtedly a great gain from the Hungarian reforms, one should not overrate its significance at this stage, for most of the managers are the same people as before the reform, and the increasing differentiation in the system of economic regulators is making it easier for managers to request — and get — special tax treatment in order to meet their own 'special' circumstances, a situation facilitated by the high concentration of Hungarian industry.

Some additional general issues arise from the Hungarian and Soviet experience of economic reform. These concern the problem of designing incentives to stimulate satisfactory long-run performance, the problem of distinguishing between the effects of enterprises' own efforts and the results of external factors, and the question of conflicting objectives in the design of incentive systems. Long-run performance is an issue which has exercised reformers everywhere; the basic idea seems simple enough but little progress has been made in identifying solutions. The success indicators employed in Eastern Europe are all based on measures of short-run performance, covering at most a single year; consequently, they tend to stimulate good performance as measured by these indicators. As a result managerial attention is diverted from those aspects of an enterprise's activity which might yield longer-term benefits, such as research and development, market research, marketing studies and campaigns, major innovations, development of exports, and so on. This is why such activities are often specified in enterprise plans in the Soviet Union, or stimulated by special subsidies or credits in Hungary. Hungary recently decided to supplement these measures to encourage good long-run performance with a new kind of success indicator: this is the so-called *complex evaluation*, whereby ministries will evaluate those aspects of enterprise activity not well reflected in the standard profit indicator. Managers judged to be successful after such an evaluation are to receive additional bonuses from special ministry funds. Since precise details of this scheme have not been published, it is hard to assess how well it might work. Apart from the development of new indicators, one might also expect that long-run performance would be stimulated simply by the ambition of individual managers seeking promotion – perhaps within a given enterprise, to a larger one with correspondingly higher pay, to establish a new one, or to a senior position within a ministry. Just as in Western firms, ambition can be an important factor in motivating managers, but its effectiveness depends on the available career structure. At least in Hungary, however, it seems that the turnover of personnel within the upper echelons of the management structure has been so low in recent years as to provide very little incentive to anyone (see Granick, 1975, ch. 10).

Since incentives are designed to reward an enterprise's performance, it would appear to be important to isolate the enterprise's own contribution from that of the various external events which may affect it. Such has certainly been the view of Eastern European planners until relatively recently, and many would still hold that view. It has entailed, for example, the use of constant prices in measuring enterprise performance; in particular, enterprises have been strictly isolated from the effects of price changes in world markets, whether favourable or unfavourable. Effectively, therefore, enterprises have been rewarded for producing efficiently in response to out-of-date prices! It is at least arguable that it would be more satisfactory for enterprises to be exposed more quickly to the impact of changed conditions to which they will one day have to adjust anyway. Along similar lines one may question the common practice of imposing special taxes on very successful enterprises, or paying large subsidies to those in difficulty, since this seems to inhibit the kind of adjustment which would be needed – expansion of production in the former case, probably some contraction in the latter. This seems to be a field in which reforms have led to the adoption of apparently contradictory positions. On the one hand, there is much public discussion of the need for and importance of greater enterprise independence, often allowing for substantial decentralisation of investment decisions; on the other hand, formal decentralisation is undermined by the lack of institutional change which is reflected in the special taxes and subsidies just mentioned, since these enable the centre to retain some control over enterprise decisions. In this context arguments about isolating the enterprise's own contribution are really arguments about the desirability of maintaining such central control.

Finally, we come to the objectives which incentive systems are designed to meet. As we have seen, much of the emphasis in the debates on incentives concerns one particular objective: namely, the promotion of economic efficiency. Thus the proposed schemes are seeking answers to the following kinds of question. How can we encourage enterprises to reduce costs of production? How can we stimulate efficient exports? How can a better adaptation of supply to meet the needs of consumers be secured? What is the best way of stimulating effective innovations? And so on. These are undoubtedly very important questions, but when one examines incentive systems in existence one does not find such a single-minded concern for economic efficiency. We have already mentioned at various points the planners' desire to maintain macroeconomic balance, and if this requirement is thought to be undermined by local (i.e. enterprise-level) efforts to raise efficiency, then intervention is certain; in practice the planners are only willing to accept fairly modest rates of change in enterprise production activities, and even in Hungary incentives are likely to be 'adjusted' to make that happen. Distribution is another issue which (quite understandably) sets a constraint on the pursuit of efficiency. The issue arises in the form of concern over diverging trends in wage and bonus payments between enterprises in different branches of the economy. For example, for a short period the economic regulators in Hungary related permitted wage increases to a measure of productivity increases which was based on performance of each individual enterprise; hence more successful enterprises could and did offer higher wage increases. Such divergences soon became politically unacceptable, and the present system now relates wage increases to a national norm specified at the start of each year; for increases in excess of this there is a steeply progressive tax on wage increases, just as before. Another aspect of this concern with distribution arose at the start of the Hungarian reforms. Under the initial proposals the upper limits on bonus payments allowed production workers to receive up to 15 per cent of the basic wage in the form of a bonus but allowed managers to get up to 80 per cent. After vigorous protests from the normally rather inactive trade unions the maximum managerial bonus was cut to 25 per cent of the basic salary; these basic salaries were raised, but managers can lose up to 25 per cent of them if their enterprise performs badly, while production workers do not face the same risks.

Thus incentive systems in practice attempt to achieve a number of rather distinct objectives, of which efficiency is only one. Indeed, other objectives often come to the fore because there is widespread mistrust of the price system as a source of reliable information for enterprises to use as guides in the search for efficiency. In addition, the retention by the central authorities of fundamental powers over the enterprise, even in Hungary — thus ministries can hire and fire the managers, decide whether an enterprise should expand or contract or be merged with some other unit, and decide whether to establish new enterprises — means that informal, often personal, relationships within the planning hierarchy continue to be an important component of any explanation of enterprise behaviour in the planned economies.

4 INDICATIVE PLANNING IN FRANCE

In this chapter we consider a form of economic planning adopted in an environment entirely different from that described in the previous two chapters. Since the war the French economy, although it has a large public sector, has been a predominantly private-enterprise economy; it has enjoyed relatively high growth rates of gross domestic product; and it has also had a system of economic planning which has now operated, if in different forms and with different objectives, for more than thirty years. The combination of these last two facts has led many economists to wonder how much of France's growth can be attributed to the French system of planning. We consider this question in the final section of this chapter. First however, as in Chapter 2, we give accounts of how economic plans are constructed in France, and how they are implemented.

4.1 Constructing the indicative plan

France's first post-war plan was compiled under the direction of the first Planning Commissioner, Jean Monnet. It originally covered the years 1947–50 but was subsequently extended to 1953. The plan provided for recovery from the destruction and dislocation of war, and was intended to prevent the French economy from relapsing into the continuous stagnation of the 1930s. By the start of the seventh French plan, in 1976, the economy had grown fivefold since 1946, France had been a member of the European Economic Community for nearly two decades, and her industry had undergone a transition from being highly protected to being open to international competition. In the course of those thirty years the organisational framework of planning had changed slightly, the stated aims of the plan and its supposed manner of implementation had altered considerably and the techniques of plan construction had become enormously more sophisticated. However, these changes of emphasis and technique should not blind us to important continuities in the planning process.

One continuing feature is the central role of the Planning Commission and the importance of the Commissioner. The Planning Commission is a relatively small organisation, staffed by as few as sixty senior civil servants, many of them graduates of the elite training schools for government officials. The staff are recruited from a wide range of organisations. The Commission was originally subordinated to the President of the Council, and then to the Ministry of Finance (the relationship between the Commission, concerned with medium-term planning, and the Finance Ministry, which makes short-term macroeconomic policy is an important one which is discussed below). Since 1962 the Commission has reported to the Prime Minister, except that from 1967 to 1972 it was subordinate to a deputy minister in the Prime Minister's office. In 1974 a Central Planning Council was created, headed by the President, with the Planning Commissioner and major economic ministers as members. The Council meets monthly to guide the Commission in plan formation and to supervise implementation.

The Commission has three functions: to compile the plan, to oversee its execution, and to advise the government on economic matters in general. The small size of the Commission ensures that the functions which it exercises are largely co-ordinating or advisory. In particular, it does not carry out large planning studies itself, but commissions them from other organisations, and makes extensive use of INSEE, the official government statistical institute, and the forecasting directorate in the Ministry of Finance. This role corresponds with the general aims and methods of French planning. The greater part of the economy is outside the control of the government, which must implement its policies, not by administrative instruction, as it does in the traditional centrally planned economy, but by persuasion and by creating appropriate incentives for the private sector. Even within the public sector the Planning Commission has to operate less by instruction than by persuasion, encouraging other government ministries to fall in with the plan. The role of the national economic plan is somehow to concert the aims and plans of the independent organisations making up the economy. The Commission's role, which is to make this possible, is best fulfilled by involving these organisations in compiling the detailed plans for subsequent integration into a national plan. This is achieved by forming commissions covering the major sectors or functions of the economy, consisting of representatives of the interest groups involved and usually staffed by Commission officials. Because of its role as an intermediary between the government and other economic agents, the Commission has tried to maintain some degree of independence from the government machine.

It is conventional to break down the planning process into four stages: analysis, dialogue, formulation of the plan, and implementation. Each plan has been characterised by a different emphasis or major objective, in keeping with the stage of development of the economy, and this emphasis has emerged partly as a result of government policy, and partly as a result of interaction between the parties involved in the planning dialogue. The main themes of the first six plans are well summarised by Siebel (1975, pp. 155–9), but for a more complete account see Ullmo (1974, pp. 5–22). The first plan (1947–53) was dominated by reconstruction; the second (1954–7) and third (1958–61) plans continued that theme and also tried to take account of the implications of France's membership of the European Economic Community, particularly the need to make industry more competitive; the fourth plan (1962–5) stressed social and regional aspects of planning (although regional planning in general has received progressively greater importance since the fourth plan, for reasons of space we do not examine this aspect in detail here); the fifth plan (1966–70) was characterised by a much greater use of monetary indices in planning, intended by the planners to obtain a closer control over wages and prices; the sixth plan (1971–5) represented a reversion to the basic goal of increasing industrial output; while the seventh plan (1976–80) was intended to allow the economy to make a recovery in the unfavourable climate created by the world recessions of the 1970s.

While the objectives of the plans have changed, major features of their compilation have been fairly consistent, change being confined principally to the tools of planning rather than basic procedures. We illustrate the process principally with reference to the sixth plan, which represented an important milestone in planning practice. Preparation of the more recent seventh plan followed the same sequence of procedures but at an accelerated pace (see Carassus, 1978, p. 63).

In the early years of the fifth plan the Planning Commission organised a number of important inter-ministerial study groups on long-term problems connected with the labour market, industrial policy and the public sector (see below), but the preliminary phase of preparation for the sixth plan really began in 1968. This took the form of a projection of the economy in 1975, based on the extrapolation of past trends. The projection was made using a large econometric model developed by a group headed by R. Courbis, known as the *Fifi* (or physical and financial) model. The structure of Fifi and of other planning models is discussed at greater length in Chapter 10 below (see also Liggins, 1975). Here we note only that Fifi is a 2,000-equation model with seven sectors, and that one of its major features is the division of the economy into a 'protected' sector of non-tradeables and an exposed sector in which prices are international prices. The original projection revealed certain unsatisfactory tendencies, and the model was also run with a number of illustrative policy changes intended to overcome the deficiencies in the economy revealed by the original projection. Then, as a consequence of the major disruptions of May 1968 in France, new projections had to be prepared by the Commission. This analysis stage was completed by the autumn of 1969.

The second stage of dialogue or *concertation* embodies the major innovation in French planning. The data prepared by the Commission are passed on to a number of commissions concerned either with sectors of the economy or with major general aspects of economic activity. Here the organisations which are intended to be the willing executants of the plan take part in its compilation. The commissions are composed of representatives of employers and unions, of independent experts and of planning officials or administrators, who often have the function of compiling the report. The proportions in which the interest groups are represented are not fixed and attempts have been made to keep the membership within reasonable bounds, though these have not always been successful. The intention is that each commission, with its special knowledge of one sector or aspect of the economy, should agree detailed targets which would overcome the problems revealed by the original 'policies-unchanged' projection. These targets would then be resubmitted to the Planning Commission for final integration into a consistent and coherent aggregate plan.

Since the dialogue stage plays such an important role in the ideology of planning, it is worth describing the operations of the commissions in more detail. The commissions have operated for as long as the planning system itself, and were instituted by the first Planning Commissioner, Jean Monnet, to prepare sectoral plans for the introduction of modern production techniques, and to provide the data necessary to co-ordinate the development of the economy. Subsequently the number of persons involved grew steadily (the commissions for the sixth plan involved six times as many people as did those for the first plan). Prior to the sixth plan a distinction was made between 'vertical' commissions, concerned with sectors, and 'horizontal' commissions, concerned with general functions such as finance. (The sixth plan introduced, and the seventh plan retained, a further confusing distinction between commissions and committees, the latter being smaller than the former, and with similar but usually more limited terms of reference.) Members of the commissions are formally appointed by the Prime Minister but the commissions have the power to form their own working groups, appointing anyone they wish.

The objective of the commissions was set out in the first plan:

> Since the execution of the plan will require the collaboration of everyone the participation in its elaboration of all active elements in the nation is indispensable. It is for this reason that the method of work proposed combines for each sector the responsible official organisation, the most highly qualified experts and representatives of professional organisations (workers, managers and owners). It is only in this way that problems will be solved by a continuous exchange of ideas between the government and the country within a *concerted* economy, and not an economy controlled bureaucratically or corporately (quoted in Atreize, 1971, p. 55).

According to Ullmo (1975, p. 40), 'for a long time one of the planners' objectives (through the commissions) was to establish a consensus. Some even hoped that the work of the commissions could give rise to a sort of contract or rather quasi-contract.' Such hopes proved unrealistic, however, and this is scarcely surprising. The commissions contain representatives of groups with conflicting interests. Employers, who are normally represented by the members of trade associations and large firms, have had a rather ambivalent attitude towards planning, and in the commissions have opposed intervention or even inquiry into their own management strategies (see also the attack made in 1967 by the CNPF, the French employers' organisation, on the plan's potential role in the economy (Ullmo, 1974, pp. 294–6)). Instead, employers have tended to interpret plan proposals and government recommendations as instructions, and have sought to gain via the commissions a *quid pro quo* for acceding to them.

However, they have consistently taken part in all stages of the planning process, and in the sixth plan particularly they used the dialogue stage to express their strong preference for a fast 'Japanese-style' rate of growth with emphasis on industry.

Union participation in the dialogue phase has been less consistent. The Communist CGT took no part in the commissions for some time, and all the union organisations have at various times refused to consider themselves bound by the work of the commissions or, as in February 1976, have withdrawn from the process entirely. In these circumstances the search for concensus has, not surprisingly, been unsuccessful. The interests of the groups represented are in fundamental conflict and the final decision, taken by the government, is a strongly political one.

What purposes might the commissions then serve? First, they facilitate the exchange of information; employers and unions are told about the possible development paths for the economy as a whole, and the planners collect information on particular sectors — a function of particular importance in the early days of planning, when statistics were poor. Second, they offer a forum for the articulation (if not the satisfaction) of interest-group demands, though consumers' interests are often under-represented. Third, it is the planners' hope that work in the commissions has an educational impact on those involved which encourages reform. Finally, the horizontal commissions allow new issues to be considered, or old problems to be viewed from a different perspective. We note that the usefulness of these functions, particularly the last three, is rather hard to evaluate.

The output of the vertical commissions is a highly aggregated sectoral growth target which may, but need not, represent the views of the sector as a whole. There can be no presumption, however, that the sectoral plans are mutually consistent in the input—output sense. The third stage of planning, which succeeds the dialogue stage, is an attempt to amend the sectoral programmes in the direction of consistency. This is done by the Planning Commission. Beginning with preparation of the second plan in 1953 input—output tables in constant prices constructed from the national accounts were used for this purpose (for more details on this technique, see pp. 25—8 above). According to Siebel (1975, p. 160) this technique had its hey-day at the time of the fourth and fifth plans in the early 1960s, when the Planning Commissioner Pierre Massé argued that the internal consistency of the plan, a consistency guaranteed by the use of input—output tables, would itself ensure that it would be implemented by creating the appropriate expectations (see Ullmo, 1974, pp. 290—4, for an account of how input—output techniques were used). Ensuring consistency between the sectors involved a further dialogue between the Commission and the commissions, described by a planner as a complicated 'process of discussion, pressure, negotiation and compromise' (quoted in Lutz, 1969, p. 109). Some adjustments might be made by the planners alone. Their views did indeed prevail in the case of any disagreement, so that in some instances in the 1960s the commissions had little impact on their sectors' final targets (McArthur and

Scott, 1969, pp. 424–8). The principal aim of this stage of the planning process was to eliminate physical bottlenecks in production by maintaining consistency between sectors in physical output.

In the 1950s and early 1960s this was a reasonable objective. But the nature of the French economy was changing. As it became more open, opportunities for overcoming bottlenecks by recourse to international trade increased and the need for detailed integrated planning, which was strongly felt in the early post-war period, largely disappeared. As a consequence the emphasis in planning shifted away from the more detailed projections in physical terms towards planning macroeconomic aggregates – a change which coincided with alterations in the method of plan implementation as well. This led to a much greater emphasis on projections of income and expenditure in monetary terms, and hence on wages and prices. At the time of constructing the fourth and fifth plans the physical projections were checked for consistency in respect of investment finance and, as part of the discussion of incomes policy, projections were made of wages and prices.

This greater emphasis on monetary variables culminated in the use for the sixth plan of the Fifi model mentioned above, which specifically integrates the physical and financial sides of the projection. However, like the earlier techniques, the model is used to integrate the reports from the sectoral commissions.

In fact, in the course of preparing the sixth plan use of the new model enabled the Commission to work out three alternative consistent growth projections, with annual rates of growth of 6.5, 6.0 and 5.5 per cent respectively, and to submit them to the government. In the event the government chose essentially the intermediate variant, and in May and June 1970 the French Parliament, in a debate on options for the plan, endorsed the government's choice. The plan itself was enacted in June 1971, six months after its starting date.

Parliamentary discussion of the plan was first introduced in 1965 for the fifth plan, in response to demands that the planning process be made more democratic. Each of the fifth, sixth and seventh plans was first approved by Parliament in outline and then enacted about a year later, but because of the requirement of maintaining internal consistency deputies have found it difficult or impossible to follow through the logic of any alterations which they might favour and the government majority should in any case ensure the plan's passage. In addition, the seventh plan was prepared in some haste, and opposition deputies criticised the lack of time available for discussion. This formal parliamentary approval, however, completes the stages of plan compilation.

4.2 Plan implementation
In the traditional centrally planned economy plans are implemented by administrative instruction. In Hungary, a socialist economy which has undergone a thoroughgoing reform, plans are implemented by a combination of market incentives and financial instruments which tend to be differentiated from enterprise to enterprise. The state, however, by virtue of its ownership of the

means of production, retains extensive reserve powers over the economy which it exercises in various ways. In a mixed economy like France, by contrast, the ability of the authorities to implement the plan is restricted. The state can in principle implement the plan in the public sector (though, as we shall see, this has not always happened), but its powers in the private sector are limited, and in any event the implementation of any medium-term plan, as the successive French plans have been, is subject to unexpected short-term events which upset both the government's macroeconomic policy and the expectations of firms. In this section we examine the procedures for implementing the plan in both the private and the public sectors. We distinguish between the direct influence of the plan and its indirect influence via specific government measures. (This is identical with Lutz's (1969, pp. 24–5) distinction between exogenous instruments and 'the logic of the plan'.)

Pierre Massé, the Planning Commissioner from 1959 to 1965, was responsible for a theory of the execution of indicative plans which had a powerful influence on the formulation of the fourth and fifth plans. Massé's concept is of a plan which complements rather than replaces the market process. He argues that the absence of futures markets imposes on firms an additional uncertainty which can be eliminated by the publication of a consistent projection for the economy. Accordingly he described the plan as a process of 'generalised market research', which carries with it its own implementation mechanism. If a sufficiently large number of agents believe in the plan — and the dialogue stage of plan construction is supposed to ensure that this condition is satisfied — then the plan is automatically implemented (Massé, 1965). (Another possible direct form of implementation, which we do not discuss further, is the use of moral incentives. This method can be illustrated by the suggestion of the French President in 1962 that fulfilment of the plan was a 'burning obligation' for all Frenchmen.)

A full discussion of Massé's view of indicative planning is postponed until Chapter 8. Here we merely list some of the problems associated with it:

(1) The 'market research' is only capable of eliminating some of the uncertainties affecting agents in the medium term. Elimination of others is beyond the power of any agent in the French economy, including the government. Yet a single plan is constructed for each period, rather than a range of alternatives corresponding to different values of the uncontrolled variables. The plan is therefore almost certainly based on false assumptions.

(2) If there are errors in the construction of any part of the plan (as is likely to be the case), they may carry over to all other sectors and destroy the coherence of the plan as a whole.

(3) It is not quite clear how a firm is supposed to react to output targets or projections compiled on an industry basis unless it also known how its market share is going to change. The publication of an industry target, even if it is generally agreed by all firms, cannot offer a guide to action at the firm level, and may even encourage perverse reactions. (This point is elaborated in Lutz (1969, ch. 11).)

(4) Finally, the output projection for any sector embodied in the final version of the plan may not have the support of all, or indeed of any, of the firms in the sector. Moreover, different agents will have different subjective probability distributions over the outcome which cannot be averaged out.

The direct influence of the plan is thus open to serious question on analytical grounds. We should hardly be surprised that the careful study by McArthur and Scott (1969) of the influence of the plan on industry reported that the direct impact was slight, even though their research was carried out in the mid-1960s, the hey-day of the Massé conception of planning. Nor is it surprising that the sixth and seventh plans have adopted a different approach, concentrating more on formulating general principles for medium-term macroeconomic management and control of the public sector, rather than making detailed sectoral forecasts.

The problem here is that short-term developments at the macroeconomic level may encourage policy measures which are in conflict with the objectives of the medium-term plan. This happened notably in 1963, when inflation and a balance-of-payments deficit led to deflationary government policies introduced as a stabilisation programme. The conflict between growth and price stability became increasingly severe in the subsequent years. Massé, the Commissioner, attempted to reconcile the two objectives by means of an incomes policy, and this attempt was one reason for the increased use of targets expressed in monetary terms in the fifth plan. However, no consensus could be established in favour of such a policy, and incomes policies in recent years have been *ad hoc* affairs, divorced from the plan.

The fifth plan, however, did provide for a system of monthly warning signals, which would indicate that the implementation of the plan was in danger and give the authorities the choice of either taking corrective action or effectively abandoning a particular target. The warning signals covered prices, foreign trade, growth of industrial output, investment and unemployment. The problem was that the Ministry of Finance tended to ignore the warning signals and continued to make macroeconomic decisions on a short-term basis (this, of course, destroyed the whole rationale of the 'direct' method of plan implementation). The warning signals flashed regularly throughout the fifth plan but little happened; in any case the events of May 1968 overturned the plan targets.

In constructing the sixth plan more attention was given to modelling short-term macroeconomic policy and integrating it with the medium-term model, and the warning-signal system was replaced by a new series of quarterly indicators and by a mid-plan review carried out in 1973 (Liggins, 1972b). The review found output growth on target but inflation running faster than expected. The last two years of the plan, however, saw the French economy plunged into serious recession, partly as a result of a set of deflationary measures adopted by the Ministry of Finance in 1974. Equally, the implementation of the seventh plan has been characterised by a macroeconomic policy which has not been based on the plan projections. Instead a set of measures worked out by the Prime Minister (the Barre plan) was effectively substituted for the seventh plan, though its success has been fairly limited.

The introduction of warning signals and a mid-plan review might be taken to herald a new approach to implementation which recognises that there are so many uncertainties over a five-year time horizon that what is needed is not a plan but a plan strategy embodying an appropriate response to the realised values of uncontrolled variables which cannot be forecast with certainty (for a discussion of this approach, see Johansen, 1977, pp. 105–24). Such an analysis was incorporated in preparations for the sixth plan, in the course of which scenarios were constructed showing possible reactions to various sets of circumstances (Atreize, 1971, p. 77; Liggins, 1975, pp. 125–8), and the seventh plan document placed emphasis on the need for adaptability in plan execution (VIIe Plan, 1976, pp. 158–60). However, such exercises are of little value unless the planners have a significant influence on short-run macroeconomic policy, and unless the latter takes the plan as a reference point. The experiences of 1963, 1974 and 1976 suggest that the plan plays no such role.

One important difference between plan execution in France on the one hand and in Hungary and the Soviet Union on the other has been the willingness of the French government, particularly in the 1970s, to accept high and persistent unemployment. In framing the seventh plan the government estimated that an additional 1,100,000 jobs would be created by 1980, thus restoring full employment (VIIe Plan, 1976, pp. 74–5, 154). In fact, in the course of the Barre plan unemployment rose from 1976 to 1979 by over one-third. In centrally planned economies, in contrast – both before and after the reforms – priority has been given to the maintenance of full employment even at the cost of efficiency in production. In France, on the other hand, balance-of-payments and inflation targets have generally been given priority over full employment and the attainment of the growth path specified in the plan (Carré *et al.*, 1972, pp. 437–92).

The above remarks refer to plan implementation at the macro level. We have yet to consider whether the plan influences government policy towards individual enterprises or organisations in the private and public sectors. The instruments used by the government in its dealings with the private sector have changed enormously in the post-war period (see Ullmo, 1974, pp. 325–69, for a full account). The original Monnet plan was implemented in its first two years as much by directive as by indicative methods. The government had extensive powers over the allocation of important materials, particularly through its control of import licences. In addition, since little investment was financed by internally generated funds, the government, which allocated Marshall aid and credits, could control the investment programme. The latter was in any case primarily directed towards heavy industry, which was highly concentrated and hence more subject to control.

The directive phase soon gave way, however, to a system in which the government sought to implement the plan by other means. These still included some government allocation of investment funds, but directives were replaced by systems of incentives and informal contacts with firms. In the language of the plan *targets* gave way to *projections*.

Most government financing of investment in both nationalised and private industry was channelled through an organisation called the Fund for Economic and Social Development (the FDES). The Planning Commission is represented on this body, and it can be used to encourage investment in conformity with the plan. However, its role in the financing of private investment had become very small by the early 1960s, and although it enjoyed a revival in the latter part of that decade its function of dealing with the private sector was largely taken over in the early 1970s by a newly created Ministry of Industrial and Scientific Development (Bonnaud, 1975, pp. 101–3). The government retained some control over capital issues and other sources of credit through the supervisory role of the Ministry of Finance and lending from state-owned banks (Lutz, 1969, pp. 36–40), but these powers have not been extensively used as a means of plan implementation. Indeed, in France, as in other countries, it has proved difficult or impossible to establish a consistent industrial policy.

Not all government industrial policy is directly linked with the publication of five-year plans, though the Planning Commission is often involved in formulating such policies. Policies to restructure industry and promote mergers have an important impact on the planning process and may further the objectives of the plan, but are often implemented independently of it. In the mid-1960s the Planning Commission played an important role in a number of inter-ministerial committees established by the government to work out policies for industrial development, employment and the public sector. It was also closely associated with plans for specific industries, such as computers, shipbuilding and the aircraft industry. Not all of these studies were published, but they were influential in shaping government policy, and the Commission was seen as having an important contribution to make in this connection.

We are left, then, with a picture of government relations with private industry in which planning plays a role of limited and perhaps declining importance. McArthur and Scott (1969, p. 26) summarise their findings on this issue as follows:

the national planning process played only a limited role in the network of continuous direct relationships between business managers and the state – a network which we found to be the most important influence of all (except market forces and competition) in shaping the strategies of industries and companies. We found in general that strategic plans for all the industry sectors we covered were decided in private and outside the official institutions and procedures associated with the national planning process.

We defer further discussion of the reasons for this state of affairs until the next section. First, we briefly consider plan implementation within the public sector.

The prospects for ensuring that government departments and nationalised industries implement the plan seem infinitely more favourable than those for the private sector. Since, moreover, the public sector accounts for about one-half of total investment and about one-third of productive investment (Carré *et al.*, 1972, p. 588), and has relations as supplier or customer with large parts of private industry, control of the public sector seems to offer great scope for plan implementation. Indeed, the Monnet plan stated that 'the adoption of the plan by the government would be equivalent to an order to carry it out for the administrations, the public services and the nationalised enterprises' (quoted in Lutz, 1969, p. 98, n. 3). However, this injunction has not been obeyed. This was recognised in 1964, when the Planning Commission and the Ministry of Equipment made it clear that the plan was indicative for the public sector as well as the private sector. In none of the fourth, fifth and sixth plans were the public-sector targets exactly met.

Relations between the state and nationalised industries were examined by a Public Enterprise Committee in the mid-1960s. The Committee recommended that nationalised industries should operate on a commercial footing, and that a contract should be drawn up between the state and each public enterprise covering the five years of a plan. Firms sould be free from continual interference, but in return they would undertake certain commitments over investment and pricing. (This system thus has something in common with the planning agreements which the British Labour government of 1974–9 sought to conclude with private and public industry.) In the event only three firms negotiated such contracts for the sixth plan (Bonnaud, 1975, pp. 99–101). Although these agreements were overturned by the unexpectedly high rates of inflation encounted in the early 1970s, new three-year contracts were negotiated in 1978 with the state airline and coal company, and in 1979 with the state railway, and the options for the eighth plan endorse this practice (VIIIe Plan, 1979, p. 46). The planners have exercised a more continuous influence over nationalised industries by virtue of their participation in the FDES, which has continued to be responsible for financing much nationalised-industry investment. Also, as in the private sector, the plan may have operated as a 'reducer of uncertainty' and stimulator of forward planning and rational decision-taking. As the nationalised industries are typically monopolies, it may have discharged this function more effectively in the public than in the private sector.

We turn finally to the plan's impact on direct spending by government departments, on such facilities as roads, schools, hospitals, and so on. The categorisation of such expenditure has varied throughout the plans, but its importance has grown (Atreize, 1971, pp. 182–91). As noted above, the projections in the plan are no longer imperative, and are subject to short-run government policy changes. In the fifth plan, for example, investments by government departments grew by less than 60 per cent of the forecast increase. This does not mean, however, that the plan had no influence. According to Leruez, public spending projects have a better chance of surviving spending cuts if they are written into the plan and 'the real influence of the planners was revealed by the way they rescued their essential investment programmes at a time when the government wanted to make cuts in public spending, in 1959 and 1963 for example' (Leruez, 1978, p. 45).

In the sixth plan attempts were made to plan public investment in a more coherent manner. A total budget of 228 billion francs was allocated in the plan to nine categories of expenditure. In addition, six priority programmes were identified (VIe Plan, 1973, pp. 138–43). The seventh plan dropped the allocation of expenditure into general categories, but increased the number of priority programmes to twenty-five, costing 200 billion francs and ranging from improvements in the telephone system to facilitating access to the courts (VIIe Plan, 1976, pp. 171–300). Each programme was made the responsibility of a minister, and criteria were established for measuring its success. The eighth plan will retain the system of priority programmes and some programmes in the seventh plan will continue to operate (VIIIe Plan, 1979).

The development of the programme approach in the plan has been accompanied by the introduction of a system for the detailed planning and control of public spending similar to the planning, programming and budgeting system (PPBS) used in the USA. The French system is known as 'rationalisation of budget choice' (RBC). (For a detailed account, see Ullmo (1974, pp. 483–523).) It began in the late 1960s, went into abeyance in the early 1970s but has since been revived. In principle RBC could be used as a micro and continuous version of the macro planning exercise carried out every five years. In practice the link between RBC and the plan has been tenuous; a French government official notes that the priority programmes identified in the seventh plan were not integrated into the programmed budgets of the ministries as established under the RBC system (though the eighth plan may correct this situation). However, the same author argues that the RBC system, with its emphasis on objectives and programmes to achieve them, has influenced the planning system more than it has affected the budget. Planning (he argues) now consists of general macroeconomic projections and a few priority programmes. The RBC system offers an opportunity for annual plan revisions as the new departmental budget is prepared each year, the whole process being presided over by the Planning Council established in 1974 (see Carassus, 1978, pp. 61–4). This role is a far cry from the conception of the plan current in the early 1960s which sought to provide a comprehensive picture of the development of the economy over a specified time period, but it is in keeping with the general tendencies of French planning, discussed below.

4.3 How well has indicative planning worked in France?

This question raises important methodological problems. To quantify the contribution of the planning system would involve a re-run of post-war French economic history without the successive plans. The problem is complicated, moreover, by certain ambiguities in terminology. To what extent have successive plans contained targets on the one hand or projections and forecasts on the other? Should different criteria of assessment be used in either case?

One piece of information which is important but not conclusive is the relationship between plan targets and fulfilment. The relevant figures for rate of growth of gross domestic product are shown in Table 4.1, but the aggregate figures even before the sixth plan disguise more substantial divergence between target and actual growth rates at the industry level (Lutz, 1969, chs 8–9; Carré *et al.*, 1972, pp. 575–6). Even so Carré and his collaborators conclude that in spite of the fact that forecasts are partly compiled by groups representing specific interests rather than discharging a scientific function, the results are still better than those compiled on an individual basis (Carré *et al.*, 1972, p. 577).

Table 4.1 GDP growth rates: plan targets and out-turn (%)

	Second Plan	Third Plan	Fourth Plan	Fifth Plan	Sixth Plan	Seventh Plan
	1952–7	1958–61	1962–5	1966–70	1971–5	1976–80
Target	4.4	4.7	5.5	5.7	5.9	5.7
Out-turn	5.4	3.8	5.8	5.9	3.7	3.9*

* 1976–9. (Plan and out-turn data for the eighth plan are not strictly comparable because of changes in national accounting conventions.)

However, it is not enough for the forecasts to furnish potentially more accurate information than would otherwise be available. They must also be disseminated and acted upon. A survey of enterprises carried out in 1967 revealed that managers in enterprises accounting for about 80 per cent of French industrial production were aware of the over-all target growth rate, the figure ranging from 55 per cent in enterprises employing between 10 and 100 persons, to 100 per cent for enterprises with more than 5,000 employees. However, more detailed information concerning projected rates of growth for output and investment in the firm's own sector was less widely known. Finally, we have to establish how much notice enterprises take of plan forecasts in taking their own decisions. In 1967 more than half of large firms (with more than 5,000 employees) reported that the plan forecasts had a significant influence on investment decisions, and more than one-third reported that production decisions were similarly affected. Smaller firms reported a much smaller direct impact but may have been indirectly influenced by the larger firms (see Carré *et al.*, 1972, pp. 577–82).

Over-all, then, Carré and his co-authors conclude that in its first years of operation the planning system made a substantial contribution to encouraging belief in the possibility of continued expansion. Later, however, during the third, fourth and fifth plans, although planning continued to have some impact on economic policy, its contribution to economic growth was reduced (Carré *et al.*,

1972, pp. 507—9). In this limited sense planning in France could, in 1970, be said to have worked.

But the conclusions are less favourable to adherents of the theory of indicative planning. If planning has worked, it seems to have done so through other and more diffuse means than those expected by planners such as Massé, i.e. by bolstering confidence rather than by reducing uncertainty. The reasons for this situation are discussed at greater length in Chapter 8. We conclude this chapter by drawing attention to changes in the French planning system in the last ten years, and this seems to involve a recognition by the planners of the limited general influence of the plan.

The transition is expressed by one commentator in the phrase that the 'plan of the nation' has been replaced by the 'plan of the government' (Liggins, 1976, p. 4). In other words, the government recognises that setting output targets for particular sectors fulfils no purpose. The targets have always (with the possible exception of the first plan) been no more than forecasts, with no satisfactory mechanism for their implementation in the private sector. Starting with the sixth plan, and continuing with the seventh, attempts to establish interlocking output targets for the major sectors have largely been dropped. Hence the apparent paradox that the sixth plan, which was compiled using far more sophisticated mathematical techniques than its predecessors, finally contained fewer numerical targets. Instead, the plan has become a technique for co-ordinating medium-term planning in the public sector, as outlined above, and a channel for passing on government medium-term macroeconomic projections. In the less predictable economic environment of the 1970s, however, medium-term planning became far more hazardous, and even this limited role is now in question.

This state of affairs is implicitly recognised in the report on the options for the eighth plan, published in March 1979 and adopted with minor amendments by Parliament in July of that year as the basis for compiling the plan itself. The document departs from previous practice in that it declines to issue a central growth-rate projection as the quantitative foundation of the plan. The reason given is the mounting uncertainty to which the economy is subject. The document asserts that to ask Parliament to approve such a projection would give the erroneous impression that the future can be fixed in advance. However, the report continues: 'this clearly does not mean however that economic policy should be made from day to day. *A fortiori* this adjustment of French planning to new realities is not an abdication: a counterbalance will be provided by the preparation and execution of programmes precisely intended to surmount difficulties, whether anticipated or unanticipated' (VIIIe Plan, 1979, p. 25).

Thus in spite of the report's assertion that the generalised market research of Pierre Massé is a continuing feature of planning, the eighth plan will cease to be based on detailed and consistent quantitative projections. This is in keeping with the government's policy of disengagement and reliance on the competitive process, which is strongly reaffirmed in the report on options.

The report claims that the plan 'gains in intensity what it loses in exhaustive-ness'. The selectivity of the new approach is shown by its concentration on six major priorities of government policy, such as reducing the country's dependence on energy, developing agriculture and improving the environment. Like its two predecessors the eighth plan will also include a number of action programmes which will give concrete expression to the government's role in the achievement of these major objectives. Ministerial budgets will list separately the funds to be expended on each individual programme. In addition, state enterprises will be drawn into a series of contracts with the government. Thus, apart from the limited public assistance to industry intended to achieve the priorities listed above, the plan aims to influence the private sector indirectly, via macroeconomic policy. In sum the eighth plan is to become even more a plan of the government than its two predecessors. The decline in the scope and ambition of French planning seems destined to continue.

Part II Issues in the Theory of Economic Planning

5 THE ECONOMY AND THE PLANNING PROCESS

This chapter analyses planning processes in an abstract way. The first section discusses how the choice of a planning process might be made. The second section examines planning as a process of co-ordinating information held by the various agents in the economy, and gives a general representation of planning processes which suggests certain principles of classification. The third section discusses the formation of administrative hierarchies, the authority relations existing within such hierarchies, and the problem of reconciling conflicting preferences. This is an aspect of planning procedures which is imperfectly captured by analyses emphasising information flows.

5.1 The choice of a planning process

Here we visualise an unrealistic situation. An economy consists of a number of primary units, which typically will be individuals or basic production units. There is one further individual, the 'Organiser' (we cannot use the term 'planner', for reasons which will soon become clear). The Organiser has the function of forming the primary units into agents, and specifying a procedure which the agents thus formed will use to allocate resources and products among competing uses. (For convenience we shall refer to this problem as that of finding a resource-allocation procedure, the meaning of the term being extended to include the partitioning of the economy.) Among the set of possible resource-allocation procedures are a number in which certain agents perform the functions of planning, i.e. co-ordinating the behaviour of other units in the economy. Such procedures are known as *planning processes*. The issue arises as to how the Organiser should choose a resource-allocation procedure.

Let us assume for the moment that the economy has a social-welfare function — which gives a relation between the quantity of output produced and an index of social welfare. Resources are limited and must be allocated either to production or to operating the resource-allocation procedure itself. The Organiser's problem can thus be represented as that of choosing from the set of feasible resource-allocation procedures that one which maximises the social-welfare function, bearing in mind the cost of allocating resources. To achieve this state the condition must be satisfied that the marginal benefit of resources used in production must equal the marginal benefit of resources devoted to operating the procedure.

(We could complicate the matter further by allowing resources to be devoted to enlarging the set of possible resource-allocation procedures.)

This formulation raises an important point in the analysis of resource-allocation procedures, i.e. that resources have to be devoted to operating the procedure, and the resources thus used cannot be devoted to production. (In conventional analysis it is normally assumed that resources are allocated costlessly.) The implication of the condition above is that it is undesirable to lavish resources on the planning system when they could be better utilised directly in production, even if the plan guiding production is imperfect, or even inconsistent. This may explain features of certain observed planning procedures, as (for example) the property of the Soviet planning system based on material balances described in Chapter 2 shows. We noted there that the system failed to take note of all the interrelations between the balances but instead tried to take into account only the most important. To do otherwise would perhaps require more resources to be allocated to planning, and this to the detriment of production itself.

Another important aspect of the approach adopted here is that the choice of resource-allocation procedure depends upon the environment in which agents in the economy operate. The term 'environment' is conceived here broadly to include certain attributes of the agents in the economy, in particular the preferences and initial endowments of households and others, and the technological possibilities of production units. The resource-allocation procedure itself is not considered as part of the environment. Rather, the choice of a resource-allocation procedure is made given a particular environment (though the operation of a resource-allocation procedure may modify the environment).

There are a number of obvious illustrations of the dependence of the choice of resource-allocation procedure on the environment. An important preoccupation of the theoretical literature is the question of *returns to scale*. A number of procedures can be shown to operate satisfactorily only in environments characterised by constant or decreasing returns to scale. Another example taken from practical planning experience is the development of the planning and management systems of the Soviet Union and Eastern Europe described in Chapters 2 and 3. As technology becomes more complex and the sectors of an economy more interdependent, it is desirable to develop a new resource-allocation procedure to replace one which may have worked satisfactorily in a previous environment. Indeed, such a change may be necessary, as the old procedure may no longer be feasible. In 1962 the Soviet cybernetician V. M. Glushkov estimated that if the Soviet management system were retained intact, then by 1980 the whole labour force would be engaged in administration with none left over for production, and observations of this kind gave an impetus to reform. The movement towards reform may well have been reinforced by another change in the environment, an increase in the weight given by the central authorities to the preferences of individual consumers.

Some Soviet economists have christened the problem described above as that of meta-planning or selection of the best planning procedure. Our formulation is not intended as a preliminary to practical solution of the meta-planning problem. It is not as though one can continually vary the attributes of the planning procedure and thereby find a maximum value for the social-welfare function. In fact, the formulation is open to the objection that one of the important variables in the social-welfare function may be the resource-allocation procedure itself. The inclusion of this variable is implicit in the work of the many writers on political and economic matters who argue that either freedom from central control or planned co-ordination is an end in itself and therefore an independent argument in the social-welfare function. Moreover, the approach sidesteps the important social and political aspects of planning. We do not go into these important issues here (see Chapter 11), but instead use the formulation set out above as a framework for the discussion of planning procedures which follows.

5.2 Planning as the co-ordination of information

As we saw in Chapter 1, a powerful argument employed by opponents of socialist planning in the debate in the 1930s revolved around the problem of co-ordinating information for the purposes of planning. Information is initially dispersed among different agents in the economy, and Hayek (among others) argued that the problem of collecting and processing that information centrally was an insoluble one which made central planning impossible in practice. The price system, on the other hand, was an impersonal mechanism which by transferring the information relevant to each decision-taker co-ordinated the separate activities of individual agents (Hayek, 1945).

In this section, without accepting Hayek's conclusion, we adopt his premise that information is initially dispersed among the various agents in the economy, and examine the planning procedures from the standpoint of the information flows they require. To do so, we use a general description of planning processes due to Hurwicz (1971).

A planning procedure is broken down into the two stages of construction and implementation of the plan. It is assumed initially that each of the agents in the economy, indexed $0, \ldots, n$, observes a part of the environment in which the economic system will operate. Firms, for example, are aware of their own production possibilities, and households are aware of their preferences or utility functions, defined over goods and services consumed and factor services supplied. We denote by e_i the knowledge of the environment e held initially by agent i.

The first part of the planning procedure consists of an exchange of messages between the agents. We suppose that planning time is broken down into a sequence of stages $s = 0, \ldots, T$, and at each stage agents send out a message, though some of these messages may be empty. The nature of the message sent depends upon the response function of the agent, which may be different from agent to agent and may vary with the stage the planning process has reached. The message sent by an agent depends, via the response function, on messages received in previous stages and upon the agent's own perception of the environment, except of course that the first message is based entirely upon the latter variable. The process can be expressed in equation form:

$$m_0^i = f_0^i(e_i) \qquad i = 0, \ldots, n \qquad\qquad (5.1)$$

$$m_s^i = f_s^i(m_{s-1}, m_{s-2}, \ldots, m_0, e_i) \qquad i = 0, \ldots, n; \quad s = 1, \ldots, T$$
$$(5.2)$$

where m_s^i is the message communicated by agent i at stage s, and f_s^i is the response function of agent i at stage s.

The final message transmitted is m_T, and on the basis of this message agents decide what course of action to pursue. The final message need not be an instruction to an agent, but it might require decoding by the agent to arrive at a possible action. Hurwicz calls the decoded final message a *paper plan*, designated by b:

$$b = d(m_T)$$

where d is the decoding function.

The formation of a paper plan completes the planning stage, and the agents may then implement the paper plan. But this may not always be possible as the planning procedure may not result in a feasible plan. Hence we need a function transforming the paper plan b into a real plan a:

$$a = r(b)$$

The last two functions can be collapsed into what Hurwicz calls an *outcome function*:

$$a = y(m_T)$$

In this representation a planning process consists of three characteristics: a set of messages transmitted by the agents, a response function, and an outcome function. Since we are concerned here with planning rather than implementation — though the two are intimately linked — we concentrate on the process down to the formation of the 'paper plan', leaving the final part of the outcome function, the emergence of the real plan, for later discussion.

Let us first consider the information flows which take place in a planning process. Hayek argued that there was a limitation on the amount of information which could be transmitted: in other words, that messages could only be of a certain size. This can be called the 'message space', and a limitation on message space will restrict the amount of information which can be transmitted in any message. One example of such a restriction which is widely discussed in the literature is a limitation of the size of message space to vectors whose dimensionality is the same as that of the commodity space. In other words, if there are n commodities or factors in the economy, no message may contain more than n variables. (In fact, the restriction should be slightly more limiting than this, as we need to eliminate the possibility of complicated information being smuggled in apparently simple messages.)

It is natural to interpret these messages as vectors of the prices of commodities and factors, or vectors of quantities to be supplied or of quantities demanded. These are examples of possible languages in which messages may be transmitted. A planning procedure may contain messages transmitted in several different languages: for example, at stage s the language may be that of vectors of prices and at stage $s + 1$ of vectors of quantities, a regime which operates in some of the procedures outlined in Chapter 6 below. Although these two types of languages naturally come to the mind of economists acquainted with the model of competitive equilibrium, there are other more elaborate alternatives. For example, the messages may be conditional in form. Firms may transmit messages indicating what course of action they will follow on certain alternative assumptions about the behaviour of other agents, or all agents taken together. In a model of indicative planning firms may transmit messages showing alternative courses of action based on different assumptions about the over-all growth rate of the economy. Other messages can convey probability distributions of variables. In still other cases agents may transmit all the information known to them, i.e. their whole environment; this will usually involve a varied language and an extensive message space.

The second characteristic of a planning procedure is the response functions of the agents. These describe how each agent forms messages on the basis of earlier messages received and the agent's own perception of the environment. Hurwicz distinguishes first-order, finite-order and infinite-order response functions. First-order functions depend only upon the message transmitted immediately before:

$$m_s^i = f_s^i(m_{s-1}, e_i) \qquad i = 0, \ldots, n; s = 1, \ldots, T$$

Finite-order response functions contain as variables messages transmitted at a finite number of previous stages, while with infinite-order functions the number of messages recalled may be infinite. These distinctions obviously determine the amount of information which must be stored by the agents in the course of the planning process.

In many of the decentralised planning procedures discussed below (in the Lange procedure, for example) the response functions are cyclical. Agents are divided into two groups, a central planning board, indexed 0, and households and firms, indexed $1, \ldots, n$. The two groups will then issue non-empty messages at alternate stages. Other more complex patterns may arise when agents fall into three or more groups — not all of which transmit non-empty messages at every stage.

The nature of the response function obviously determines the amount of data stored and the complexity of the calculations performed in the planning process; the size of the message space determines the amount of information transmitted. These two characteristics, and of course the number of stages of the planning process, thus determine the quantity of resources used up in planning. Some attempts have been made to explore these cost relationships (see Marschak,

1959) but they are not conclusive. Indeed, since the technologies of collecting, storing and performing computations upon data are changing so fast, largely as a result of computer developments, such cost relationships are extremely volatile. Accordingly we confine ourselves here to a purely definitional question of the meaning of the term 'centralisation'.

This is an issue which has occupied a disproportionate space in the literature. The problem has revolved around the ambiguities of the terms 'centralised' and 'decentralised', but it has now largely been resolved by the recognition that centralisation is a two-dimensional concept. On the one hand, we may speak of a planning process as being either centralised or decentralised with respect to authority, indicating thereby the extent to which the agents in the economy are obliged to follow instructions from other agents. This is the most natural interpretation, and probably what most people have in mind when they speak of the Soviet economic system as being an example of centralised planning. We consider this aspect further in the following section.

The second aspect of centralisation relates to information, and systems are classified as more or less centralised on the basis of how much of the information in the system is concentrated in the hands of a single agent. A system is said to be centralised if all information is collected by a single agent. This will happen if agents, either at the first stage or in the course of a planning procedure, transmit the whole of their environment to the central planning board, and it is this kind of system which Hayek rightly described as being impracticable. In fact, no observed economic system beyond the simplest has been centralised in this respect. All the planning systems discussed here which are observed in practice, or even proposed, fall into the category of being non-centralised with respect to information. It can be argued that as a consequence they are non-centralised with respect to authority as well, on the grounds that where superiors' information is incomplete their control must be incomplete as well.

An informationally centralised system is at one end of the spectrum of informational centralisation and decentralisation. The other extreme is an informationally decentralised system. This could be defined as a system in which no communication between agents occurred, but such a definition is not helpful, as the economic system so described would be chaotic. Instead, economists have tried to define informational decentralisation with reference to the model of general competitive equilibrium. This system is co-ordinated entirely by transmission of messages of price vectors and of vectors of quantities demanded and supplied at those prices. Attempts have been made to define as informationally decentralised those procedures which require the transmission of no more information than, or of information of the same type as, that transmitted in the model of competitive equilibrium. We return to this issue in the following chapter, which discusses a number of planning procedures which are decentralised according to alternative definitions.

One of the dangers of devoting too much space to a discussion of centralisation and decentralisation is that it creates the impression that one kind of system is preferable simply on the grounds of being more or less centralised either with respect to *authority* or to *information*. The fact that the model of competitive equilibrium, traditionally the system against which other arrangements are compared and found wanting, is informationally decentralised often creates the impression that decentralised procedures are automatically preferable to non-decentralised ones. As noted above, it is quite legitimate to argue that properties of the economic system such as the degree of centralisation themselves enter the social-welfare function, or to seek to demonstrate that decentralised procedures are cheaper to run, but by and large no presumption should be made in favour of decentralised systems unless either or both of these conditions is satisfied.

5.3 Hierarchy and authority

We now turn to an aspect of the Organiser's problem which in the previous section we had assumed resolved. This is the formation from the basic units in the economy of agents which will operate the planning procedure. This leads naturally to a further consideration of authority relations within the planning system, as an agent in the planning process normally has relations of superordination or subordination with other agents.

The partitioning of the economy is an issue of great importance, and one often overlooked in the literature on economic planning, where the identity of agents is assumed to be given. Yet in the socialist economies, as Portes (1971, p. 425) has observed, 'planners have a great degree of latitude in this regard. . . . They are relatively free to reshuffle ministries, dissolve or create industrial associations, break up or amalgamate enterprises and reorganise the lines of authority and communication defining the administrative hierarchy.' A conspicuous example of such a change was Khruschev's reorganisation of 1957 which switched the whole economy from a ministerial to a regional system of administration (for an analysis see Keren, 1964), but there are many less thoroughgoing changes taking place at any time in many of the socialist countries, and, indeed, in capitalist economies as well. Our discussion is restricted to reorganisation of the production sector. Although alternative partitionings of the household sector are theoretically possible, in practice such reorganisations have not been undertaken. We should recognise, however, that even within the production sector different planning functions may require different partitionings of the economy.

We assume that there are a given number of basic production units from which the agents operating in the planning system are formed; these might be individual plants or factories, for example. One organisational structure is formed simply by establishing each unit as an agent, but in practice it may be desirable to form agents for production by amalgamation of the basic production unit. This immediately introduces the notion of different levels in the system, with a number of primary units comprising a single agent in the planning process (though for the purposes of describing the planning process, arrangements internal to the lowest-level agent are ignored). However, lowest-level agents may themselves be included in or associated with other agents at a higher level, and so on until the highest level is reached, which may consist of a single agent. In this case the organisation system will correspond to a pyramid. Even on simple assumptions the number of possible permutations of organisational structure is enormous, and enumeration and examination of all possible structures is a hopeless task; some organisational principles are required to restrict the problem to manageable proportions.

In some circumstances features of the environment may simplify the problem of organisation. Let us take the case of an economy which is decomposable into a number of separate sectors. This may arise if the objective function is of an additive kind – for example, maximisation of the value of outputs (measured at some given prices) of particular sectors, and where each sector uses no factor of production which could be transferred to another sector, and uses none of the output of another sector as an input. In this case the economy can obviously be decomposed into a number of sectors which then operate independently. The condition of full decomposability is obviously an implausible one, but attention has also been paid to systems which are nearly decomposable, in the sense that interactions among sub-systems are weak compared with interactions within a given sub-system (Simon and Ando, 1961). In certain cases sub-systems can be aggregated into single units for the purposes of high-level co-ordination, while for lower-level control interaction between sub-systems can be ignored. This property suggests a natural partitioning of the economy and a corresponding hierarchy of management and is the basis for a number of planning algorithms used in practice (see Chapter 10).

The discussion above has not specified the authority relations existing between agents at different levels. In practice, of course, hierarchies are arranged on the basis of relationships of super- and subordination, with higher-level agents controlling lower-level ones. It is difficult to capture the extent of centralisation of authority using the representation of a planning process in terms of exchanges of information among agents. (There is obviously a substantial difference in nature between, say, a message in the form of a legally binding annual plan handed down to a Soviet enterprise and publication of an indicative plan providing a consistent forecast and a (non-irrevocable) statement of government intentions in a private-ownership economy.)

In the representation of planning given above centralisation of authority had two aspects. At the state of plan formulation agents exchange messages in accordance with response functions. These response functions can be either imposed on individual agents by higher authority (possibly sustained by an incentive system) or accepted voluntarily by them. In the Walrasian model of competitive equilibrium households follow the logic of rational behaviour by maximising their utility functions at successive vectors of prices, and firms follow the logic of competitive behaviour by maximising profits. In other procedures agents are instructed to adopt particular response functions, even though they may not always obey the rules. A system with imposed response functions is more centralised with respect to authority than one without.

The second aspect relates to the decoding of the final message. A procedure with two levels can be said to be centralised with respect to authority if (when the process of exchange of information is complete and the final message decoded) the only argument in the decoding function of the ith agent, $i = 1, \ldots,$ n, is the final message received from the central agent, indexed 0:

$$b_i = d^i(m_T^0) \qquad i = 1, \ldots, n$$

In this case the 'paper plan' b_i is simply a decoding of the final message from the centre; it ignores the environment (including the preferences) of the ith agent. More generally, the degree of centralisation of authority (or of coercion, as it is sometimes described) can be shown by the size of the set of paper plans from which the lower-level agents can choose. Of course, the implementation stage may reveal a different picture, especially if the paper plan is infeasible. This situation often arises in the Soviet Union, where enterprises receive mutually inconsistent compulsory plan indicators and are thus forced to exercise authority themselves in choosing which target to fulfil.

It is clear why the two aspects of centralisation of authority — obedience to response function rules and acceptance of the centre's final message — must be taken together: otherwise agents may, by systematically distorting messages in the plan-formulation stage, be able to influence improperly the final message sent by the centre. This phenomenon is illustrated by the 'safety margin' retained by the Soviet enterprise director at the stage of plan formulation (see Chapter 2).

Centralisation of authority, then, consists essentially in one agent imposing his will upon another or others. Thus we are led to a discussion of the preferences or objectives of the agents in the system. The simplest case is one in which all agents share the same objective, and have common preferences. A set of agents sharing a common objective has been christened a 'team' by Marschak and Radner (1972), who have conducted extensive analysis of such groups. Members of a team differ in that they may (initially at least) have different information and may control different action variables, but the assumption that they share a common objective vastly simplifies the analysis of alternative resource-allocation procedures.

However, in normal cases there are divergences between the preferences of different agents in the system. In some cases the authorities may set themselves the task of aggregating individual preferences into a social-welfare function, in which case they will face the familiar difficulties described by Arrow's theorem that it is impossible to establish a social decision rule meeting certain desirable conditions. The requirement which for our purposes is most relevant is that of non-dictatorship — a condition that no individual agent's preferences should always determine the alternative chosen (Heal, 1973, ch. 2).

In practice, however, Arrow's theorem is of limited relevance. The authorities in planned economies regard themselves as being placed in power through some political or historical process which entitles them in principle either to impose their own preferences or to take account of the preferences of other agents as and when they choose. In such cases they try to gain the compliance of other agents either by sanctions or by imposing an appropriate incentive system which encourages subordinate agents to behave as their superiors would like them to. (The Soviet economist Novozhilov (1970) has characterised the latter kind of system as being indirectly centralised with respect to authority.)

This task may be difficult or impossible. Johansen (1977) has well illustrated some of the difficulties involved. The essence of the matter is that it is not a team problem in which all agents share the same objectives but a game played by agents with conflicting interests. Consider Figure 5.1. The planners' preferences are represented by a function with two arguments, a and d. This function reaches a maximum at W^{max}. The contour lines for W are planners' indifference curves; the further they are from W^{max}, the lower the planners' welfare level. A subordinate agent (say an enterprise) has a utility function in the same two arguments, but with a maximum of U^{max} and different contour lines. If the planners controlled both variables a and d, there would be no problem as they would immediately adopt the optimal values of these variables. However, if planners control one variable, a, and the enterprise another, d, a more complicated situation arises.

What will be the outcome in this case? If the parties act in isolation, without communication or agreement, the non-co-operative solution to the game is point

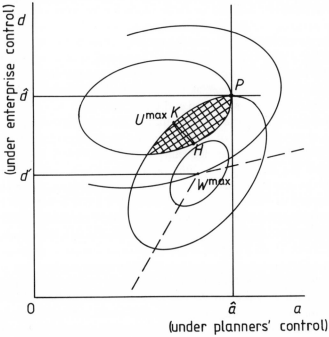

Figure 5.1

Source: Johansen (1977, p. 78).

P. At P the enterprise finds that it has chosen the best value for its variable, $\hat{d}$, given its expectation of the value which the planners will choose for their variable, $\hat{a}$. Equally the planners, expecting the enterprise to choose $\hat{d}$, find that in choosing $\hat{a}$ they have chosen the value which is the best possible one in the circumstances. Yet for both players, P, the non-co-operative solution, is inferior to all the points in the shaded area in the diagram.

This situation can be avoided if the planners can alter the rules of the game. By altering the enterprise's preferences through a suitable revision of the incentive system, they could shift U^{max} to coincide with W^{max}, and turn the problem into one of teams whose members share the same preferences; or, by trying to turn the game into a co-operative one, they can seek a solution along the line HK of points which are Pareto optimal and an improvement for both players on P. A final alternative, which could be adopted if the enterprise declares the chosen value of its decision variable first, would be for the planners to make a conditional declaration in advance stating how they will respond to any value of d chosen by the enterprise. If they announced in advance that their response to any value of d would be as shown by the dashed line in the diagram, and then the enterprise, if it believed them, would choose d' and the outcome would be W^{max}. However, complications arise if the enterprise does not believe that the planners will act according to their declaration.

Johansen's interesting formulation of the problem of reconciling conflicting interests is applicable both to centrally planned economies and to those with indicative planning. In the former the authorities have more scope for operating directly on the preferences of subordinates and, of course, for direct intervention in their affairs, while indicative planning can be seen as an attempt to introduce more co-operative elements into the economic system by exchanging information and forming coalitions. However, as other chapters in this book amply document, in neither case have the results been entirely satisfactory.

The above problems arise from conflicts in objectives. Other difficulties arise from the sheer difficulty of communicating preferences from one agent to another. We noted above the possibility that the authorities may wish to take into account the preferences of other agents in compiling the plan, with the difficulties this may cause. According to Drewnowski (1961), state and individual preferences in socialist economies are combined in a way which over time gives increasing weight to the latter in the determination of the relative proportions in which consumer goods are produced. The problem is therefore a growing one.

The shift to a more individualistic preference function obviously imposes further informational requirements on the planning process. One way of circumventing some of these difficulties is by substituting specification of target values for variables which appear in the objective function in place of an approach starting from the formulation of the function itself. The choice between these two alternatives became the subject of a disagreement between Frisch and Tinbergen, the latter favouring the targets approach on practical grounds.

There are two major arguments for an approach which *starts* from targets rather than *derives* them through explicit optimisation. First, it is argued that in practice the objective function cannot be formalised. Frisch (1976, ch. 2) himself devised a technique for establishing the objective function through careful interviews with ministers or officials, and starting from another angle attempts have been made to infer the preference function underlying the decisions embodied in the sixth French Plan (Guesnerie and Malgrange, 1972). However, it is apparent that an objective function thus established can only contain a few arguments. Compiling a detailed central plan will require substantial further disaggregation of the initial variables, and choices of considerable magnitude will have to be made. In the Soviet literature some initial attempts have been made to solve the problem in this way by establishing a hierarchical system of objectives under the title of the 'tree of goals' (Cave, 1980, pp. 62–3) but no significant practical applications have been reported. When optimising methods have been used in practice within centrally planned economies the problem has been circumvented by employing various objective functions, and using the calculations as a way of exploring the feasible area, rather than selecting the optimal plan directly. This is akin to what Johansen calls the 'preference-constraint approach', in which some arguments are taken out of the objective function, assigned specified values, and reinserted in the model as constraints on the optimisation of the remaining variables (Johansen, 1977, pp. 249–55).

The second major argument in favour of the 'targets' approach is that it facilitates the link between plan construction and plan implementation. This is achieved by means of Tinbergen's well-known result on economic policy: i.e. that if target values are selected for a given number of variables, then an equal number of independent instruments is sufficient to implement the plan (Tinbergen, 1952). (This formulation ignores certain complications, such as the possibility that achievement of the targets may require infeasible values for the instruments. See Chapter 8 for further discussion of this approach.) This is certainly an important result for macroeconomic planning – for the co-ordination of fiscal and monetary policy, for example. But it is less suggestive for the more disaggregated planning which is the principal subject-matter of this book. If the target approach is generally used in preference to an explicit welfare-maximisation exercise, it is because of the difficulty or impossibility of formulating the latter rather than because the target approach solves the problem of implementation.

Of course, the problem of communicating preferences operates in both directions. Even if lower-level organisations share the preferences of or are willing to subordinate their own preferences to those of their superiors, there is still the problem of communicating those preferences. We saw in Chapter 2 that the Soviet annual planning cycle began with the stipulation of a small number of highly aggregated output targets for the following year. These targets are then broken down successively by lower-level agents until they reach their executants, the enterprises. The disaggregation is undertaken by agents without a precise knowledge, or even with no knowledge at all, of the preferences underlying the original choice of targets at the highest level. Even an idealistic enterprise manager may have no alternative but to use his discretionary powers to maximise his bonuses, hoping that the system has achieved indirect centralisation by making his own self-interest congruent with the preferences of the highest-level agents.

In this chapter we have tried to identify at a fairly abstract level some of the major difficulties involved in choosing planning procedures and using them to compile plans for subsequent implementation. The basic questions we have considered are the criteria for choosing a resource-allocation procedure, the nature of the information flows required for the operation of the procedure and the allocation of authority within the system. These issues are fundamental to any economic system, and it is hardly surprising that economic analysis has failed to resolve them. Hitherto economists have been more successful in describing and classifying alternatives than in proposing means of choosing between them.

The matter to which we draw particular attention is the far-reaching effect of the incomplete centralisation of information. No agent is able even approximately to accumulate and process all relevant information in an economy. In these circumstances delegation of authority is inevitable. All planned economies incorporate this property, and so should all models of planned economies. Simon (1972) has called this limited ability of agents to process information 'bounded rationality', and the consequences of bounded rationality for economic planning are enormous. First, it rules out full optimisation except on a very limited scale. Second, planners and managers must allocate their time and effort in ways which take account of their limited information-processing capacity, and 'satisficing' behaviour becomes rational. Some formal attempts have been made by both Western and Soviet economists to analyse such procedures (Radner, 1975; Makarov and Perminov, 1979), with limited results to date, but any analysis of planned economies and any proposals for improvement must take account of the problem.

6 DECENTRALISED PLANNING PROCEDURES

This chapter is concerned with a topic which has dominated the theoretical literature on economic planning, i.e. the design of procedures for compiling a plan which are decentralised in some precisely specified sense. In Chapter 10 we examine the use to which these procedures have been put in planned economies. Here we confine ourselves to giving an outline of the procedures proposed and making a preliminary assessment of them. The first section discusses some of the requirements which have been made of planning procedures; the second discusses the first and best-known such procedure originally proposed by Oscar Lange in the 1930s; this is followed by sections outlining other procedures, including some which meet the special problems which arise in the presence of economies of scale. (For a more advanced treatment the reader is referred to Heal (1973).)

6.1 Characteristics of planning procedures

The first problem is to define the criteria by which a procedure for compiling plans will be judged. When this problem was posed in Chapter 5 the approach taken was to choose from the set of procedures which were feasible in a given environment (i.e. compatible with the given preferences, endowments and production possibilities of the economy) that one which maximised the value of a social-welfare function defined over the economy's possible output vectors. At the same time, account was taken of the fact that resources used up in operating the procedure could not be used for production. Thus there is a trade-off between choosing a more elaborate and complete procedure and having more resources available for production itself. This means that the 'best' plan is not necessarily a perfect one.

Applying such an approach requires precise knowledge of (i) the social-welfare function, and (ii) the costs of operating alternative procedures. Neither of these is readily available, so the approach taken in the literature is to apply a more general criterion for the final outcome of the planning process, and to supplement it with some further requirements relating to the process by which that outcome is reached. The need for some kind of decentralisation springs from the recognition that information is initially dispersed throughout the economic system, that concentration of all information and calculation in the hands of the central planning board is infeasible, and consequently that the final outcome of a planning process is reached through an iterative process involving exchanges of messages between agents. We shall be concerned below with certain characteristics of the iterative process. First, however, we stipulate some requirements on the final outcome of the planning process.

Hurwicz has proposed a triple requirement for the outcome of a planning procedure. First, he requires that it should be not only feasible but also optimal in the sense, for example, that no more of one good can be produced without producing less of another, and that no consumer can be made better off without making another worse off. This requirement he calls *non-wastefulness*. Second, Hurwicz requires that the procedure should not systematically favour some individuals or groups at the expense of others; this property is known as *unbiasedness*. The third requirement is that the procedure yield a *single-valued* or *unique* solution. If these three requirements are fulfilled, the procedure is in Hurwicz's terms *satisfactory* (see Arrow and Hurwicz, 1977, pp. 22–4).

Like so much of the discussion of planning procedures, these requirements draw inspiration from the concepts used in the analysis of general equilibrium in a competitive economy. (The link is made even more explicit in the discussion of the planning procedure proposed by Lange, described below.) We may recall here two basic results in welfare economics: first, that a competitive equilibrium is in certain environments Pareto optimal; second (and this result is valid under more restrictive conditions), that any Pareto optimum may in certain conditions be attained by a competitive equilibrium after a suitable redistribution of initial resources. In both cases the conditions which must be fulfilled are conditions concerning the environment of agents in the economy.

Now clearly the non-wastefulness requirement is inspired by the first welfare property of competitive equilibrium, i.e. it yields a Pareto optimum. The requirement that the procedure is unbiased is inspired by the second result, i.e. any Pareto optimum can be achieved by a suitable reallocation of initial endowments; in other words, there is no systematic bias in favour of particular agents.

However, Hurwicz's requirements of a planning procedure are more general than the standard Pareto-optimality criterion, though they include it as a special case. A planning system presupposes some conscious direction of economic processes which may either breach the condition of Pareto optimality or adopt a less generally specified objective function than that implied by Pareto optimality. Thus in many of the procedures outlined below the objective function assumed is a scalar one, rather than the vector-valued function implied by the criterion of Pareto optimality. In other words, we assume that alternative allocations, Pareto-optimal or otherwise, can be evaluated and compared.

We have now discussed the set of requirements made concerning the *final* outcome of the planning procedure. However, in practice, the *intermediate* stages of operation are frequently of equal interest, because the procedure often has to be halted before the final outcome is reached, and the properties of the resulting plan are therefore significant. Hence we should be interested not only in whether the procedure converges, and how quickly it does so, but also in certain aspects of the convergence process.

Malinvaud (1967, pp. 177–9) has proposed two criteria for judging the convergence of planning procedures. He requires first that the procedure be *feasible*, in the sense that it is possible to implement plans thrown up by the iterative process before it arrives at the final outcome. This requirement will be breached, for example, if firms in intermediate stages are required to produce at points outside their production sets, or if demand for some products exceeds supply at intermediate stages. Second, Malinvaud requires that the process of iteration be *monotonic*, in the sense that successive iterations yield successively higher values of the objective function. The knowledge that a procedure is monotonic gives planners the confidence to go on with further iterations of the procedure in the knowledge that the extra resources thus expended will not be wholly wasted. Clearly this requirement is only of interest for procedures which are feasible. If an intermediate plan is infeasible, then the associated value of its objective function is of no interest.

The final aspect to be considered is a precise definition of decentralisation. The ambiguity in this term was discussed in Chapter 5. Here the relevant concept is *informational* decentralisation, and recalling the discussion in Chapter 5 we describe as *decentralised* any procedure which satisfies the following two properties:

(1) The messages transmitted by agents in the planning procedure depend only on their own environments and relate to their own proposed actions. This requirement is often known as *privacy*.

(2) There is some limit on the size of messages which can be transmitted; in particular, the messages must consist of *points* (i.e. specified values of the components of the messages) rather than, say, sets or functions.

The first aspect is fairly straightforward. It effectively eliminates procedures in which agents must have information about the environments of other agents. The second follows on from the first. Its purpose is to prevent agents from transmitting to one another all the information at their disposal — to prevent a firm from transmitting its production function or a consumer his utility function. Clearly in these cases the messages are not points in space. On the other hand, messages consisting of a vector of prices or of a vector of quantities of goods demanded or supplied do meet the requirement.

We note in passing that the model of competitive equilibrium is decentralised in the terms of our definition. However, the model of perfect competition also meets an additional condition, i.e. that the size of the message is no larger than the number of goods in the economy, as each message is a vector *either* of prices *or* of quantities to be supplied or demanded. In fact, as we shall see below, a procedure involving the transmission of larger messages will still count as decentralised, provided that each message is point valued — in other words, provided that it indicates only points in space rather than complete sets or functions.

We have thus accumulated a set of questions to ask of any planning procedure: In what environments is it satisfactory, in the sense of being non-wasteful, unbiased and single-valued? If it is an iterative procedure, does it converge, is it feasible and is it monotonic? And finally, is it (informationally) decentralised? We now ask this set of questions of a number of particular procedures.

6.2 The Lange procedure

Historically the first decentralised planning procedure is due to the well-known Polish economist Oscar Lange (Lange, 1938). It was developed in the special historical context of the 1930s in response to the debate on the possibility of planning which we briefly recounted in Chapter 1. Essentially the opponents of planning at that time, principally Ludwig von Mises, argued that an efficient allocation of resources was impossible without prices and markets. Such an allocation depends upon a knowledge of marginal rates of substitution and of transformation, and without prices, it was argued, such knowledge could not be achieved.

This argument was readily answered by the demonstration that a model for the efficient allocation of resources could be formulated and solved in a central-ised way, the solution then being implemented directly by administrative methods. In such a case no reference would be made to prices nor use made of them. However, the optimal central solution would implicitly evaluate alternative uses of resources and choose directly the one which equated marginal rates of transformation and of substitution. This procedure would comprehend, in Lange's words, prices in the broader sense – i.e. the terms on which alternatives are available – but not prices in the narrow sense, money prices at which goods are available in an actual market.

However, the centralised solution imposes very severe informational problems. All information about preferences, production possibilities, endowments, etc. (the environment of each agent, in our terms) would have to be transmitted to the central planning board. Much of this information is hard or impossible to formulate, and the data once arrived at the central planning board would present acute problems of storage and of computation. There would be, as Robbins has observed, millions of equations to solve (see Hayek, 1935; Dobb, 1969, ch. 9).

Lange was able to show that a decentralised procedure would overcome these problems of information collection, transmission and storage and the associated problem of computation. In this section we begin by describing Lange's conception of how a planned economy might operate in a decentralised way; we then examine more formally the mathematical basis of the procedure and identify the set of environments in which it will perform satisfactorily.

What Lange proposed, in essence, was that the planned economy should mimic the procedures for reaching an equilibrium outlined by Walras in his model of general competitive equilibrium. In Walras's model the procedure for reaching an equilibrium is by means of a *tâtonnement*, or trial and error. It is assumed that in addition to the consumers and producers there is another agent in the economy, known as the *auctioneer*. That agent's function is to get the process of finding an equilibrium started by announcing a trial set of prices which may be chosen randomly (or, more plausibly, may be the prices prevailing in an earlier period). Consumers then maximise their utility subject to these prices, which, as they include factor prices, also determine consumers' incomes. Producers calculate their profit-maximising output levels and input demands at those prices. Each agent communicates his net supply or demand for each good or factor to the acutioneer, who calculates total supply and demand. When supply is greater than demand for a commodity or factor the auctioneer lowers its price; when demand is greater than supply the auctioneer raises the price. The whole process is repeated until demand is equal to supply for all goods and factors. It can be shown on certain assumptions that a set (or sets) of equilibrium prices exists, and that the procedure outlined above will converge to that equilibrium. Thus the market can be interpreted, as Pareto observed, as a gigantic computing device, finding equilibrium prices by a process of trial and error.

Lange's model simply replicates this process within the framework of an economy with social ownership of the means of production. In fact, Lange's formulation for a planned economy is in many ways a more convincing one than Walras's formulation for a capitalist economy. In the latter the auctioneer is a shadowy figure, performing the essential function of adjusting prices but having no equivalent in an actual economy. In a planned economy, on the other hand, there is an agent — the central planning board — outside the groups of producers and consumers who could quite naturally assume the role of price-adjuster. Second, in Walras's formulation of the trial-and-error method no transactions can take place until the equilibrium prices are reached; otherwise, with trade allowed at non-equilibrium prices, there would be redistribution of income in favour of those receiving above-equilibrium prices for their products or factors, and the process of adjustment would influence the final outcome. Again, in the context of a planned economy, such a period for calculation has a quite natural interpretation as an organised period of planning preceding the planned period in which transactions actually take place.

Lange's discussion of how his proposal would operate contains a whole variety of interesting observations — on how a socialist planned economy would deal with problems of income distribution, on how economies of scale would be dealt with, and on how investment would be allocated. In the treatment of consumers he advances alternative models. In one, consumers express their own preferences in the market, as they do in the Walrasian model; in the other, the central planning board substitutes its own preferences for those of consumers (the nature of these two alternatives was discussed in Chapter 5). The second model is more practicable, as using an iterative method with millions of households clearly presents many more problems than the same method used with the many fewer units of the production sector. In the more formal account of Lange's model which follows we adopt this second formulation, with the state adopting a single utility function to represent the interests of consumers. Goods would then be distributed among consumers either by rationing or alternatively by establishing a set of prices which would equate demand to the supply fixed by the central planning board. (These prices would not necessarily, and would not normally, be the same as the equilibrium prices resulting from the trial-and-error process in the production sector.)

Formally the model of resource allocation can be presented as follows. (Here we follow Arrow and Hurwicz (1977, pp. 41–76.) The economy has a utility function $U(y_1, \ldots, y_n)$ defined over quantities demanded, y_i, of n goods. The production sector consists of m firms, and the level of activity in the jth firm is represented by x_j. The net output of the ith good by the jth firm is given by a function $g_{ij}(x_j)$ of the level of activity of that firm. Where a firm uses good i as an input, net output is negative. Where it has good i as an output, net output is positive. Net output of good i for the economy as a whole is given by $\Sigma_j g_{ij}(x_j)$. For some goods the economy may also have an initial endowment, which can be represented as ξ_i.

In our notation the planning problem reduces to the following:

$$\text{maximise } U(y_1, y_2, \ldots, y_n) \tag{6.1}$$

subject to

$$y_i \leqslant \sum_{j=1}^{m} g_{ij}(x_j) + \xi_i \qquad i = 1, \ldots, n \tag{6.2}$$

$$\left. \begin{array}{ll} y_i \geqslant 0 & i = 1, \ldots, n \\ x_j \geqslant 0 & j = 1, \ldots, m \end{array} \right\} \tag{6.3}$$

Expression (6.1) is the objective function. Expression (6.2) represents the constraint that for each good final output can be no greater than the sum of total net output, produced by all firms, and initial endowments. There are also non-negativity constraints (6.3).

We now consider alternative methods of solving this planning problem. If the utility function U and the functions g_{ij} are concave and differentiable (this corresponds to cases where indifference curves have the normal shape and returns to scale in production are constant or decreasing), we can solve the problem centrally by forming the Lagrangean

$$L = U(y_1, \ldots, y_n) + \sum_{i=1}^{n} \lambda_i \left(\sum_{j=1}^{m} g_{ij}(x_j) + \xi_i - y_i \right) \tag{6.4}$$

where λ_i is the Lagrangean multiplier corresponding to the ith constraint in (6.2). (The technique employed here is discussed in Dixit (1976, pp. 1–12).) For a maximum of (6.1) subject to (6.2) and (6.3) the first derivatives of (6.4) should satisfy the following conditions:

$$
\left.
\begin{aligned}
&\frac{\partial L}{\partial y_i} = \frac{\partial U}{\partial y_i} - \lambda_i \leqslant 0; \quad y_i \geqslant 0 && i = 1, \ldots, n \\[2mm]
&\frac{\partial L}{\partial x_j} = \sum_{i=1}^{n} \lambda_i \frac{\partial g_{ij}}{\partial x_j} \leqslant 0; \quad x_j \geqslant 0 && j = 1, \ldots, m \\[2mm]
&\frac{\partial L}{\partial \lambda_i} = \sum_{j=1}^{m} g_{ij}(x_j) + \xi_i - y_i \geqslant 0; \quad \lambda_i \geqslant 0 \quad i = 1, \ldots, n
\end{aligned}
\right\}
\tag{6.5}
$$

These equations can be solved centrally to find the optimal values of the unknowns. This corresponds to a centralised solution.

Before going on to consider Lange's alternative procedure, let us note one further point. It is well known that Lagrangean multipliers in constrained maximisation problems can be interpreted as prices. Thus associated with each constraint i in (6.2) there is a multiplier which can be interpreted as the shadow price of the corresponding good. Now solving equations (6.5) would yield values for the λ_is as well as for y_is and x_js: that is, the solution would include shadow prices as well as optimal quantities. The interesting point is that if these prices are used in a market, and if firms maximise profits at them, then the resulting levels of activity will be the same as those found in the direct solution of the problem. In other words, when the optimal plan has been found it can be implemented either by direct quantitative instruction to firms on what to produce or by use of the price mechanism. This is the familiar result that under certain conditions a quantitative allocation can be sustained by an appropriate price system.

The previous paragraph describes a way of implementing an already calculated optimal plan by means of the price mechanism. But Lange's proposal extends to using the price system to discover the optimal plan as well as to implement it. Formally the procedure would work like this. The central planning board would issue a set of prices. If firms find that they would have positive profits at that set of prices, they increase their planned scale of activity in proportion to the marginal profit. If they would suffer losses, they reduce the scale in accordance with the loss, except that if the level of activity is already zero it cannot be further reduced. Denoting the profit of the jth firm as π_j, this gives:

$$
dx_j/dt =
\begin{cases}
0 & \text{if } x_j = 0 \text{ and } d\pi_j/dx_j < 0 \\
d\pi_j/dx_j & \text{otherwise}
\end{cases}
\tag{6.6}
$$

On the demand side, quantity demanded y_i is increased if the marginal utility of the good exceeds the trial price for it announced by the central planning board; if the price is greater than the marginal utility, demand is reduced unless it is already zero. Formally:

$$dy_i/dt = \begin{cases} 0 \text{ if } y_i = 0 \text{ and } \partial U_i/\partial y_i - p_i < 0 \\ \partial U/\partial y_i - p_i \text{ otherwise} \end{cases} \tag{6.7}$$

This adjustment is done within the central planning board, which in our case determines the utility function. Finally, the central planning board adjusts prices in accordance with the over-all demand situation, raising prices of goods in excess demand, lowering those of goods in excess supply (to a minimum of zero):

$$dp_i/dt = \begin{cases} 0 \text{ if } p_i = 0 \text{ and } g_i > 0 \\ -g_i \text{ otherwise} \end{cases} \tag{6.8}$$

where $g_i = \Sigma_j g_{ij}(x_j) - y_i + \xi_i$, the excess supply of good i.

The three adjustment rules (6.6)–(6.8) now define a process in which supply is adjusted in accordance with marginal profit, demand in accordance with the relation between marginal utility and price, and price itself in accordance with excess supply or demand. This is essentially a continuous version, with adjustment taking place the whole time, of Lange's informal account of a possible planning procedure. It can be proved that if the utility function and the functions g_{ij} are strictly concave (the latter assumption corresponding to strictly decreasing returns to scale), then the process will converge to the optimal solution.

We have described the general case of the procedure, and we consider some of its properties below. However, it could be specialised or modified in a number of ways. An example of a specialisation would be to cause output and demand to be adjusted instantaneously to maximise respectively firms' profits and consumers' utility, rather than merely moved in the direction of an improvement, as prescribed in (6.6) and (6.7). In this case only prices would be gradually adjusted under (6.8).

The procedure can also be represented formally in a discrete version rather than the continuous version shown above. In this case adjustments take place in discrete steps rather than continuously. (The continuous version can be seen as the limiting case of the discrete version, as the duration of a step goes to zero.) The discrete case raises the question of the size of adjustment at each step. For example, if demand exceeds supply for a commodity at any stage, by how much should the price be raised? (This is sometimes known as the 'pitch' of a procedure.) There is a dilemma here because a narrow pitch may lead to slow convergence, while a large pitch may, in the discrete case, cause the procedure not to converge at all. A procedure should ideally at each stage adopt the maximum pitch consistent with convergence. Some progress has been made in finding the optimal pitch and incorporating it into a procedure, but a different procedure than that originated by Lange (see Henry and Zylberberg, 1978).

How does the procedure formally outlined above rate by the criteria set out in section 6.1. Clearly it is decentralised with respect to information as it meets the *privacy* requirements and the messages are restricted to *points* rather than functions or sets. (In this case the central planning board enunciates trial sets of prices and the other agents in the economy respond with quantities demanded or supplied at those prices.) The procedure can be shown to converge to the optimum under certain conditions but intermediate steps are clearly infeasible as demand and supply are out of balance. The chief advantages of the procedure are (i) the ease of calculation offered by the straightforward adjustment rules (6.6)–(6.8), and (ii) the fact that there is no need for storage of data at the centre, as all adjustments are based on immediate information. The chief drawback is the assumption of strictly decreasing returns to scale, which must be made to guarantee convergence. But as we shall see, this restriction on permissible environments is a feature of many decentralised planning procedures.

Lange clearly intended his proposal as a polemical rebuttal of the opponents of economic planning rather than as a blue-print for the operation of an actual planned economy. However, the procedure brings out an interesting feature of the operation of markets. In its iterative search for an optimal allocation of resources the market can be viewed as a giant analogue calculating machine, achieving the same solution as that achieved by centralised calculations made on a computer within the central planning board. When Lange returned to the subject thirty years later (it was his last article) he pointed out that the comparative advantages of market and centralised solutions had changed rapidly with the development of computer technology (Lange, 1967, p. 158). We return to the issue of the practical impact of computers on economic planning in Chapter 10.

6.3 Other decentralised procedures

The Lange model of decentralised planning, as subsequently refined by Arrow and Hurwicz, is the first but by no means the only decentralised procedure to be developed. The last fifteen years have seen the emergence of a range of other procedures, differing in the information transfers and computations they require and in the range of environments in which they can operate successfully. In this section we examine two procedures, the first due to Weitzman, the second to Malinvaud. As each lends itself to diagrammatic presentation, we use this method of exposition.

The Weitzman (1970) procedure is designed to capture one particular aspect of planning behaviour in Soviet-type economies, i.e. that the iterations between central planning board (CPB) and subordinate production units typically take the form of the CPB proposing a series of ambitious plans to which lower-level units respond with counterplans which scale down the CPB's initial target. (The rationale for this behaviour is to be sought in the incentive systems under which production units operate, as described in Chapter 2 and to be analysed in Chapter 9.) Weitzman has shown how this behaviour could be used to construct an optimal plan in a decentralised way.

The CPB is assumed to begin with an over-optimistic conception of the production possibilities of each firm. By aggregating its (false) estimate of the production sets of all firms it constructs an aggregate production set, chooses the optimum point within that set in accordance with its utility function, and then breaks down the optimal quantities among the firms and communicates them as individually specified output targets, one to each firm. Thus the first message the firm receives is a provisional output target which is, in fact, infeasible because the CPB's conception of what each firm can produce is exaggerated.

The process so far can be represented for the two-good case in Figure 6.1. The CPB's initial estimate of the firm's production-possibility frontier is CC, and the initial target it sends down as a result of the process described above is T_1. The firm's true production-possibility curve, however, is DD. Hence T_1 is infeasible, and the firm responds by scaling down each component of the initial target T_1 to a feasible plan by selecting any point on the segment PQ. The first counterplan, say R_1, is communicated to the CPB, together with another piece of information, the marginal rate of transformation at R_1, or the slope of the tangent to the production-possibility frontier at that point. The firm's response to the CPB thus consists of a counterplan in quantity terms, supplemented by information of a 'price' type — the marginal rate of transformation at that point.

After the first exchange of messages the CPB knows a point on the firm's actual production-possibility curve, and it also knows the slope of the curve at that point. Now *if there are constant or decreasing returns to scale*, the firm's whole production set must lie below the tangent to the production-possibility curve at R_1. Knowing this the CPB is able to revise its estimate of the firm's

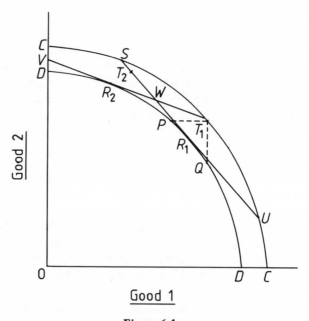

Figure 6.1

production-possibility frontier from CC, its initial estimate, to $CSR_1 UC$. With reduced, but still optimistic, estimates for each firm, the CPB repeats its over-all maximisation procedure, finds new targets for each firm, and the process is repeated. Our firm may receive target T_2, to which it responds with counterplan R_2 and the slope of the production-possibility curve at R_2. With this further information the CPB revises its estimate of the firm's production-possibility curve to $VR_2 WR_1 UC$, and selects a further target for the firm. The process continues until in the same iteration the CPB sends each firm a feasible target which lies on its production-possibility curve.

Essentially the CPB is building up from above a picture of the firm's production possibilities which is accurate within the relevant area close to the optimal point. Typically the successive targets set by the CPB and the counterplans proposed by the firms will eventually cluster in a relatively small area, and in regions of the production-possibility curve away from that area (near either axis in Figure 6.1, for example) the CPB may have a wholly inaccurate conception of what firms can produce even at the end of the procedure. The point is that this does not matter provided that the CPB has an accurate picture within the relevant area.

Weitzman's procedure can be shown to converge to an optimum. If the production-possibility curve of each firm consists of a series of linear stretches, convergence takes place in a finite number of stages. One adaptation of the procedure which may speed convergence is for the CPB, at the same time as it assigns targets to firms, to specify its own marginal rate of substitution between goods at the provisional optimal point. Firms could then choose a counterplan on their production-possibility curve where the marginal rate of substitution specified in the previous message from the CPB and the firm's own marginal rate of transformation are equal.

The procedure is informationally decentralised by our two criteria specified above: firms are required to issue messages based only on their private knowledge of what they can produce and on previous messages, and those messages themselves consist only of points rather than complete sets or functions. The size of messages is larger than in the Lange procedure, as firms communicate not only the quantities of goods they would produce but also 'price'-type information in the form of marginal rates of transformation. The information storage and computational requirements at the CPB are also greater. The CPB is building up a picture of what firms can produce; hence it needs to store previous messages, and to identify each message with a particular firm. It also has to solve a large constrained maximisation problem at each iteration. (In the Lange procedure, on the other hand, the CPB is interested only in aggregate supply and demand information communicated in the previous set of messages from the firms.)

The second procedure to be discussed in this section, which was developed by Malinvaud (1967), is in important respects the obverse of the Weitzman procedure. Where in the Weitzman procedure the CPB starts out with an over-optimistic view of what firms can produce, in the Malinvaud procedure the CPB begins with an underestimate. Where Weitzman has the CPB sending out messages consisting of quantity targets and receiving messages consisting of revised targets and 'prices', in the Malinvaud process the CPB issues prices and receives back quantity proposals.

In Malinvaud's procedure the CPB begins with a picture of the firm's production set which is less than what the firm can actually produce. This initial image of the true production-possibility frontier DD is represented by ABC in Figure 6.2. (In other words, the CPB knows that B is a feasible point, perhaps as a result of experience in the previous year.) When the CPB maximises its utility function subject to the constraint of what it *believes* firms can produce, it derives a provisional plan and the associated common marginal rate of tranformation and substitution. The CPB communicates this common marginal rate as a price ratio; and firms calculate the output levels which maximises their profits at those prices. If the price ratio is S_1T_1, then the firm illustrated in Figure 6.2 would maximise profits by producing at R_1. The CPB now knows that R_1 is on the firm's production-possibility frontier and is able to expand its estimate of the firm's production set to include any point in the area ER_1BC. It repeats its over-all maximisation exercise to find a new optimal point based on revised estimates of what firms can produce and communicates the associated marginal rate of transformation S_2T_2. The firm now finds a new profit-maximising point, R_2, which it communicates to the CPB. The CPB now increases its estimate of the firm's production set to ER_1R_2BC. This process continues until the CPB receives the same proposals in successive rounds from each firm. This occurs

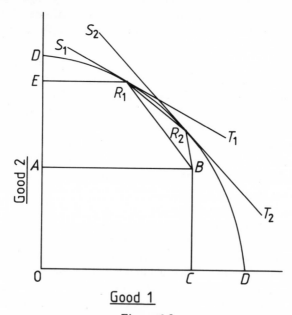

Figure 6.2

when the CPB has built up an accurate picture of the production possibilities of each firm (and hence of the economy as a whole) in the neighbourhood of the final plan. Implementation of the plan can then be achieved either by instructing firms to produce output equal to their last reply, or by telling them to maximise profits at the final set of prices.

The Malinvaud process can be shown to converge to an optimum, provided that firms work under constant or decreasing returns to scale. The computational load is equivalent to that in the Weitzman model, but the size of messages communicated is smaller, since in the firm's responses quantity data do not have to be supplemented with price-type information, as is the case with the Weitzman process. Moreover, each message from the CPB, since it is a set of relative prices, is identical for each firm. A more important difference, however, is that intermediate plans prepared in the course of the Malinvaud process are feasible, and can therefore be implemented even if the process does not reach a final conclusion. Moreover, each successive iteration yields a higher value of the objective function, thus satisfying the property of monotonicity. These desirable properties are present because in the Malinvaud process the CPB builds up its view of the firm's production possibilities from the inside of the production set, whereas in the Weitzman procedure the CPB successively reduces its estimate of what firms can produce. Both procedures, however, share the property that the CPB acquires in the process of communication with firms an image of what they can produce which, while not being wholly accurate, is accurate in the neighbourhood of the final optimal point.

6.4 Increasing returns to scale

Each of the three planning processes outlined above will only function in an environment characterised either by decreasing returns to scale in production (in the Lange case) or by non-increasing returns to scale (for the Weitzman and Malinvaud processes). The problems created by increasing returns for the Weitzman process are illustrated in Figure 6.3. Suppose the firm's true production-possibility curve is represented by DD. In the Weitzman procedure the CPB will set a target T_1 for the firm, which will respond with a counterplan R_1, and information specifying the marginal rate of transformation at R_1 — the tangent SU. The CPB will now presume that the firm's product set lies wholly below SU, but this will clearly exclude parts of the production set which lie above that line. The CPB will reach a false conclusion and the procedure will not work. A similar problem arises with the Malinvaud process, with the CPB again drawing a false conclusion from the firm's messages (the reader is left to work out this example for himself).

The restriction of many processes to environments not characterised by increasing returns to scale is a serious matter, as there is substantial evidence that increasing returns are prevalent in industry. Attention has naturally been focused on developing procedures which can also work successfully in environments with increasing returns. These fall into two categories: those which, like

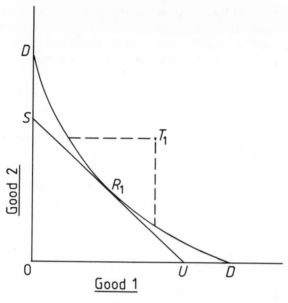

Figure 6.3

the three procedures discussed above, use prices or price-type information (marginal rates of transformation, etc.); and those which rely wholly on exchanges of messages in terms of quantities.

The first category includes a modification proposed by Arrow and Hurwicz to their version of the Lange procedure which we described above. The modification ensures convergence to a local optimum (i.e. to the best point within any specified neighbourhood, which need not, however, be the global or over-all optimum) (see Arrow and Hurwicz, 1977, pp. 76–88). Heal (1971) has developed an alternative procedure which uses prices in a rather ingenious way. It operates successfully because firms move continuously *in the direction of* an improvement rather than directly to an optimal point. This is illustrated in Figure 6.4 for the case of an economy with a single firm. The firm's production-possibility curve is CC, and community indifference curves are represented by I_1I_1 and I_2I_2. At point R_1 the marginal rate of substitution – the slope of the indifference curve – exceeds the marginal rate of transformation – the slope of the production-possibility curve. This implies that a movement down the production-possibility curve is advantageous. In Figure 6.4 the direction of movement from any starting-point would be towards R_n, the global optimum. However, the process starting from R_1 would stop at R_n even if the transformation curve were represented by CC' in the figure, where R_n would be a local but not a global maximum. In other words, convergence to the global optimum is not guaranteed.

There are three further problems. First, the point to which the Heal process converges may not be even a local maximum but a criticial point where the slopes of the indifference curve and production-possibility curve are momentarily equal. (It can, however, be shown that the process will not converge to a local minimum.) Second, in a multi-firm context local utility maximisation by each firm may result in a situation in which the final outcome is inefficient, in the sense of being inside the aggregate production-possibility frontier for the economy. This may arise if each firm converges to a point where it produces balanced quantities of all goods, when it would be a better solution for each firm to specialise in the production of a single good. Third, it is difficult to sustain a point such as R_n with a price mechanism. A firm maximising profits at given prices will choose a boundary point on either the horizontal or the vertical axis. If a point like R_n is to be sustained by a price system, prices would have to vary with output levels, producing iso-revenue curves like the indifference curves in Figure 6.4 rather than the standard linear iso-revenue curves.

The second category of planning procedures operating under increasing returns to scale uses no price-type information at all. We take as an example a procedure due to Cremer (1977). The firm's production-possibility curve is represented by CC in Figure 6.5. The CPB has initial knowledge of upper bounds

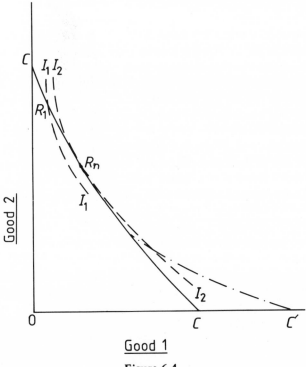

Good 1

Figure 6.4

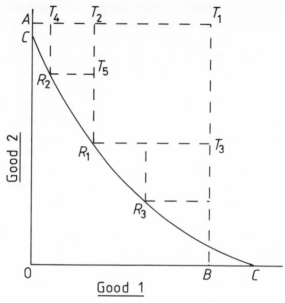

Figure 6.5

for the firm's production of the two goods, represented by point T_1 lying outside the firm's production-possibility curve. It sets T_1 as the firm's first target. The firm responds with R_1, an efficient feasible point strictly smaller than T_1.

The CPB now knows that any point to the north-east of R_1 is infeasible. It therefore knows that the firm's production set lies in the region $AT_2R_1T_3B$. The best point in this set will be either T_2 or T_3. The CPB chooses the better of these , say T_2, which it sets as a new target for the firm. The firm responds with R_2, a scaled-down version of T_2, and the CPB adjusts its estimate of what the firm can produce to $AT_4R_2T_5R_1T_3B$. This set is dominated by one of T_4 or T_5 or T_3. The CPB chooses the best of these — say T_3 — and issues that as a target. The firm's response of a feasible point, R_3, slices a little more away from the CPB's estimate of what the firm can produce. The process continues until the CPB issues a feasible target. It will then have approximated the firm's production-possibility frontier in the relevant area.

As the two examples given here show, increasing returns present grave difficulties for decentralised planning procedures. In one case the procedure can only be shown to converge to a local maximum, and in the other the informational and computational load becomes extremely burdensome. Indeed, it has been proved that no planning procedure which is decentralised in a rather more restrictive sense that the one used here can operate successfully with increasing returns (Calsamiglia, 1977; Cremer, 1978). The problems are multiplied further when we introduce additional difficulties such as externalities and indivisibilities, both of which are likely to be present in practice. Thus the limits on the environment in which decentralised planning processes can operate successfully do seem to be fairly tight.

6.5 A provisional assessment

The properties of the planning procedures discussed above are summarised in Table 6.1. Generally there is a trade-off between a procedure's environmental coverage and the complexity of the messages and calculations which it requires. There is no reason, of course, why a single procedure should be used throughout the whole economy. For example, plans for sectors with increasing returns to scale could be compiled with different procedures than those used for sectors with decreasing returns (for an example, see Portes, 1971, pp. 426–8). However, in spite of this possibility computational requirements and doubts about the convergence of the processes described above have contributed to discouraging their use in practical planning work. Where such processes have been used they are normally special (usually linear) versions of the processes outlined above. This simplification often reduces the computational burden substantially.

However, these are essentially technical problems which will gradually be solved with the introduction of cheaper and more powerful computational facilities. But the operation of decentralised procedures comes up against another obstacle, that of establishing a framework of incentives in which the firms in the economy can operate. We can illustrate this point with the Weitzman procedure, which requires each firm to respond to an infeasible target from the CPB with a point on its production-possibility frontier. We have seen in Chapter 2 above that when a procedure of this kind is used in the Soviet Union firms respond with a point strictly inside the frontier which enables them to retain a 'safety margin'. In other words, the system of incentives has to be integrated with the system of information flows if firms are to transmit accurate information.

This problem goes some way to explaining why decentralised procedures are often used within a CPB just as a computational device which breaks down a large problem into a number of smaller ones, rather than as a genuine means of decentralising the planning process within an economy. As shown elsewhere in this book, the problem of devising appropriate incentives for compiling and implementing plans is a difficult one.

Table 6.1 Properties of five iterative planning procedures

Properties	Lange	Malinvaud	Weitzman	Heal	Cremer
(1) Requirements on environment					
(a) Production: returns to scale must be	Decreasing	Decreasing or constant	Decreasing or constant	Increasing, constant or decreasing	Increasing, constant or decreasing
(b) Utility function must be	Concave	Concave (usual shaped indifference curves)	Concave	Concave	Non-decreasing in all arguments
(2) Convergence: is optimal plan finally achieved?	Yes	Yes (some minor differences)	Yes	Normally (local optimum)	Yes
(3) Feasibility: are intermediate plans feasible?	No	Yes	No	Yes	No
(4) Monotonicity: do successive iterations yield a higher value of the utility function?	Not applicable	Yes	Not applicable	Yes	Not applicable

(5) Information and computation					
(a) Are the requirements for decentralisation of information satisfied?	Yes	Yes	Yes	Yes	Yes
(b) Does the CPB need to know the source of the messages it receives?	No	Yes	Yes	Yes	Yes
(c) Must CPB remember information from previous iterations?	No	Yes	Yes	No	Yes
(d) Quantity of information transmitted at each iteration (i) by CPB	Vector of prices	Vector of prices (finally production targets)	Individual production quotas	Allocation of inputs to firms	Individual production quotas
(ii) by firms	Production programmes (CPB needs only know aggregate)	Production programmes (CPB needs individual knowledge from each firm)	Production programmes and marginal rates of transformation	Production programmes and marginal productivities of inputs	Production programme
(e) Must CPB solve large mathematical programming problems?	No	Yes	Yes	No	Yes

7 THEORY OF INDICATIVE PLANNING

7.1 Information and expectations under competition

In Chapter 1 we took as our starting-point the general-equilibrium model of perfect competition and discussed the possibility of planning by referring to certain drawbacks of this model. Two further shortcomings or difficulties with the model were alluded to but deferred until this chapter for an adequate treatment. These are the unsatisfactory formulation of the investment decision-making process within the general-equilibrium model, resulting from the standard assumptions made about intertemporal transactions; and second, the neglect of expectations and their effects on current decisions. Thus may be summarised the theoretical focus of this chapter, which leads on to the development of a theory of indicative planning. But we should also recall the more concrete examination of French experience with indicative planning which occupied Chapter 4. Much of the theory to follow has an empirical counterpart in this experience which we shall try to make clear as the argument proceeds. Moreover, some of the theoretical arguments which have been critical of the concept of indicative planning have been at least in part based directly on the French efforts in that field (see, for example, Lutz, 1969; and Richardson, 1971).

It is as well to begin by suggesting some of the questions which a theory of indicative planning might hope to answer. First of all, does the approach we are proposing to use actually yield a coherent theory of indicative planning? Second, what sort of indicators can help firms (and possibly households as well) to make decisions which are economically rational from a long-term point of view? Third, how should the rate of investment be determined? Fourth, how far does the theory of indicative planning suggest that it would be possible to reduce the uncertainty which firms face, and what economic effects are to be expected from an enduring reduction of uncertainty? And finally, what are the implications of the theory of indicative planning for the conduct of macroeconomic policy? Obviously this is not a complete list of possible questions but it does include some of the major ones. Let us therefore proceed to the analysis.

Strictly interpreted, the perfectly competitive model extends over an indefinite number of future time periods, which analytical tractability normally confines to a finite number of periods. This observation entails that great care should be taken in interpreting the equilibrium set of prices which emerges from the model (see Bliss, 1975). Take, for example, a simple everyday commodity like a pair of shoes, neglecting the fact that they come in numerous styles and sizes and are available in many different locations; for the moment the essential variable is time. Thus shoes available in the first period are not the same as shoes available in the second or tenth. Hence for each time period the set of equilibrium prices will include a price for shoes, these prices forming a vector: $p_1, p_2, \ldots, p_{10}, \ldots$ (p_i is the price of shoes in period i).

Now, p_{10} is the price payable at the start of period 1 for shoes to be delivered in period 10; that means we must regard p_{10} in present-value terms. In the model all transactions for all time are decided at the start — this is what a full general-equilibrium implies — so that p_{10} is the only price which will ever arise for period 10 shoes. More realistically one might expect it to be possible to regard p_{10} as the actual price of shoes which will rule in period 10 discounted by some factor common to all period 10 goods and services (the discount factor would depend on the choice of a *numéraire*). Even this is not quite correct, however, as p_{10} may well be the equilibrium price based on the information available before period 1, but if expectations are not fulfilled then p_{10} may not be 'verified' by the market economy. What is perhaps worse than this, it is rather likely that the real costs of operating numerous, possibly thin markets, which are neglected in the formal model, will preclude the emergence of a market which could even begin to generate a price like p_{10}: there simply is no forward market for shoes!

The general-equilibrium model also has implications for savings and investment, though these do not appear explicitly as part of the solution. Consider first a typical household. Over the periods covered by the model the household faces a single budget constraint to the effect that the present value of its consumption stream should not exceed the present value of its income stream. Such a household can borrow to finance present consumption with no restriction related to its current income; similarly, it can choose to save. As a matter of definition, $s_1 = y_1 - c_1$, where s_1 is period 1 savings (borrowing if negative), y_1 is income accruing in period 1, and c_1 is the value of consumption then, all evaluated at the equilibrium prices. All these savings or borrowings earn or pay interest at the rates implicit in the equilibrium price system, with no difference between borrowing and lending rates. In practice, as we all know, households do not have access to the kinds of borrowing facility suggested here, and for fairly obvious reasons.

Second, consider a typical firm: its objective is the maximisation of the present value of its profit stream (according to standard assumptions; but other objectives have often been suggested in the literature, such as sales maximisation or growth maximisation — see Baumol, 1962; Koutsoyiannis, 1975; Marris and Wood, 1971, ch. 10). Provided this is positive, it is of no consequence that the firm may incur negative profits, as these would be measured by normal accounting conventions, in one or more of the model's years: that is, our model firms can suffer from no liquidity problems. Firms can of course invest, and these investments are financed partly from their own resources, partly from net savings by households. Again, all their production and investment programmes are determined by the start of period 1: the 'market' does not re-open.

From these remarks it seems that the general-equilibrium model allows far too much intertemporal flexibility, far more than exists in any actual economy. It should be pointed out that some of the apparent flexibility is really an illusion: for example, if budget constraints allowed everyone to buy all their shoes in period 4, say, it would still be impossible for them to do so, because of production constraints and capacity limitations. And equilibrium prices would therefore be established in such a way that households would not collectively choose to make these impossible demands. Nevertheless, it is apparent that many restrictions on transactions which exist in all real-world economies are not present in the model; making allowance for some of them changes the nature of the model's equilibrium as well as the latter's implications for planning.

Returning to the first point the non-existence of futures markets creates obvious difficulties for investors. Very few forward markets operate on a regular basis, and those that do rarely extend beyond securities markets, the money market and the so-called 'commodity' markets. To the extent that employment contracts cover several years (e.g. for apprentices, management trainees, senior management, lecturers, etc., in the United Kingdom) they are apparently another form of forward market; however, wage scales specified in employment contracts are normally superseded by the results of subsequent collective bargaining so that we do not have a true forward market in labour, only a sequence of spot markets.

Now if, for the most part, forward markets do not exist, then the information they provide to investors, namely the relevant prices (expressed in present-value terms), is also not available. But investors need these prices in order to evaluate, by means of computing their present values, the relative profitability of the alternative investment projects under consideration. Even when less sophisticated investment-appraisal techniques are used, some prices for goods which will only be available at a future date, after new capacity has been installed, are required. Plainly, therefore, some substitute has to be found for the missing prices. Mirrlees (1969) suggested that current prices may serve to provide estimates for these prices, and, moreover, that this is one of the major functions of the price system. Alternatively, entrepreneurs could use other information, for example to do with foreseeable developments in the technology of production and distribution, or recognised possibilities for organisational improvement as the foundation for their price-forecasting exercises. Yet a third procedure would be to estimate the required prices by some form of extrapolation from the experience of the recent past. For the last two cases different entrepreneurs would form different expectations about future prices, either because technical information is not typically uniformly accessible to everyone at a given moment of time, or because there are numerous ways of performing extrapolations. Thus there are practical means of avoiding the problems resulting from the lack of forward markets, but the effect of their use is to generate a considerable diversity of price expectations; consequently some entrepreneurs will turn out to have forecast correctly, while others will turn out to be mistaken. Such diversity may in fact be helpful for the establishing of equilibrium, as argued by Richardson (1960) and Loasby (1976, 1977).

So much for prices, but what can be said about the corresponding quantities or outputs? In principle, firms in perfect competition can sell what they choose at prevailing prices, so that there is actually no need for them to forecast market size. Over a long enough period of time, when equilibrium prices are firmly established, this may well be correct, but normally firms do need to estimate their potential market quite carefully: partly because of cyclical factors, partly because Arrow's concept of competitive firms behaving like mini-monopolists away from equilibrium captures an important aspect of market adjustment, and partly because of widespread attempts to deviate from perfect competition through product differentiation.

Rather paradoxically, although the model of perfect competition assumes economic agents to have complete information about the prevailing prices, the view it takes about other types of information is quite different. For example, technical information concerning production possibilities resides in individual firms and is their property, not being transferable at all between them. Since firms observe prices, however, they can deduce that certain (probably most) goods are being made more profitably by other firms than they could manage themselves, which is evidence that these other firms have different knowledge of technology. Despite this the model allows no technology transfer in response to incentives produced by such price and cost observations. Technical information is simply dispersed among the firms in a manner given initially and is unaffected by any decisions firms might take. Apart from the need for drastic reformulation of the model in order to explain research and development (R & D) outlays the basic model somewhat overstates the technical secrecy which characterises a private-enterprise economy. Indeed, many firms incur costs to preserve their secrets against other firms acting on the incentives mentioned above, but much information is still transferred. In contrast, such information is normally freely transferable within a socialist economy (except information obtained under a co-operation agreement with a Western firm), but the incentives for its actual transfer are different; hence the net effect is not certain.

Another kind of information which is crucial for everyday economic management of most firms, even new ones, is information about the past; in the formal competitive model such information is non-existent except in so far as it is embodied in technology and preferences. We already saw earlier that the past could provide some guidance for forecasting prices. And past economic experience, especially of prices, provides a basis for developing expectations about what the current equilibrium prices should be. If these expected prices were established, it might well turn out that they do not yield an equilibrium, for the present is not merely an extrapolation of the past. But given their expectations, firms are unlikely to start adjusting prices straightaway, or certainly not substantially; instead they would accept quantity adjustments, some producing more than expected, others less, while waiting to see how the market situation develops.

(There is a rapidly developing theoretical literature on quantity adjustments; see, for example, Barro and Grossman (1974, 1976).) And a world in which quantities are adjusted like this is a world in which firms should also be making forecasts about quantities, contrary to the standard assumptions of the competitive model.

Let us first try to see why firms' quantity forecasts might turn out wrongly, which should suggest the types of information needed to improve the forecasts. There are two principal sources of error: namely, incorrect expectations about the equilibrium relative prices, and failure to judge correctly the prospective general level of demand. Now, at equilibrium, there are intimate connections between the price and quantity descriptions of the equilibrium. These connections arise from what are called *duality theorems*, for some analysis of which see Dixit (1976). The point is also referred to in Chapter 6, where we introduced planning procedures. The implication is that as an alternative to our earlier suggestions for improving price forecasting one might also get closer to equilibrium by improving the forecasting of quantities, branch by branch, or product by product. This use of quantity indicators as a basis for indicative planning is examined more closely in section 7.2 below.

The general level of demand refers to what is normally called *aggregate demand* and immediately calls to mind the standard monetary and fiscal policies employed in its regulation. For the present argument the relevant point to note is that government activities, whether to do with taxation or expenditure, are rarely motivated by considerations of profit maximisation, so that they do not give rise to conventional supply and demand functions. From the private sector's point of view, government demands for goods and services are simply additions to demands arising from households and firms themselves, while government supplies of services, for example education, also affect demands for privately produced goods and services through relations of complementarity and substitution; for example, provision of state education affects both the demand for books and the demand for private education. Hence demands and supplies in the private sector depend not only on the prevailing prices but also on the level and structure of government activities. As a result, private-sector forecasting and planning will be the more reliable, the better informed it is about the government's intentions for developing its own activities; total government expenditure would be a helpful indicator for some industries, but others could more usefully be provided with much greater structural detail.

By now we have probably said enough about informational aspects of the competitive model to illustrate some of its weaknesses. We have proposed ways in which firms and households can 'construct' the information which the model assumes them to have, and make use of other information neglected by the model which they do have. This is a step forward and begins to demonstrate what we believe to be one of the major features of indicative planning: namely, its constant striving to 'patch up' the real world (in our case the French economy) by improving the information flows to firms and households in a fashion designed to achieve a closer approximation to a competitive equilibrium. To take the argument further requires a more careful examination of the investment process and some comments on uncertainty. Before passing on to these issues in the following sections, however, we add a brief remark on *optimality*.

As noted already, in the introductory chapter, the competitive model has the appealing optimality properties of technical and Pareto efficiency, both of which are considerably weakened in practical interpretations when we take account of those aspects of real economies not properly described by the model. Although suggesting that pure concepts of efficiency might be hard to apply to the econ-omies we are studying, we are not thereby prevented from attempting to make any forms of welfare judgement about alternative economic systems – for it is always possible to compare realisations, even though there may be no warrant for comparing realised outcomes with some theoretically ideal models of the econ-omic systems concerned. Thus analysis of income distribution, living standards, productivity, and so on, can often be guided by economic theory, but we should beware of casually assuming that one or other system being compared actually satisfies strictly some standard set of optimality conditions. On the other hand, to the extent that an indicative planning system succeeds in providing the very information (or good approximations to it) needed to achieve a full competitive equilibrium, optimality conditions could be (approximately) restored.

7.2 Co-ordination of investments
It has been argued that a market-type economy is unlikely to generate 'enough' savings in the absence of government intervention to impose a higher savings rate; in addition, the uncertainty faced by firms about their prospective growth rates makes them 'unduly cautious' about committing resources to new invest-ments. An appropriately organised system of indicative planning can apparently solve both these problems simultaneously and help to get the economy on to a self-sustaining path of faster growth. The aim of this section is to evaluate these claims in the light of some of the more critical literature on indicative planning (see Dobb, 1960, 1969; Marglin, 1963; Meade, 1970; Massé, 1965; Beckerman *et al.*, 1965; Lutz, 1969; and Richardson, 1971).

Why should a market economy give rise to less than optimal rates of saving and investment? Consider savings first of all. Part of this is done by firms in the forms of depreciation provisions and retained profits, and part by households. Typically each household arrives at its decisions about savings independently of decisions made by other households. Together these savings sum to a total amount for the economy which, in Marglin's view, falls short of the total which households would have chosen if they had determined their savings plans collect-ively. He claims that aggregate savings takes on the character of a public good with its attendant free-rider problems. It is argued, essentially, that people want to see their society progressing and are quite willing to contribute their share but not to bear a disproportionate part of the burden. Thus all might feel better off if savings were higher, but no individual is willing to save more himself since this would confer most of the benefit on to others. The implication is that government must take on the task of raising the over-all savings rate to a satisfactory level, using taxation to distribute the burden reasonably equitably. It must be admitted that it is rather hard to be more precise, either in theory or in practice, about the identification of a satisfactory level of savings.

A quite different argument, leading to the same general conclusion, suggests that all households discount the future more than society as a whole should do. Individual households do not expect to live indefinitely, and given their expectations they can make consumption and savings plans to cover the relevant period. Personal savings in the economy then depend on the distribution of the population between different stages of the life cycle. (For discussion of the life-cycle approach to savings, see Ando and Modigliani (1963). The argument of this paragraph is not absolutely rigorous since precise conclusions depend on the detailed formulation of a life-cycle model.) For a slowly growing population net savings (from the early part of the life cycle) will typically outweigh net dissavings (e.g. of pensioners) so that savings would be positive in total. Also, if people expected to live longer, they would probably choose to save more at early stages in their lives. Society has to adopt a longer time perspective than any particular household in order to provide capital stock and other resources for the future generations, which again suggests a case for government to raise savings above the levels which individuals would themselves have chosen.

Now savings are only desirable in so far as there are sufficiently productive investment projects waiting to be taken up, either in the public or private sectors of the economy. It is obviously important to judge correctly the appropriate balance between public and private sectors, and to direct investment accordingly, but there are reasons for believing that the private sector is often too cautious or risk-averse in its investment decisions. Let us now consider why the private sector might invest too little, as it is frequently said to do in the United Kingdom, and as used to be argued in France. The standard explanation for low rates of investment is that investors face too much uncertainty. In order to analyse this issue it is helpful to distinguish between two principal forms of uncertainty, which Meade (1970, 1971) calls *environmental* uncertainty and *market* uncertainty.

The former, environmental uncertainty, is that unavoidable or largely unavoidable uncertainty resulting from natural phenomena (e.g. the weather) and factors external to the economy of interest. Its effects can often be mitigated by means of suitable investments (e.g. irrigation schemes, flood-control projects) but the underlying uncertainty remains. The latter, market uncertainty, however, concerns the problems which arise when one group of economic agents does not know the market-induced decisions of others; thus enterprises do not have enough information about the intentions of their competitors, nor do they always know enough about government policies or intentions.

Being unavoidable to a large extent environmental uncertainty can hardly be held responsible for low rates of private investment, unless it is claimed that entrepreneurs have suddenly begun to worry about it much more than in the past. This would amount to a shift in entrepreneurs' utility functions in the direction of an increase in risk-aversion. (See Arrow (1970) for a formal definition and analysis of the concept of risk-aversion.) Alternatively, a model in which entrepreneurs basically behaved in a way which ensured the continued viability of their firms would have the same outcome if perceived costs of bankruptcy increased or changes in tax laws made it appear more probable. Neglecting such complications, we can concentrate attention on the more interesting problems raised by market uncertainty.

In several recent works Nickell (1974, 1977, 1978) has studied various aspects of the investment decision at the level of the individual firm in situations where the firm's environment is changing. Part of the analysis considers a firm which is subjectively certain about the course of development of the economic variables which determine its profitability, and on the basis of which it formulates an investment plan. The environment then changes unexpectedly, and the firm has to adjust to the new conditions, while continuing to believe that there will not be further changes (somewhat implausibly, admittedly). The context is one in which the changes being analysed are best understood as resulting from government policy operating to expand or contract the economy.

Another strand of the analysis considers a firm which expects its environment to change in some particular way, but it is uncertain about the time at which the change will occur. In the model the change examined is a shift in the firm's demand curve, which could again result from shifts in government policy. A further complication is the existence of lags between decisions and the coming into operation of new plant and equipment (delivery lags), which means that the firm is committed to some projects even if demand changes in an unfavourable direction while being unable to respond immediately to a favourable change.

The upshot of all this is that profit-maximising firms are typically adjusting their capital stock cautiously and gradually in response to current or expected future developments in their environment. It turns out that even large changes in current demand only lead to substantial increases in investment if they are expected to endure for a significant period of time. Moreover, if government policy is directed at getting the economy out of a slump, firms' reactions are likely to be especially sensitive to their expectations about the duration and severity of the slump. Overall it seems to be much easier for governments to discourage than to stimulate investment by its policy measures. This should not be taken as an argument against all intervention by governments, but it does strongly suggest that such interventions are most likely to be successful if they take account of the current state of expectations held by firms. In addition, over a longer period those policies are likely to be most effective which help to generate or sustain favourable expectations about the future growth in demand. And a stable and therefore predictable environment is more conducive to investment than one which is erratically shifting in response to the changing views of policy-makers.

So much for the effects of government policies on investment. Unfortunately, the practical situation is somewhat more complex than Nickell suggests, for in his models government policies impinge directly on the demands of individual firms, whereas these policies actually affect industry demands first of all, and only subsequently or indirectly act on the demands faced by individual firms. And within the literature on indicative planning there is a lively debate about this problem of the links between firm and industry demand. The problem arises as soon as we attempt a complete specification of the information needed by firms as a basis for their investment decisions. Except in the extreme and unusual case of a pure monopoly, the effects of government policies on industry demand are not the same as their effects on the demands facing firms. Firms may perfectly well estimate what is happening at industry level but they still meet with great difficulty in estimating how their competitors might react.

Given the expectation of an increase in total market size, resulting from the general rise in incomes as the economy grows, specific government policies, or shifts in consumer preferences, any given firm can only predict the extra demand it will face if it also knows or can estimate the demand which would be met by competitors. Consequently its own investment to increase capacity will only turn out successfully if it judges correctly the investment decisions of competitors. But how do firms get the information to make such judgements? According to Richardson, the standard stories we tell about the market mechanism do not provide a convincing answer to this question. Firms are supposed to invest in response to price signals which make some lines of activity seem relatively profitable, others not. But if one particular firm, or potential firm in the case of a new entrant, observes the signals and considers investment, then why not others? Yet if all such firms go ahead and invest, none will prove to be profitable and the market may well be oversupplied, for each is able to recognise the investment opportunity but no one knows how many others will avail themselves of it, nor to what extent: the price signals presage an increase in market demand but not necessarily in the demand for the products of each firm in, or potentially in, the market. Thus a firm's investment decisions depend not merely on the ruling prices which it observes but also on additional information or expectations.

There are two extreme cases, resulting respectively in no investment and too much investment, which illustrate the problem facing individual firms. In the former situation each firm believes that information about the investment opportunity is widely and easily available to potential competitors, encouraging the expectation that many others will take advantage of it. Hence our initial firm is likely to regard the project as too risky and refrain from investment all together. Conversely, in the latter situation, each firm considers that it is the only one which recognises the new opportunity, and proceeds to invest only to find that many others have behaved in a similar way. Thus in Richardson's words, 'an opportunity for all is an opportunity for none'.

What follows from this is that standard views about perfection of information under perfect competition do not lead to a determinate equilibrium of investment activity at the level of the firm. Somewhat paradoxically it seems that equilibrium is only likely to emerge from the normal operation of market forces if one postulates some imperfections in information flows, ensuring that some but not all firms recognise any particular investment opportunity. (For more details of this argument, see Loasby (1977) and Richardson (1960).) In this context the initially appealing proposal to operate a system of indicative planning in order to 'co-ordinate' the investment plans of different firms and branches of the economy can turn out to be positively harmful in practice, for such 'co-ordination' modifies information flows – we do not immediately regard the modification as an obvious improvement – without imposing the corresponding allocation of resources, since obligatory targets and instructions are not a feature of indicative planning, either in theory or in the French experience of it. Yet a satisfactory allocation of investment requires either some imperfections of information (market) or some degree of centralised control (central planning), while indicative planning seeks some middle ground which may be worse than either of these.

Indicative planning can be set up in two possible ways, called by Richardson *analytic* and *synthetic*. The synthetic approach starts from the views and expectations of individual firms in each industry or branch and builds up from these some common prognosis for the industry as a whole; naturally firms' opinions may well take into account likely changes in government policy, but the emphasis remains with the firms' own forecasts about developments. In contrast, the analytic approach takes as its starting-point official predictions or desires about the development path of the economy. Given expectations about the path of total output, employment, consumption, and so on, the next step is to estimate their implications for the pattern of output by the main branches of the economy. The outcome is once again a set of proposals for economic growth in various branches, with attendant implications for investment, employment and pricing policy. If both approaches to indicative planning are pursued simultaneously, it is rather likely that their results – an indicative plan broken down to branch level – would be very different in consequence of the substantial differences in information and incentives between the agents involved in the planning process in each case. Presumably, then, there would be some attempt at reconciliation in order to secure an agreed plan. But from the preceding arguments it follows that this whole procedure is beset by immense conceptual and practical difficulties which make us doubtful whether much significance can be attached to the resulting indicative plan.

In order to convince the reader of this we should examine the following two questions. First, is there any reason to expect that the outcome of an indicative planning exercise would actually be a feasible or desirable allocation of resources for the economy as a whole, or even a useful guide to such an allocation? Second, given that an indicative plan is obligatory for no one, for whom might it provide helpful information, and whose decisions are likely to be affected by such a plan?

The first question concerns the quality of resource allocation to be expected from carrying out an indicative plan. Now a plan based only on the expectations or intentions of individual firms, suitably aggregated, is unlikely to be consistent with the economy's over-all resource availabilities, essentially because the proposals from different firms will typically derive from imperfect and incomplete information about what these constraints actually are. If each firm pursued its own plans, such inconsistency might not matter greatly, simply implying that some would succeed in carrying out their plans while others would fail. For example, some firms would judge correctly which kind of new product could succeed on the market, while many others would try out new products which did not sell. Similarly, firms' decisions might depend on their expectations about future wage rates, which at least in part depend on the balance between supply and demand for labour: different firms would normally hold different expectations about the likely development of the labour-market balance. Again, some firms would make mistakes, while others would turn out to have their judgements vindicated by the actual course of development followed by the economy.

An indicative plan attempts somehow to reconcile all these incompatible expectations. The aggregate of firms' proposals therefore has to be adjusted to render it feasible from the point of view of economy-wide constraints on resource allocation. The resulting plan is convenient for certain purposes of government, like estimation of the government's budget balance, and allows the production of a series of tables showing the economy's proposed growth path along which the major resources – labour, capital, foreign exchange, and so on – are all 'properly' allocated. As a public-relations exercise this is ideal. For the general public, who are not concerned to make production decisions, indicative plans may well be judged rather favourably, at least initially, since they suggest that the government has a coherent view about the economy's development and create the impression that what is actually a crudely adjusted forecast will become the reality. Firms themselves know better, and are unlikely to be misled, which evidently raises some problems of controlling plan implementation as far as the government is concerned (these problems are surveyed in the following section). But in the absence of any mechanism or organisation for imposing the allocation on firms it is difficult to take it very seriously beyond that. Clearly the aggregate of original proposals from firms cannot actually 'happen' because it is generally known to be inconsistent overall. But there is no warrant for adjusting this aggregate to secure formal consistency when the result corresponds to nobody's concrete expectations, except perhaps the expectations of a government powerless to act! Planners always assume quite casually that consistency is not only attainable but highly desirable; in our view, however, it is a grossly overrated feature of any economic plan, especially an indicative plan.

Consistency is always relative to some model of the economy's functioning. Consequently, to claim that a given plan is consistent merely asserts that it is compatible with the constraints of the prevailing economy-wide model, given suitable assumptions about values taken by whatever variables are deemed exogenous. It does not guarantee that the plan can actually be implemented, though one might expect that only small modifications would be required to secure feasibility. Nor is the averaging of diverse expectations and the imposition of consensus a convincing way of securing allocations of resources which are either technically efficient or satisfactory in welfare terms.

And even without these doubts it is not easy to think of firms which could use an indicative plan in their investment planning process, as Richardson and Lutz have both made clear. For example, suppose that the output of the mechanical engineering industry is expected to rise by 4 per cent per annum over the next five years according to the plan. What implications does this have for a firm specialising in the manufacture of valves for use, say, in chemical-industry construction? The answer, of course, may well be very little! The firm cannot just assume that output of its own specialised products will also grow at the industry average rate of 4 per cent per annum, yet the plan itself provides no basis for a more complex analysis. On the other hand, our firm may be interested in plans for the chemical industry since these affect the likely demand for valves. But even that information might be of limited value if, as is rather likely, the valves being made are only needed for certain types of chemical-industry construction. Moreover, if our firm were less specialised, the growth targets of the plan might be more meaningful indicators of market prospects, but the firm's situation would be complicated by competition from others. As we have already seen, such competition, especially if we assume 'perfect information', makes it almost impossible for firms to formulate rational investment decisions; the indicative plan 'improves' the information available to firms, and by doing so may only make matters worse. Thus most firms would find it very difficult to make use of the quantity indicators provided by an indicative plan, as is borne out by the French experience.

This distinctly negative appraisal of indicative planning started by assuming a plan built up from enterprise proposals, initially inconsistent but somehow reconciled – i.e. Richardson's synthetic approach. The argument would go through in a very similar way for a plan based on the analytic approach, leading us to conclude that for private-sector agents (firms and households) an indicative plan has little practical significance except as a public-relations exercise, and in particular provides very little information of value to investors; it does, however, provide information in a form useful for the kind of economic analysis and regulation with which governments are often concerned.

It would be unfair to supporters of indicative planning to leave the argument at this point, so we conclude the section by commenting on some recent work of Kornai (1971) which adopts what may be called a *systems theory approach* rather than a general-equilibrium approach to analysis of the economic mechanism. This implies a slightly more favourable appraisal of indicative planning by suggesting that the above argument was somewhat overstated. Kornai emphasises the importance of information flows in modern economic systems, especially their potential role in reducing the uncertainty which economic agents, mainly enterprises, face. For example, he points out that firms are often uncertain about the demand for their products, so that even when the market provides signals about current sales and prevailing prices there is still the need for further information to guide investment decisions. It is in this context that Kornai sees a system of planning indicators playing an important role.

One way of reducing uncertainty is by improving the information flows generated by market operations themselves; this might be done by devoting some resources to market research, or by developing market models to yield more reliable price forecasts, and so on. But an alternative response to uncertainty is what Kornai calls the 'multiplication of information channels'. In any communication system random disturbances generate uncertainty and distort signals. If such uncertainty is significant and an accurate signal is required, then just as in the economic case there are two possible approaches: either improve the original signal, or send several signals independently. It is the latter which corresponds to the multiplication of information channels; in the economic context it involves some combination of information provided by the market, the plan, the credit system and perhaps from elsewhere. Moreover, these alternative sources of information do not merely repeat the information provided by the market.

Plan indicators in particular are supposed to give firms more confidence in their expectations about the economy's likely growth path which, by reducing uncertainty, could be helpful to investment even if the indicators were not detailed enough to include specific output targets for each firm. The precise means whereby plan and market information might be combined and reconciled would not be easy to formalise in a simple model, but Kornai's general point is that such disparate types of information can indeed be combined and used by enterprises. For example, the enterprises' past experience would sometimes enable them to do this. Thus, despite earlier arguments about the problems faced by firms in using indicative planning targets and indicators to guide their investment decisions, Kornai is claiming that that information can actually still be helpful, presumably by reducing firms' uncertainty about the general economic trends likely to be experienced in their environment.

7.3 Problems of control
In the preceding two sections we have examined, albeit somewhat sketchily, some of the ways in which markets might fail to provide enterprises with sufficient or the right kinds of information to determine a reasonably coherent set of investment decisions. It was also suggested that matters might not be greatly helped by the formulation and dissemination to individual firms of consistent branch targets for the economy's development. Nevertheless, systems of indicative planning can do rather better than these arguments would lead one to believe by employing certain techniques of economic regulation which link the activities and decisions of particular enterprises to some of the plan targets. Naturally the result is a highly differentiated and, indeed, quite messy regulative system, whose effectiveness depends on the care with which significant structural features of the economy are allowed for. Such differentiated regulation has

certainly been a feature of French indicative planning and, while not referred to as indicative planning, some elements of official industry policy in the United Kingdom illustrate a similar approach. Moreover, even in Hungary's investment policy it is easy to discern elements of the same spirit. though the over-all pattern of investment is imposed much more strictly than has been the case in any market-type economy.

Rather than dwelling at length on each of a long list of possible controls, we restrict attention here to some brief comments on some of the major ones which have been considered and/or applied in either France or the United Kingdom. The instruments and policy approaches to be surveyed are the following:

(1) Concentration on major firms and key sectors.

(2) Agencies such as the National Enterprise Board (NEB) or the Scottish Development Agency (SDA).

(3) Taxes and subsidies related to investment decisions.

(4) Direct controls over investment in nationalised industries and publicly provided services (e.g. education, health, roads, etc.).

(5) Other macroeconomic instruments.

The starting-point for successful control of the microeconomic structure of a market economy is the recognition that such control may be achieved quite effectively by concentrating attention on key firms and sectors. Many branches of the economy are characterised by the predominance of one or a few large companies, regulation of which largely determines the pattern of development in their respective branches. Thus although the market may be supplied by a few large firms together with numerous smaller ones, in many cases it turns out that policy towards the former is what really matters.

An important example recently has been UK price policy, in which different rules applied to firms in a number of size categories but with the most stringent requirements imposed on the largest firms. They had to notify proposed price increases, which were subject to strict rules on allowable costs and controls on unit profitability. The object of the differentiation, of course, was to reduce the number of firms with whom the Price Commission had to maintain close contact while enforcing an effective degree of regulation; spot checks and regular monitoring, plus publicity for offenders served to regulate most of the small firms. No doubt, the Price Commission would also be aided by competitive pressures: if the market leader's price were held down, then smaller and probably relatively high-cost competitors would not be in a position to raise their prices. At least part of any cost increase had to be absorbed. This case illustrates the important principle that regulation can be enhanced and strengthened if it can be performed in a way which allows normal market forces to reinforce rather than oppose it.

Even in cases when the policy affects or is available to all firms it is quite likely that the large firms will be in a better position to take advantage of it than smaller ones. For example, investment grants in development areas of the United Kingdom (before 1970; since replaced by various provisions of the 1975

Industry Act) were largely taken up by a few of the biggest firms in each area, so that the main impact of the policy on, say, employment was the outcome of these firms' decisions combined with local linkage effects. For very small firms it may well be far too costly for them to keep track of, and therefore respond appropriately to, every shift in official policy; this is especially likely to be the case in the United Kingdom, where policy changes have been quite frequent, as compared with France, which exhibited greater stability, at least until the 1970s.

The identification of key or leading sectors raises somewhat more complicated and controversial issues. The very attempt seems to rest on the view that in any given period some sectors will need to expand significantly faster than others, and that over-all growth will be largely governed by the performance of these so-called 'leading' sectors through their direct and indirect linkage with the remainder of the economy. Models where changes in the pattern of demand are determined by income elasticities, which then influence production levels through an input–output system of relationships, tend to suggest this view of development, but they are not, however, especially easy to apply. Moreover, such models are subject to some severe limitations, among which the following are particularly important.

First, demand for many products is very dependent on export markets, so that domestic income elasticies may not be the relevant ones. Second, the presence of demand (or potential demand) has little immediate implication for domestic production, for one can always choose to import, though not everything of course. Hence even given the demand, there is still the question of how much to produce domestically and how far to engage in international trade. Consequently one cannot immediately decide on the basis of demand studies which should be the leading sectors, for it is not merely a matter of prediction but one of very tricky choice depending on domestic resources and costs at least as much as on demand.

Third, the approach is beset by extremely serious aggregation problems, for even if it is agreed that some branch such as small electric motors is to develop especially rapidly this is a long way from identifying exactly which types of motor should experience the greatest expansion. There is obviously no warrant for assuming that the output of every product in the branch should grow at the same rate, and the pattern of investment required in it must depend on more detailed information than the average growth rate unless all new capacity is sufficiently flexible to be able to produce a wide range of products. Moreover, the extra detail is not such as can be provided by the standard kinds of input–output tables. But planned economies do manage to find solutions to these difficulties – clearly, since plans often contain at least a few specific investment decisions – so we should not exaggerate them here.

The experience of the planned economies suggests that the difficulties are greater in some sectors than in others. For example, in the case of organic chemicals it may be clear that demand for ethylene is rising and it would not be too hard to compare domestic production costs with the costs of additional imports in deciding whether to install new domestic capacity. Some other types of chemical plant, or capacity used for, say, food-processing or textiles manufacture, may be easily adaptable to a variety of specific products, and hence do not require detailed product-mix information before their installation. In between these extremes come projects to build plant which has to be tailor-made for the particular product, like factories making televisions. Even here the enterprises concerned should either have some knowledge of demand (though, as we discussed earlier, it may be virtually impossible for them to predict their market share) or the resulting structures might at a cost be adaptable to the manufacture of something else in the event of forecasting errors.

Thus at least in certain branches of the economy the details of new projects have to be decided by individual firms; there will naturally be mistakes, but at least firms themselves are possessed of the precise market information and experience of specific products which governments are unable to obtain themselves. How well the information is used is a different matter, and here governments can help. Uncertainties about possible future tax changes can inhibit firms with basically efficient projects from going ahead with them. Consequently one means of providing greater security to certain firms would be for the government to guarantee to maintain the tax rates applying to newly proposed projects for a number of years, as happens in the United Kingdom to some extent now as a result of the 1975 Industry Act. The government is not prevented from changing the general tax rates but the tax environment is left unchanged for projects already being supported.

Going beyond this, the government may feel that investment in certain fields should be encouraged. In the United Kingdom several sectors were identified in 1975 (e.g. machine-tools) as meriting support, not so much on leading-sector arguments, but more on the argument that these were important sectors in terms of ongoing technical developments in which the United Kingdom seemed to be having difficulties in meeting foreign competition. In part, therefore, the case for support depends on the desirability of import substitution, as well as the view that the United Kingdom should play an active role in sectors experiencing the most rapid technical improvements. Support took the form of earmarking resources, again under the Industry Act, for new projects proposed by firms in these branches of the economy.

Another approach pursued in France and the United Kingdom is the use of tax concessions and sometimes subsidies to stimulate investment. France has used these means to stimulate investments which are in line with the plan. In the United Kingdom such instruments — investment grants, accelerated depreciation, building and machinery grants, and so on — while not tied to a specific plan, have often been differentiated not by sector but by region, being intended particularly to promote projects in the so-called Assisted Areas.

Such agencies as the NEB or SDA are essentially organisational forms through which government policy towards investment may be implemented (see Radice, 1978). Similarly, the government's direct influence over or regulation of investments in the nationalised industries can be seen in the same light. All these arrangements take us far from the standard view of a competitive economy which has illuminated much of the formal theory of indicative planning. Or perhaps more correctly one should say that the rather complex arrangements which Western governments have instituted to regulate the level and pattern of investment reflect the widely appreciated inadequacies of perfect competition in the sphere of investment. As we have seen, much of the theory of indicative planning leads us to be very sceptical about its possibilities for success, so we should not be surprised to see governments tackling the immense problems of investment co-ordination in rather different ways.

7.4 Indicative planning and macroeconomic policy

So far we have concentrated on examining indicative planning from the point of view of individual enterprises; thus indicative planning is regarded as a means of generating information which these agents may find helpful in coming to decisions about production, though in earlier sections we expressed some scepticism about its likely value. In this brief concluding section we now consider indicative planning from the government's point of view — by asking whether it may lead to improvements in the practice of macroeconomic policy. Some of the points mentioned here are discussed more fully in Section 4 of Chapter 8.

By macroeconomic policy we mean the standard combinations of monetary and fiscal policy which are thoroughly discussed in textbooks on macroeconomics (see, for example, Branson, 1979; and Chrystal, 1979). Such policies are to be distinguished from structural or regional policies in that they apply to all agents in a particular category rather than only to some sub-set. For example, income tax applies to every individual earning in excess of the tax threshold, and is certainly not limited to workers in certain industries or locations. This feature of macroeconomic policy suggests that it is likely to be based on indicators which describe aggregate characteristics of the economic situation, such as the level of employment, the level and rate of growth of GNP and its main components, consumption, investment, exports, and so on. Also, indicators measuring the balance of payments, and the rates of change of wages and prices can be expected to be important. Given these assumptions, it would appear that the more detailed indicators of the economic situation which would be generated by a system of indicative planning can only hope to improve macroeconomic policy if some additional conditions are satisfied.

If some of the more detailed indicators are known by experience to be highly correlated with the aggregate measures which the government would prefer to use, and because of their more limited scope are available sooner or more frequently, then indicative planning can help. It may be the case, for example, that trends in employment or wages in particular industries can be recognised before the general trend is at all clear; if the position in these industries typically reflects what is happening in the economy as a whole, this information is obviously useful in relation to possible proposals for amending whatever form of incomes policy happens to be in force. Similarly, it may be known that certain branches of the economy are increasing their levels of investment, and this, too, may provide valuable guidance about what is going on elsewhere. In other cases, when rapid structural change is known to be taking place, information about the newly developing branches may be hardly correlated at all with the situation in the rest of the economy; a notable example of this is the development of North Sea oil in the United Kingdom.

It therefore seems that, under the conditions outlined above, the information collected as a result of a system of indicative planning may be able to contribute in a modest way to macroeconimic policy. It should be added, however, that these possible benefits are in the nature of a by-product of the system; even without developing all the institutions and practices associated with a fully developed indicative planning system it would be possible to achieve the macro-economic benefits at lower cost. The government would simply have to study a variety of partial indicators of the economic situation in order to discover which turned out to be most highly correlated with the over-all measures in which it is really interested. Then after a suitable period of study the statistical services would be assigned the task of collecting data on the partial indicators which appeared to be the most promising, and the resulting series would be fed into the macro-policy process in the usual way. A procedure of this kind has actually been adopted in a number of countries, for example the USA, which are in no sense planned economies. These countries have constructed sets of indicators to help them recognise turning-points in trade cycles before they are reflected in the economy-wide statistics on the economy; such indicators are often called 'leading indicators', for obvious reasons. While the importance of indicators of this kind is clear in principle, the practical experience in their use is somewhat mixed. However, the idea is an important one and will no doubt be developed further.

8 PLAN IMPLEMENTATION

8.1 Instruments and types of control

In this chapter we discuss some of the principles of plan implementation and the practical issues to which they give rise. The present section begins by outlining the basic concepts required for the analysis, and then comments on the main instruments and forms of economic control which are available. Two caveats are in order before we proceed. First, while much of what follows is based on our earlier examination of the Soviet Union, France and Hungary, it is convenient to develop certain points in a relatively general manner without worrying too much about the precise institutional details. However, we shall attempt to indicate the major implications of the analysis for the individual countries. Second, parts of the more formal treatment may give the impression that we regard plan implementation as a purely technical matter; but we should emphasise from the outset that this can never actually be the case. In any particular country the feasible and relevant economic instruments always depend on institutional and political considerations, but it is beyond the scope of this book to dwell on such issues, except briefly in Chapter 11.

Plan implementation was described in Chapter 1 as the second phase of planning, following on from plan construction. As such it consists of the set of techniques and policy measures, as well as the organisational and legal forms, which serve to translate the plan from paper into practice. As emphasised earlier, one should not regard plan construction and plan implementation as totally separate activities. For one thing the formulation of the next plan takes place while the present one is being implemented; and for another the process of plan implementation itself generates information used in the construction of the next plan which itself entails making modifications to the current plan. This last point means that plan implementation is not just a matter of ensuring that some plan is carried out in every detail, for in most cases that would be undesirable, or absurd or simply impossible. Circumstances are continually changing, and the original plan undoubtedly contained imperfections to begin with, so that part of the task of plan implementation consists of providing some means of adjusting plans to meet new conditions in a reasonably efficient and smooth manner.

The term 'instrument' is widely employed in the literature on economic policy to refer to any individual policy measure available to the government, and we shall adhere to that usage here. It is convenient to distinguish between a number of different types of instrument, and the subsequent sections of the chapter are ordered according to these distinctions.

(1) *Microeconomic instruments affecting the current period.* These are directed at individual economic units, product groups or regions, and fall into two broad classes: namely, price-type instruments, and quantity-type instruments. The former includes prices themselves, tariffs on specific products, special taxes and subsidies on production, and so on, while the latter includes direct administrative orders about production, trade quotas, prohibitions of various kinds, and so on.

(2) *Instruments relating to investment.* These include both quantity- and price-type instruments, for example detailed instructions about particular projects, and the regulation of prices and enterprise incomes to affect investment choices. In addition, it involves important organisational measures concerned with the preparation, analysis and financing of individual projects, from the work of project-design institutes to the operation of the credit system by banks.

(3) *Macroeconomic control.* Here we are concerned with instruments which have a general, economy-wide character, such as the exchange rate, the income-tax schedule, or the volume of public expenditure. Such instruments affect the environment within which enterprises function but do not presume to dictate directly how any individual enterprise should respond.

Section 8.2 examines instruments in category (1) from the point of view of individual enterprises, while section 8.3 is concerned with investment and section 8.4 with macroeconomic control. Before embarking on that analysis we must introduce the idea of economic objectives, comment on organisational and legal aspects of plan implementation, and draw attention to some general issues in the choice of instruments.

As the term suggests, instruments are not usually ends in themselves, but are better regarded as means to an end. The ends, or objectives, embodied in plans include such things as:

(a) growth targets for individual industries or sectors;

(b) growth targets for real incomes;

(c) growth targets for the main macroeconomic aggregates — consumption, investment, exports and imports;

(d) targets concerned with balances — the balance of payments, the government budget balance, the balance between income and expenditure of the population, balance between the demand for and supply of labour (full employment); and

(e) targets concerned with prices and wages (avoidance of inflation).

This is already a long list, and could easily be extended; but if these are the objectives which the planners, acting on behalf of the government, are seeking to achieve, then one might well wonder why they are not implemented directly, rather than indirectly by means of a complicated set of economic instruments. The answer to this is quite simple: namely, that there is no one in the economy who can be instructed to achieve any particular target from the above list in any meaningful way, which brings us to the so-called *address* principle of planning.

Let us consider, for example, a particular target specifying that the chemical industry should increase its output by, say, 7 per cent in the coming plan year. Under Soviet conditions such a target would be implemented by breaking it down to plans for each separate enterprise in the industry; plan fulfilment by every enterprise would then secure fulfilment of the industry's plan. Thus the over-all industry target is met by means of detailed quantity targets addressed to the enterprises capable of achieving them; in this case these detailed targets are the instruments. In contrast, plan implementation in the Hungarian (or French) case would be less direct; to achieve the desired 7 per cent growth rate might require certain credit guidelines to influence investment, special taxes or subsidies to modify enterprise incomes, and an export subsidy. Consequently instructions about these instruments would be addressed to the appropriate functional bodies. No one could be told directly to grow at 7 per cent, and so no one can be held responsible for failure to do so; instead, functional bodies can be held responsible for setting the correct values for the instruments under their control.

These two procedures have something in common which is worth spelling out explicitly. They both involve the determination of values for a set of instruments designed to secure the achievement of a given goal, implying that the planners must have in mind some definite relationships between objective and instruments in order that they can choose the latter sensibly. The particular relationships relevant for the Soviet and Hungarian cases, respectively, are not the same, of course. The Soviet case involves little more than addition: the sum of the instruments (enterprise plans) should equal the over-all objective (industry target). In practice, matters are never so simple, because of errors in plan construction and unexpected events occurring during the plan-implementation period. However, the basic idea is certainly straightforward and we are quite justified in regarding the Soviet procedure as a form of direct plan implementation. The Hungarian case is somewhat more complicated, involving the specification of relationships between the industry growth target and the proposed instruments which are indirect, subject to considerable uncertainty, and hard to estimate. For example, one relationship might link credit policy and enterprise income to the volume of investment, while a second one might relate the latter and some demand variable to the volume of output in the period of interest, and so on. In both cases, however, what is required is some theory about the functioning of the relevant parts of the economy which allows predictions to be made about the effect of the various instruments on the objectives of interest. And these remarks hold whether we are considering some partial objective, as in this example, or the whole set of objectives embodied in a national plan; they also apply to situations where plans and/or other economic instruments have to be modified in the course of plan implementation.

How do we know what kinds of instrument to employ in a given situation, or what criteria to use in modifying them? It is possible to suggest a few guidelines here, but it is not so easy to provide detailed advice. First, we know from the early work of Tinbergen (1952) that in order to achieve some list of targets specified in a plan it is normally necessary to employ at least as many independent instruments as the number of separate plan targets. Thus if the plan specifies as many as 200 targets, then at least that number of instruments have to be determined to ensure their realisation. Under Soviet conditions that is no problem, since each output target is broken down into sub-targets for individual enterprises, and plans based on these provide plenty of instruments. This does not mean that the targets must always be fulfilled, only that the theoretical condition is satisfied. Since the Hungarian reforms it was expected that objectives would be expressed in a more aggregated form, so that fewer, and mainly macro-economic instruments would be required; but it seems that the planners are still concerned with the output in particular enterprises or branches, and this might explain the increasing differentiation of regulators to provide enough instruments.

Second, the question of modifying instruments has given rise to an extensive literature on what has come to be called the *assignment problem*. Imagine some plan with its set of targets being implemented by means of a variety of instruments under the control of a number of different institutions in the economy; for example, prices are controlled by a price office, taxes by the ministry of finance, trade controls by the ministry of foreign trade, enterprise plans by the industrial ministries, and so on. Now as time goes on observations may be made about the progress of the plan, but any particular agent or organisation will only be in a position to make partial observations — concerning the balance of payments, production in some industry, progress with certain investment projects, and so on — and it will usually be difficult or impossible to co-ordinate all the available information in order to calculate the best way of modifying the original plan and its corresponding instruments. Instead of such a comprehensive adjustment, what often happens is that the task is decomposed into a set of partial adjustments: each control organisation is assigned the job of modifying part of the original plan and instruments in response to observations of a small sub-set of economic indicators. Accepting that complete co-ordination is likely to be impossible, one can then enquire what form of decomposition would be most efficient from the point of view of promoting flexible adjustment to changes in the economic environment without inducing instability. This is the assignment problem. (See Mundell (1962), Meade (1951) and Spraos (1977) for discussion in the context of macroeconomics; related issues in a planning framework are discussed in Johansen (1977, ch. 3).)

In the context of conventional Keynesian macroeconomics this problem arises in a particularly simple, and perhaps more familiar form. In the simplest case there are two objectives, namely full employment and a satisfactory balance of payments, and two instruments, namely the exchange rate and fiscal policy, the objectives and instruments being connected through some macroeconomic model. The assignment problem then consists in deciding whether the exchange rate should be adjusted to meet the balance-of-payments objective or the internal-balance objective, and similarly for fiscal policy. Conventionally the exchange rate is assigned to the balance of payments and fiscal policy to the internal objective, but the matter is controversial, and some Cambridge economists in particular would reverse the assignment. It all depends on the model of the economy one cares to accept.

The problem becomes significantly more complicated in planned economies, since we normally think in terms of many more objectives and instruments. However, the main point about the need to find some form of decomposition remains, and we merely note some examples from the experience of the Soviet Union and Hungary. Thus in the former country industrial ministries can modify enterprise production plans either to meet additional demands which were not recognised when the plan was formulated or to incorporate new information about enterprise capacities. But the ministries are not usually able to ensure that all the necessary materials will be available to make extra output possible, so that enterprises often have to rely on their own reserves, informal contacts with supplying enterprises, or over-fulfilment of plans in other enterprises. The procedure is rather *ad hoc*, probably quite inefficient, but almost certainly better than not attempting any adjustment at all. The assignment of such powers to adjust plans to the industrial ministries therefore seems quite sensible, despite its inevitable imperfections.

In Hungary the power to change the domestic prices of imported raw materials was not assigned to enterprises; instead, the responsibility was shared between the price office and the foreign trade ministry. As a result, when world prices of raw materials rose sharply in the early 1970s, there was no immediate effect on enterprises. The central authorities initially interpreted many of the increases as temporary fluctuations of a kind with which they were familiar, but even when the trends became clearer they preferred to allow the fourth five-year plan (1971–5) to proceed on course. Major, and fairly well co-ordinated, adjustments only came in 1975, as we noted in Chapter 3. Had the power to respond been assigned to enterprises themselves the adjustment would have come much sooner, but could well have been less well organised and may even have led to a slump as in many Western countries. The actual assignment was certainly not efficient in microeconomic terms, since it permitted producers to treat energy and certain materials as relatively cheap for at least two years after large price increases in the rest of the world; however, an efficient slump is not obviously an improvement over the Hungarian procedure. This particular example illustrates the general point that any given assignment rule is likely to have both costs and benefits which the planners should try to estimate as well as possible – and so should the critics of any policy.

The above discussion of the assignment rule presupposed that the planners knew what instruments were available to them. But more basic questions frequently arise concerning the set of instruments which it is appropriate to use. There has recently been an extensive debate on one aspect of this issue, following an interesting paper by Weitzman (1974). In this paper Weitzman concentrated on the question whether, given the planners' objectives, it would be best to bring about the desired allocation of resources by issuing direct instructions about quantities of output to the producers, or whether price signals would prove more satisfactory. Perhaps surprisingly this fundamental question had not attracted a great deal of prior attention in the literature on planning.

Much of modern microeconomics continues to make extremely strong assumptions about the information available to economic agents; for example, general-equilibrium theory often assumes that agents have perfect information about their own production possibilities and/or preferences, and complete knowledge of all the prevailing prices. Under such circumstances it becomes a matter of complete indifference whether the equilibrium allocation is achieved by means of profit-maximising or utility-maximising agents responding to these prices, or whether the centre merely instructs each agent to perform his own part of the optimal plan. Consequently, in order to explore questions about the desirability of price or quantity signals as instruments of plan implementation, it is essential to develop a model which does not assume perfect information. Weitzman restricted attention to a single market, but allowed for unexpected, random shifts in demand and costs, and sought to maximise the difference between a measure of the social benefit of the output and total cost.

In response to some price signal enterprises will adjust their production so that their actual marginal cost – unknown at the time the price had to be fixed – equals that price; and the marginal social value of the output will depend on the actual level of demand. Thus the planners should seek to set the price in such a way that, allowing for the reactions of individual enterprises, the expected net social benefit from the resulting allocation of resources is maximised. This sounds as if it might be a difficult task, but it is perhaps worth remarking that problems with this structure – some government agency attempting to select the optimal value for a certain policy instrument, taking into account the optimising decisions of other agents – arise very frequently in economics nowadays, and Weitzman's example is relatively straightforward to analyse.

If, instead of price signals, the planners had relied on quantity signals, the outcome would be somewhat different; for a given set of output instructions, the social benefit depends on the actual levels of demand and cost, which are not known until after the quantities are determined. In this case, therefore, the planners can choose the optimal quantity signals in order to maximise the expected value of the net social benefit, and there is no need to take into account any subsequent reactions on the part of the individual firms. As one might expect, it turns out that one's preference between price and quantity signals depends on the precise shape of the cost and demand curves, and how these are affected by the prevailing uncertainty. For example, if cost curves are fairly flat (approximately constant marginal cost) and the benefit curve falls sharply beyond a certain level of output (the marginal value of output declines rapidly after a certain point; or, reversing the signs, one could think of a pollution example in which small amounts of pollutant were harmless but beyond some critical level it would be very harmful), then quantity signals are almost certain to be preferred. In contrast, if cost curves rise steeply and benefit curves are fairly shallow, perhaps reflecting the availability of substitutes, including imports, then price signals will be most satisfactory; this is because the level of output actually achieved is not especially crucial, but the costs of producing at an inefficient level are high. Using this approach, therefore, one could analyse the characteristics of individual products and decide in each case whether price or quantity regulation would be the most suitable. In practice, the situation would be more complicated because a lot of important interdependencies between products and sectors have been ignored. Nevertheless, it does suggest that one should think in terms of a mixed form of regulation, involving some price controls and some quantity controls, as the best; proposals to concentrate on one or the other are probably far too simplistic.

Finally, we comment briefly on some aspects of economic organisation and law relevant to plan implementation. Organisational issues usually receive attention when considering plan construction. The particular way in which production units are arranged into enterprises, trusts, associations, ministries, and so on, affects the information flows involved in formulating a plan, and constrains the linkages which can easily be taken into account in the plan calculations, as we have shown in Chapter 5. But the same is true at the implementation stage, since adjustments to the plan are often required, as we have already mentioned; the particular organisational structure which is chosen will certainly affect the set of adjustments which are perceived as feasible, and will also influence the available instruments to some extent. In addition, the ability to create new organisations or modify the relationships between the existing ones in order to promote plan fulfilment, or simply a better economic performance in general, is always severely constrained by various legal provisions.

In the Soviet Union ministers alone are empowered to establish new enterprises, order some form of merger, or compel some enterprise to cease production. Enterprise managers can at most make suggestions in these areas, but in the absence of definite instructions from above they cannot act. Similarly, an enterprise may not independently begin producing a product which falls within the domain of another ministry; such production may often be efficient but it complicates the task of co-ordinating plans. In practice, of course, despite formal regulation, and to circumvent supply shortfalls, many products are produced by several different ministries and the result does complicate planning, for it must be virtually impossible to rationalise production to the extent required to avoid the problem. However, the practice of forming enterprises which span a wide range of product groups is undoubtedly much more widespread in France, where there is no legal restriction, and vertical integration may well facilitate plan construction there. In Hungary enterprise managers have a little more room for manoeuvre, since they are permitted to form associations and can also set up new enterprises, though in principle some ministerial clearance is still required. Not much advantage has been taken of the greater freedom, presumably in part because of the restrictions on the profits which may be taken out of the new unit. Moreover, when Hungarian enterprises are loss-making, it is entirely up to the minister to decide on the appropriate form of reorganisation.

The law also contributes to plan implementation by specifying the procedures involved in forming commercial contracts, the rights and duties of the contracting parties, and liability rules to be applied in the event of breach of contract or any failure to perform as required. (For a thorough discussion of this area, see Eörsi and Harmathy (1971).) We commented on this role of the law in Chapters 1 and 3, and its importance is considerable even in the Soviet Union, where the plans are already moderately detailed, for it is important to make contracts in order to settle delivery dates, precise specification of goods, product mix, and so on. Unfortunately, there are always factors which operate to negate some attempts to meet contractual obligations. The planners in the Soviet Union can simply order a firm to carry out different tasks from those for which it has contracted; this can also happen in Hungary to some extent, though in this case compensation must be paid to the enterprises involved. The Soviet Union also has provision for penalty payments in the event of breaches of contract, but Berliner (1976) emphasises the ineffectively low levels at which they are set. In France a firm is always free to decide that some other contract would be more profitable, though in reaching such a conclusion it would have to take account of possible penalties for breaking the original contract. But whatever the legal provisions it is likely that the effective penalties would depend on the state of the market, a point which would hold for Hungary as well. For example, in a sellers' market any individual seller can choose to sell to someone else and there is little the original buyer can do — if he wants the good at all, he must accept it when some supplier is willing to provide it or he risks not getting it at all; this is particularly true if there are few suppliers and imports are fairly restricted, as would be the case in Hungary. In the case of a buyers' market it would be the buyer who could break a contract with impunity; and Kornai (1971), among others, has argued that under such conditions enterprises would have a strong incentive to improve their products and offer better service to customers in order to avoid such situations. Thus contractual arrangements are useful lubricants of the transactions which serve to implement a given plan, but their beneficial effects are frequently undermined either by administrative interventions or by imbalances between over-all demand and supply in particular markets.

8.2 Control at enterprise level

Enterprises are the basic organisations which actually produce the goods and services which the economy requires; consequently, in so far as plans are fulfilled, it must be the result of enterprise decisions which are broadly in accord with the plans. These decisions are affected by the information flows impinging on the enterprise, the incentives which motivate it, and the relevant internal constraints (e.g. production possibilities), as we will discuss in general terms in Chapter 9. However, it is worth while developing a number of additional points in this section. Given the limited space available, the analysis focuses on the following specific issues: competition, monopoly and the nature of the budget constraint; problems of centralisation and the aggregation of controls; vegetative, or autonomous control; and the interactions between plans and enterprise decisions, depending on plan tautness.

Kornai (1980) has argued that enterprises in socialist economies operate with what he calls 'soft' budget constraints; this means that such enterprises are not particularly concerned about their costs, and are likely to react fairly sluggishly to changes in relative prices which would induce a cost-conscious capitalist enterprise to adjust its input structure quite rapidly. It is certainly the case that in both Hungary and the Soviet Union the central planners think in terms of quantities of outputs first, and only secondarily in terms of costs and profitability. This kind of output orientation, which the Hungarian reforms were supposed to do away with, is well understood by enterprise managers, who appreciate that, provided they produce satisfactory amounts of output, they are unlikely to be penalised for failing to meet profitability goals. In terms of more familiar Western concepts Kornai's idea of soft budget constraints is quite similar in its implications to Leibenstein's notion of 'X-inefficiency' (Leibenstein, 1978).

It is not hard to explain the planners' output orientation, given their historical experience. As explained earlier, the traditional techniques of plan construction always involved the preparation of so-called *material balances* for the major products, and their elaboration and disaggregation to enterprise level. This is still, broadly speaking, the procedure followed in the Soviet Union, while in Hungary some central balances are still calculated but not broken down to enterprise level. However, the concentration of Hungarian industry is such that for any particular central balance only a handful of producers are likely to be involved; it is therefore an easy matter for the ministries to communicate informally with their enterprises and suggest appropriate output levels. The managers need not obey, of course, but pressure can be put upon them, should they require credits or other forms of centrally regulated support. Thus managers continue to get the 'output' message, even though not so forcefully as before the reforms; the result is to make them somewhat less concerned about profitability than a survey of the formal regulations might lead us to expect. To some extent the increasing unreality of the price system merely exacerbates this tendency.

Many Hungarian economists appear to believe that competition should be fostered in order to break down the emphasis which enterprises place on output *per se* and to make them put more weight on profitability considerations. This raises two questions: could it be done, and would it actually have the desired effect? In a trivial sense it could obviously be done, namely by dismantling some of the huge trusts which currently dominate Hungarian industry, as was indeed quite seriously suggested in 1968. But it seems doubtful whether this alone would have a significant effect. In the Hungarian case even a doubling of the number of state enterprises from around 800 to over 1,500 would hardly make a qualitative difference; the planners in the industrial ministries would still be familiar with each one individually, and could still exert the same kind of informal control. Perhaps a better solution would be to take the power to start up new enterprises away from the ministries, and then one could expect to see more small- and medium-sized enterprises being set up. Yet that is a rather fundamental change for a socialist country to adopt, since it could make it harder for the planners to regulate the economy in the detailed manner they are accustomed to, though it may well bring gains in efficiency and flexibility. In the Soviet Union increasing the number of enterprises would do nothing to improve competition, unless buyers were given freedom to choose their sources of supply; and as we have already commented, that would only be effective if the general pressure of demand were reduced. A similar point could also be made about Hungary.

Another way of stimulating competition is by relaxing controls over imports, and this, too, was proposed in Hungary in the late 1960s. In principle, domestic buyers would be able to choose their source of supply not only from within the country but also from foreign suppliers; such an opportunity would compel domestic producers to meet foreign cost and quality levels in order to retain their market, or reorganise their output profiles to specialise in a limited range of products in which they could compete effectively. No doubt this all sounds very fine, but there are serious problems which limit the practical applicability of such a policy. For Hungary it was recognised straightaway that many products could not compete with imports at the proposed exchange rate, so it was obviously unacceptable to open the economic reforms with a string of bankruptcies. Accordingly some imports were taxed and part of production was subsidised in order to make most of the existing production viable in the new market environment; it was envisaged that most of these taxes and subsidies would be reduced in a phased programme over a few years, in order to compel enterprises to adapt their production and lower costs. Having accepted the principle of special supports, however, it then turned out to be politically impossible to withdraw them — the likely dislocations in domestic production would always appear to be too great. In addition, the use of imports as a competitive weapon requires that exports should be buoyant; but although export performance was initially quite good, depression in Western markets following the oil price increases, and the slow development of new exportable products, have turned the trade balance sharply into deficit. As a result, there is little more discussion of import competition, and the present policy involves moderately tight import controls on most products; rather than stimulating competition, the usual approach now is to import that part of any product group which is not being produced by any Hungarian enterprise. A similar approach is adopted in the Soviet Union, where again there is little trace of effective import competition.

In contrast to Hungary and the Soviet Union, France has neither planners who are excessively output-orientated nor any significant import restrictions except those which result from EEC policies, mainly in the agricultural sphere. Plans do seek to balance domestic supply and demand for various products, as we explained in Chapter 4, but it is left to the market to determine the division between domestic output and imports in the supply of any particular product. Plan implementation is therefore much more concerned with macroeconomic issues, and only to a limited extent with the details of production in individual enterprises or industries; the exceptions here are industries which are regionally concentrated and suffering particularly badly from the depression in world demand, for example steel and shipbuilding.

The above discussion of competition suggests that it is basically incompatible with the traditional approach to planning in Eastern Europe. If the planners see their role as that of regulating the development of production (rather than, say, ensuring the satisfaction of demand), then they can hardly permit a great deal of real competition, for that might fail to validate the centrally determined output targets. On the other hand, as we have repeatedly emphasised, it is impossible for the planners to accumulate enough information for the computation of an 'optimal' plan; there is too much information to collect, the incentive system encourages firms to distort some of this information, and in any case there is likely to be serious disagreement about the appropriate optimality criterion. So if perfect planning is impossible, and competition unacceptable, the planners have to find some partial, limited forms of decentralisation of economic control to enterprise level which will allow plans to be implemented in a reasonably flexible fashion without departing too far from the planners' original intentions. Montias (1976, 1977) has developed a simple model which allows some aspects of this method of plan implementation to be illustrated very neatly. In the analysis which follows some of the issues raised are closely related to the more detailed discussion of incentives in the next chapter.

It is easiest to present the model for a single enterprise producing two goods, which we shall call y_1 and y_2, respectively. Figures 8.1 and 8.2 show the production function of the firm, for given inputs. If the planners were able to obtain complete information about the enterprise's production possibilities in the course of plan construction, then they would be able to issue the instruction that it should produce at their preferred point, shown as point A in Figure 8.1. However, the enterprise will never reveal enough information for that, and the planners might have to be satisfied with the plan (y_1^p, y_2^p), shown as point B in Figure 8.1. Assuming that the firm is paid bonuses based on its profits as measured in terms of the prevailing producer prices, such iso-profit lines being indicated on the diagrams by the label π, then it would not actually choose to produce at B; instead, for the case shown on the diagram, it would produce at D, overfulfilling the plan for y_1, and exactly fulfilling that for y_2. This outcome should be acceptable to the planners.

But it is costly to calculate and monitor plans expressed in this degree of detail, and one object of economic reform has been not only to reduce the number of indicators which firms must achieve but to make the remaining ones more comprehensive, or synthetic. In the present model this means that the firm would receive a single aggregated target instead of separate output targets for each of the two products. How should such an aggregated control be formulated if the planners are still to secure an outcome satisfactory to themselves? Two possible modes of aggregation are shown in Figure 8.2. According to the first, and in some ways the most natural, the planners would simply take the original plan targets, use the ruling producer prices, and instruct the firm to produce at least the resulting value of output. The constraint implied by this procedure is the line *FBG* in Figure 8.2, which makes it clear that the firm would then choose to produce at point *E*; this produces more bonuses for the firm, but is actually a less satisfactory outcome for the planners than arises from their disaggregated approach.

The planners can improve their control in two ways, without returning to a very detailed plan: they can either revise producer prices, or they can modify the weights they use to determine the plan target (in aggregated form) which the firm is supposed to meet. The former of these is not shown on either diagram, but is not hard to explain. It merely involves shifting the lines labelled π until the firm's optimal response to the plan lies in the original acceptable region *BCD* in Figure 8.1. Such price adjustments are always possible, but could be extremely complex administratively, especially as the planners are actually dealing with a large number of firms, not just one.

The latter is administratively less demanding, and is the second of the aggregation procedures illustrated on Figure 8.2. The line labelled λ has a slope corresponding to the planners' new choice of weights for y_1 and y_2; when optimising at the prevailing producer prices the firm will then choose to produce at point *H*,

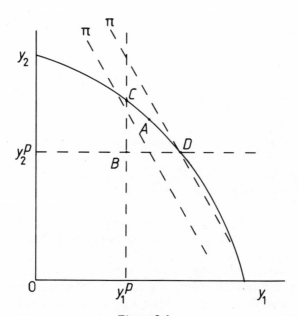

Figure 8.1

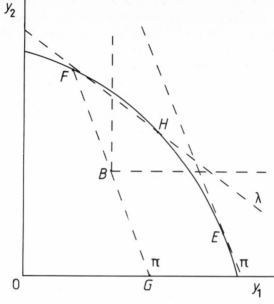

Figure 8.2

which is quite acceptable to the planners. Notice, however, that this result could not have been achieved by any target passing through B. The aggregate output constraint imposed on the firm, labelled λ, is really seeking to solve two problems at the same time. First, the planners realise that any form of aggregation which involves a constraint passing through B leads to control loss, in the sense that it offers firms a large region within which to make their optimal choice: the area to the right of FG in Figure 8.2, as compared with BCD in Figure 8.1. Control loss can be reduced by demanding a stricter target, one which lies to the right of B. Second, the planners are aware that producer prices to which the firm will respond are not good measures of the marginal social costs and benefits associated with the various goods; the planners therefore attempt to compensate for this by using different 'prices' to construct the target for each firm. Hence λ has a different slope from π.

This rather cumbersome procedure is a consequence of one of the assignment rules mentioned in the last section: namely, that there is a price office with responsibility for price-fixing and price adjustment, and industrial ministries with the power to determine current plans for enterprises. Thus planners have to take prices as given when deciding how to induce the enterprises under their control to implement the current plans, and this leads naturally to the kind of approach just discussed. Of course, in practice the planners would often simply accept some control loss without worrying too much, leaving it to detailed negotiation between producer and customers to determine the actual product mix. In many cases the planners would not have enough information to enable them to judge what control loss or other distortion was likely to arise, so that their possibilities for detailed intervention would be rather less than the model above might have suggested.

Let us turn now to consider another of Kornai's ideas which might not only be relevant to the centralised form of planned economy such as the Soviet Union but also help us to understand some aspects of economic behaviour in Hungary and France as well; this is the concept of *autonomous*, or as Kornai himself often calls it, *vegetative* control (see Kornai and Martos, 1973; and Kornai, 1980). It is not an easy concept to explain briefly, and it grew out of a comprehensive study of economic systems and control, much of which involved some quite complex mathematical models. As a starting-point we may observe that if, in a centralised type of planned economy, the central planners suddenly ceased to issue the usual 'tons' of orders, the economy would not immediately grind to a halt. This is obvious from the experience of many countries where plans for some year may sometimes not be issued until as late as half-way through the year, a situation which causes no apparent difficulty for most producers. From this it is clear that most producers, and also their customers, know roughly what they should be doing in the coming plan period, with or without a plan to tell them.

The normal continuity of most economic activity accounts for this behaviour. Production is guided by many forms of information, among which the plan is only one. Other forms are predominantly horizontal in character – demands from customers, the supply situation for various inputs, normal delivery and queueing times, and so on. Enterprises have to adapt to these features of their market situation and over time develop expectations about them. In addition, even if the expectations are not entirely correct, enterprises learn how to respond appropriately to restore equilibrium. In this context, equilibrium does not of course mean the standard competitive equilibrium of neoclassical theory but allows for persistent shortages and other constraints to which enterprises must adapt. Enterprises' responses would include attempts to build up stocks to protect themselves from risks of shortage or longer-than-normal delivery lags, forced substitution to enable production to carry on even in the presence of shortage, and so on. This kind of behaviour – a combination of expectations about the so-called 'normal' state of the economy, and attempts to restore the normal state whenever there are departures from it – is called *autonomous control*.

Some understanding of the autonomous control processes in a particular economy is thus essential for successful plan implementation, unless the plans are merely instructing enterprises to do what they would have done in any case. Even for the Soviet Union it is probably more accurate to regard plans rather as interventions in the normal, autonomous functioning of enterprises than as the overwhelmingly dominant input which determines excatly what they do, for from an enterprise's point of view the planners must often appear to behave capriciously, with their frequently changing plans, and probably imperfectly balanced ones at that! Enterprises must give some weight to their longer-term relationships with, and the expectations of, their suppliers and customers, and this prevents them from blindly obeying the plans sent down from on high. And plans which instruct the enterprise to depart substantially from its established practice, perhaps by introducing new products to modernise its product range, or by developing new designs which economise considerably on materials or introduce the use of unfamiliar ones, are likely to meet with the greatest resistance. Only when the planners make clear that their intentions are not just some passing whim but are part of a sustained effort to transform production can they realistically expect enterprises to take them seriously. All this suggests that in many cases the more interesting question is not 'Why do enterprises fail to fulfil plans', but rather 'Why do the planners not learn more about the economy's autonomous functioning?'

Considered fairly superficially the Hungarian reforms have occasionally been regarded as a basically simple, though major reform of the economy's control mechanism — from control by means of quantity instructions to individual enterprises, to control by means of price signals and 'normal' market forces. However, in conditions of persistent excess demand in several sectors this is a misleading simplification, but one which can be avoided by employing once again the notion of autonomous control. Before the reforms enterprises became accustomed to a situation in which some markets experienced shortage conditions, while in others there might be over-supply from time to time. The reform certainly changed the means whereby the centre could intervene in enterprise operations, but the national five-year plan was quite deliberately left unchanged, so enterprises had no particular reason for expecting that their market situation would be different in the future; moreover, there were almost no changes of personnel among the senior ranks of management, and many probably suspected that the reforms might not endure. Accordingly it is not really surprising that the enterprises were slow to respond to the new market signals; at least initially control by plan instructions was replaced by autonomous control.

In France the same idea explains why enterprises do not instantly respond positively to new government initiatives. For example, special taxes or subsidies to encourage firms to locate new projects in certain areas, or to stimulate investment in some fields preferentially, can only have a limited effect unless firms expect the policy to be sustained. From this point of view it may often be better to retain an imperfect policy for a considerable period, rather than introduce 'improvements' every few months. Since this example concerns investment, it leads us on quite naturally to the next section.

8.3 Control of investment
The investment plan sets out the major structural changes which the economy is expected to experience in the coming plan period; it includes a specification of

certain key projects, some indication of the desired branch pattern of development, and some additional guidelines to assist in the preparation of projects
within individual branches. Given some of our remarks about enterprise plans in
the last section, the reader will not be surprised to learn that we attach particular
importance to investment planning. However, the implementation of investment
plans is both more complex a task, and frequently less successful, than the
implementation of current output plans, for reasons which should soon become
clear.

Investment plans seek to answer three types of question which it is useful to
distinguish straightaway (these questions are also emphasised in Ellman, 1979,
ch. 5):

(1) What should the volume of investment be, both in absolute terms and in
relation to national income? This question is partly to do with macroeconomic
balance, an aspect discussed in the next section, and partly determined by the
desired growth rates, given some relationships postulated to hold between the
rate of investment and the resulting growth rate. There is a vast and often highly
technical literature concerned with this question, but since in practice it is often
resolved through the political process there is no need to dwell on the details
here.

(2) What should the branch structure of investment be, and how should it be
decided which branches should expand and which be encouraged or permitted
to contract? Also, which new branches should be established? To some extent
such questions can be answered by using growth rates from (1) above as a basis
for forecasting the development of final demand; then, in conjunction with
projections for imports and exports, it is possible to determine how domestic
production should develop. Some models available for performing such calculations are discussed in Chapter 10. Inevitably, however, models can only provide
partial solutions and consistency checks, leaving many details to be determined
by judgement and debate.

(3) How should individual projects within a branch be selected? This involves
both the specification of criteria, and the determination of financial provision
for investment. The relevant criteria may be very general – such as those specified
in the official investment methodology for the Soviet Union – or they may
reflect particular priorities – for example, preferences for renewals rather than
completely new construction at certain times, or preferences for greater use of
domestically produced rather than imported machinery.

The construction of an investment plan usually answers questions (1) and
(2), but it only partly answers question (3). The remainder of question (3)
forms part of the process of plan implementation, and it is on this that we shall
concentrate below. It may be helpful if we outline briefly the main features of
investment plans in the countries studied in this book, and so we consider the
five-year plans in particular:

Soviet Union. The investment plan consists of a list of major projects to be
started, and specifies progress on those already begun. In addition, it assigns

branch targets for investment to the various ministries, and they have to select projects to provide the required new capacity from suggestions which may emanate from enterprises but which more usually come from project-design organisations. There is limited scope for some relatively independent enterprise-initiated investment, for which the plan makes often inadequate provision (see Berliner, 1976; and Jackson, 1971).

Hungary. The investment plan consists of a list of major projects to be started, and specifies progress on those already begun. Branch investment targets are assigned to ministries, but most initiative for investment comes from enterprises which use their own funds, budget grants, credits and subsidies; the need to use external sources of finance naturally permits central agencies to exercise some control over the investment process (see Hare, 1979).

France. The investment plan lists certain projects which will be carried out by the nationalised industries but is otherwise restricted to a limited number of branch targets which influence credit policy, and other forms of central intervention (see Cazes, 1969).

With the above introduction in mind it is clear that the tools required to implement a given investment plan should involve a combination of quantity- and price-type instruments. Thus projects identified individually in the plan are carried out by issuing the appropriate orders and by providing the necessary funds to the enterprises involved. It is not necessary to give budget grants in all cases, though that has tended to be the Soviet practice until relatively recently; it is, however, quite feasible to implement even this part of the investment plan by providing repayable credits or even by insisting that enterprises use their own funds. Other projects may also be implemented at some stage during the plan period by issuing instructions once the decision has been taken to go ahead. But price-type instruments are also likely to play a part, and these include prices themselves (including factor prices), taxes and subsidies on production, credit policy, and in some cases exchange-rate policy. Of course, these instruments are of greatest importance in France, of lesser significance in Hungary, and still relatively unimportant in the Soviet Union.

In order to consider how these instruments interact to determine whether or not particular investment projects should be carried out, it is convenient to introduce some simple ideas from the theory of investment appraisal. According to the most usual approach, investors should compute the present value of each project being examined, which may be expressed by the following formula (see Bliss, 1975, chs 3, 13; Hirshleifer, 1970):

$$\text{NPV} = -I + \sum_{t=1}^{T} (R_t - C_t)/(1 + r)^t \tag{8.1}$$

where I is the initial investment outlay (or the present value of investment outlays if construction takes several years), R_t is the revenue earned by the project in year t, C_t is the total cost associated with the project in year t, r is the discount rate, and T is the expected economic life of the project.

Having calculated the net present value of the project it should be accepted if that value is positive but otherwise rejected. This means that the acceptability of some investment may be affected by the prices employed to measure revenues, costs and investment outlays, and by the choice of discount rate. In practice, it is very doubtful whether formal criteria have ever been so important as theorists often suggest, though they may well serve to eliminate some really bad projects, and they certainly help to identify the factors which affect profitability and choice of technique. From a theoretical point of view the reason for adopting a criterion such as formula (8.1) in investment appraisal is that if the prices involved are correct — namely, efficiency prices — its use supports intertemporally efficient production. Let us now look at the variations on this approach employed in our three examples of planned economies.

In the Soviet Union the official investment methodology prescribes the use of a present-value type of formula in which the discount rate is called a *coefficient of effectiveness*, and used to be differentiated between branches of the economy; however, according to the 1969 version of the methodology, the coefficient required in various branches should be uniform at a value of 0.12, except in special cases (Abouchar, 1973). Despite this, the coefficients in different branches still differ substantially. The capital-intensive nature of developments in certain branches is frequently cited as the reason for some degree of diversity, though presumably in the very long run it would be more efficient to demand the same rate of return in all branches, by permitting the prices of such capital-intensive products to rise relatively to most others. Current producer prices, or producer prices of some fixed date (planning prices), are to be employed in the efficiency calculations, with almost no special provision for building into the analysis the prices of comparable imports or prices obtainable in export markets.

Since the great majority of projects in the Soviet Union are initiated and funded mainly by the state, it should not be too hard to check that the officially approved criteria are indeed being used. But the five-year plan specifies what new capacities are to be created during the period in question, and if projects which create this capacity do not look very profitable in terms of these criteria they may still be accepted on the grounds of 'necessity', or the need to fulfil the plan. Despite calls for more efficient production, the output orientation of the planners often leads them to overlook the formal criteria, especially as it is so easy either to exaggerate the returns to certain projects to make them appear satisfactory, or to excuse low returns because of the well-known deficiencies of the price system.

Hungary also employs a criterion like formula (8.1), though it is not usually expressed in quite the same way. The so-called 'D-index' is computed as the ratio between the present value of revenue and the present value of costs (including investment outlays). Fairly obviously the condition that the net value of the project be positive is precisely equivalent to the condition that the D-index should exceed unity. The Hungarian criterion is as far as possible, to be calculated at the prevailing world prices, reflecting the importance for Hungary of promoting investments which are likely to improve foreign trade performance. Application of the criterion is only compulsory for very large projects, usually the centrally financed ones, but it is recommended more generally. For example, agencies considering loans, credits or even some form of subsidy for a project may insist that it should satisfy the official criterion. Aside from the persistence of the same output orientation in Hungary that we have just remarked on for the Soviet Union, reflected in the Hungarian case in an increasing tendency to pre-allocate credits to the industrial ministries before they are made available to particular projects, there are other reasons for being somewhat sceptical about the role played by the official investment criterion.

The main problem is that the official criterion conflicts with the incentive system, for while the former prescribes the use of world prices the latter normally rewards enterprise management and workers on the basis of indicators which depend on profitability measured in terms of the prevailing domestic prices. Enterprise managers consequently have no apparent reason for using world prices in their evaluations. Without dismantling much of the existing mechanism of price control, it is hard to see how this situation can be avoided. What it means is that domestic prices are likely to have the predominant influence on choice of technique, in so far as prices rather than persistent shortages are important at all.

Another reason for scepticism regarding the D-index is the lack of financial or other sanctions against unsuccessful enterprises. On the whole enterprises can be quite confident that they will not be permitted to go bankrupt, a situation considered to undermine financial discipline; in the investment sphere enterprises begin projects with their own resources, then secure state support to complete them even though they may be rather inefficient projects. Why should the state permit and even support such behaviour which apparently has such harmful effects? This behaviour may be tolerated partly because many branches only contain a single firm, or at least very few firms, so that one bankruptcy would appear relatively serious. Moreover, it is probably a mistake to regard the Hungarian central authorities as completely unified; more accurately, there is a coalition between the various interests competing for resources, and it is a typical feature of such struggles that the existing resource shares exert a considerable influence on future allocations. In these circumstances the individual ministries are reluctant to allow bankruptcies which effectively reduce their resource endowment, unless there is an extremely compelling reason for doing so.

In France market forces tend to make private-sector firms seeking profits select investment projects which would be judged acceptable in terms of the present-value criterion based on formula (8.1), though profits would naturally be measured after tax and r would be a market discount rate. Public firms should, in principle, adopt a similar approach, but use pre-tax profits as the measure of social return, and a discount rate prescribed by the government. As in the United Kingdom, there has been lively debate about the appropriate value for the social discount rate, with a corresponding lack of definite conclusions. (See Rees (1976, ch. 2) on the United Kingdom; while Levy-Lambert (1977) discusses French approaches.) All that seems to be accepted is that the rate should lie somewhere between one based on estimating a social time preference rate, and one based on the marginal return on capital in the private sector, suitably adjusted for risk conditions and taxation. In addition, there has been some discussion about the desirability of employing shadow prices to replace certain market prices – particularly wage rates in regions of high unemployment – for purposes of project analysis.

The prevailing prices evidently affect the particular techniques of production which will prove to be profitable when formula (8.1) is used, but they also affect the distribution of incomes between the various agents in the economy, and hence the ways in which investment activity may be both financed and regulated. Let us consider both these points, taking Hungary as our source of examples, since the issues have arisen most sharply there. In recent years controversy has raged among Hungarian economists concerning the appropriate relative price between investment goods and labour. Given the persistent shortages of the latter, it is widely argued that investment should be more capital intensive, but stimulating this presumably requires investment goods to become cheaper relative to labour. At present, enterprises pay a 35 per cent tax on their wage costs and a capital charge equal to 5 per cent of the net value of capital assets; these are both built into the prices, together with a fairly high rate of profit which is subject to the normal form of profits taxation, the result being a level of producer prices which is high in relation to wages. Hence the producer price reform planned for 1980 will reduce the wage tax, abolish the capital charge, and build a lower general rate of profit into the price system. This, it is hoped, will encourage the desired reorientation of investment by making investment goods relatively cheaper.

Unlike their Soviet counterparts, Hungarian enterprises can take considerable initiative in the field of investment, constrained only by the incomes – in the form of development funds – which the price and tax system permit them to accumulate. The general rules of taxation and price formation would tend to distribute development funds between enterprises roughly in proportion to their existing capital stocks; then, if credit conditions were applied with equal strictness in all branches, enterprises would be able to expand their capital stocks at about the same proportional rate. In practice, such a regular development would not be desirable, and the plans normally envisage some branches growing faster than others, with some perhaps even declining. This outcome is achieved by state investment concentrating in certain branches, and by the preferential granting of credit for various approved types of project; indeed, the so-called 'credit preferences' multiplied rather rapidly, with over sixty types of investment being eligible by the late 1970s. At times, however, even these interventions are insufficient to bring about the desired structure of investment. This is when special taxes and subsidies are introduced to modify enterprise incomes directly.

These measures partly serve to correct or compensate for various distortions in the price system itself, and partly act as an information channel transmitting central desires and intentions about investment to individual enterprises. For example, an enterprise subject to a special production tax, and therefore able to accumulate a smaller development fund than its market situation alone would permit, finds its possibilities for investment severely restricted. It is understandable that the central agencies should wish to retain this kind of control over the direction and structure of development; but it is not without its disadvantages, for the approach encourages enterprises to look to central guidance to indicate the approved areas of investment, yet this appears to conflict with the stated aim of relying much more on local initiative and market signals to influence such investment decisions. Perhaps it is hard to find the right balance here between central control and local initiative, while the concentration of Hungarian industry and the absence of competition tend to shift the balance in the centre's favour.

In the Soviet Union the significance of enterprise investment is quite minor, though it is increasing slowly, and the disposal of enterprise incomes is already tightly circumscribed by complex regulations and taut planning. In France the centre is less ambitious about the degree of control over structural developments which it can or should assume. Consequently, for very different reasons, the regulation of the income earned by individual enterprises plays a much less important role in the investment process in these two countries.

8.4 Macroeconomics of plan implementation

So far, our discussion of plan implementation has concentrated on issues related to the behaviour of individual economic agents, mainly enterprises. But we have already pointed out that this is not an especially fruitful way of treating plan implementation in France, and even for Hungary and the Soviet Union it neglects some important questions. In particular, although planners in the latter country intervene in enterprise activity on a day-to-day basis in order to secure plan fulfilment in terms of indicators relating to the individual enterprises concerned, some of the more significant interventions derive from aggregate measures of economic performance.

In the process of plan construction we saw earlier that a large number of economic balances are formulated, some of these being material balances relating to product groups or branches, while others are more 'synthetic', in the sense that they cover a wider sphere of the economy and are usually, therefore, expressed in financial terms. The most important such balances are the following:

(1) *The balance between the income and outlays of the population*, which was introduced in section 2.4 above. In the planning process it is assumed that full employment will be maintained and that real incomes should maintain a fairly steady rate of increase, though Hungary is the most successful of our three

countries in this respect. The levels of money wages, state benefits of various kinds, consumer prices, and the supply of consumer goods have to be planned in such a way that consumer-goods markets do not suffer from substantial or persistent shortages and surpluses.

(2) *The balance of payments.* As noted in Chapter 3, for Hungary and the Soviet Union this actually amounts to two separate balances, one with socialist countries, the other with the West. The former is based on long-term trade agreements, and is conducted at prices derived from prices prevailing in Western markets, with about a year's lag and some 'smoothing' to eliminate fluctuations. It is sometimes jokingly suggested that there would always have to be at least one capitalist country to provide the data on which these prices are based. The Western trade balance, at the planning stage, depends on projections of exports to the West over which the Eastern European countries have little control; given these projections, the permissible level of imports can be determined, and subdivided into imports of consumer goods, investment goods, raw materials, and so on.

(3) *The balance of the government budget.* Hungary and the Soviet Union both plan for balance or a small surplus, arranging their expenditure and tax plans accordingly.

(4) *The balance between investment demand and the available construction capacity.* Given the pressures in their economies to expand the rate of investment to maintain or accelerate the growth rate, both the Soviet Union and Hungary include this balance in their plans, which makes clear the volume of investment which can be absorbed, given other constraints and objectives.

France is concerned about the same four balances, but controls them in very different ways, and accepts different constraints on their realisation. For example, France is unable to take full employment as a starting-point in her plan-formulation process, and has only limited direct control over the process of price and wage formation. Similarly, except in rather limited areas, import controls are not available as an instrument in regulating (2), while as far as (3) is concerned balance would be relatively rare, with changes in the planned deficit being employed in the conventional Keynesian manner as an instrument of stabilisation policy. Similarly, while French plans do provide some investment targets and relate them to other macroeconomic balances, their importance has nothing to do with tendencies in the French economy towards over-investment; quite the reverse, in fact! Thus an interest in more or less the same macroeconomic balances does not imply either that the basic problems are the same, or that the planners' responses to them are likely to be similar; it simply reflects the fact that virtually the same macroeconomic framework of relationships and variables offers a satisfactory means of describing and analysing certain problems of plan implementation in both West (France), and East (Hungary and the Soviet Union).

As we move from the period of plan construction to the implementation period, the planners begin to observe the development of the above balances. In practice, there are always lags and delays in the collection and processing of the necessary data, but after a few months some of the main trends should be discernible. If it turns out that all balances are developing according to plan, then no action is required; and even small departures from the plan – the precise significance of the word 'small' depending on experience of earlier years – should not call for any intervention. However, if it becomes clear that departures from the course originally mapped out when the plan was formulated are going to be substantial, then something may need to be done. Naturally it is neither possible, nor especially interesting, to give a complete list of the ways in which one or other balance may fail to be achieved, though we mention a few examples.

Given some evidence that the original plan is not going to be fulfilled – perhaps because exports are not increasing as planned, or because enterprise incomes are rising more rapidly than expected, with consequential effects on the volume of investment – it may be thought that the planners could just take out of their filing cabinets another variant of the plan which fits the new conditions. There is certainly a school of thought represented in the planning literature which seems to assume that plan variants are not only calculated as part of the plan-formulation process, to assist in the exploration of the main alternatives, but are available to facilitate adjustments later. But in practice this is rarely a possibility, for plan variants normally refer to the entire plan period, and they may not provide helpful answers to problems arising over half-way through the period. Moreover, there are so many possible problems that one cannot really imagine a set of plan variants calculated in advance which allows for them all. Thus one might compute a variant for the Soviet Union which included a bad harvest in two years out of five instead of one, but who would have been taken seriously in 1970 if they had suggested a variant with the oil price rise which came about in 1973, and which is still continuing today? Similarly, it is surely not worth while calculating variants to cover all the possible natural disasters which might befall the country in question, though that seems to be an implication of some work on planning.

Nevertheless, even without their plan variants, the planners do respond to evidence of fundamental disequilibria. Some recent work – both theoretical and empirical – has suggested that such responses by the planners are quite systematic and coherent. Subject to the over-all resource constraints, when deviations from the plan become too great the planners can impose adjustments either by various forms of quantitative restrictions on resource allocation, or by tightening the financial constraints operating on some group of economic agents, like enterprises. Some econometric work on the Soviet economy, involved in building the SOVMOD model, incorporates some behaviour of this kind, though not particularly systematically (see Green and Higgins, 1977; and the critical discussion contained in Portes, 1978a). In addition, the study of Gács and Lacko (1973) contains an empirical study for Hungary which seeks to identify relationships between various macroeconomic indicators and the planners' response. Its most interesting finding is the correlation between the planned volume of investment and the trade deficit in the previous period; what this means is that the planners respond to a favourable trade balance by expanding investment plans and importing more capital equipment, while the opposite happens in the case of a deterioration.

Using a general theoretical model for studying equilibrium and disequilibrium in planned economies Portes (1978b) has examined some of these relationships more carefully. Since his interest has been mainly with the consumer-goods markets, he has left foreign trade out of his model and formulated the supply side in such a way that the key variable which adjusts to accommodate shortfalls from the original plan is the supply of consumption goods to households. The behavioural relation which emerges from this approach takes the following form, after linearisation:

$$c^s = c^p + a_1(m_0 - m_0^e) + a_2(i_0 - i_0^e) + a_3(y - y^p) \qquad (8.2)$$

where c^s is the actual supply of consumption goods, c^p is the planned supply of consumption goods, m_0, m_0^e are the actual and expected real money balances of households, i_0, i_0^e are the actual and expected initial inventories of consumer goods, y, y^p are the actual and planned aggregate output, and a_1, a_2 and a_3 are coefficients to be estimated.

Formulation (8.2) implies that the planners adjust the supply of consumption goods in response to household money balances, inventories of consumption goods and the level of output in the economy. This kind of adjustment can be seen as a planners' rule of thumb designed to maintain equilibrium in consumption markets; it is really an elaboration of what we discussed in section 2.4 above. Portes and Winter (1980) have actually estimated equations such as (8.2) as part of their study of equilibrium in consumer-goods markets in planned economies. Rather to their own surprise, they found very little evidence for that over-all excess demand in consumer-goods markets which has become part of the folklore in discussions of the planned economies. Indeed, they concluded that on the whole the planned economies have maintained a reasonably satisfactory degree of macroeconomic equilibrium; this suggests that when the planners have had to deviate from an initial plan, they have usually managed to do so without unduly disturbing the main macro balances.

This relatively satisfactory position should not, however, make us too complacent, since all the planned economies have experienced severe macroeconomic 'shocks' in recent years, and even if the over-all response has been sensible the resulting problems do not just disappear. Two particular problems may be mentioned here which are common to both Hungary and France, though of somewhat lesser significance for the Soviet Union; these concern investment cycles and pricing in foreign trade.

The French economy has experienced business cycles of the familiar kind, perhaps smoothed out to some extent by fiscal and monetary policy; these cycles involve not only peaks and depressions in the volume of investment, relative to trend, but also fluctuations in the rate of unemployment and in the output of various industries. There are many theories of such cycles, but this is not the place for a survey (see, for example, Rau, 1974). The role of government policy in damping the cycles, or, as some would say, *destabilising* them, is also widely discussed in the literature, with earlier discussions concentrating on cyclical variations in unemployment, and more recently giving greater attention to variations in the rate of inflation.

For many years the very possibility of economic cycles under socialism was simply denied, but the clear evidence for investment cycles in the published statistics of several Eastern European countries has obliged officials to take the idea more seriously. As already noted, the cycles have some connection with fluctuations in the balance of payments, but (unlike the French case) they do not generate open unemployment. Thus the impact of the cycles is typically confined to the investment process itself, with fairly well-recognised cyclical variations in such indicators as average construction periods, the volume of uncompleted investment, the frequency of starting new projects, and so on. What seems to happen is that, despite all the controls, the economy generates périodic over-investment, to which the planners eventually respond; this sequence yields the cycles, usually of about four years' duration (see Bajt, 1971).

There are many reasons for the tendency to over-investment in some of the Eastern European economies, including Hungary. The most obvious is over-optimistic planning, though that is probably less important now than it used to be. Other reasons are the lax financial arrangements under which enterprises often act as if investment were virtually costless, and the lack of alternative outlets for enterprise development funds combined with fears that the use of these funds may be restricted in the future. In addition, the state frequently underestimates enterprise financial resources (because the incentive system induces systematic over-estimation of costs by the central agencies), while insisting on carrying out its planned part of investment; and the costs of individual projects are often underestimated, either by the state authorities or enterprises themselves. In this situation the only effective constraints on investment demand result not from price and cost signals, which probably function least effectively in the investment sphere, but from physical capacity constraints and direct interventions by the planners. This argument is closely related to that elaborated in Kornai (1980).

One may wonder why the planners do not intervene earlier to prevent the emergence of investment tension: but how could they? As Sóos (1975–6) has pointed out, it is not until the symptoms are clear to everyone that the planners can recognise the existence of a problem, for at any earlier stage any small deviations from the planned path of development can be attributed to many possible causes, and would be hard to blame on the investment process. Essentially the planners cannot respond to over-investment until they recognise its existence, and this is delayed until the relevant statistics are available – otherwise, the planners would be reduced to making wild guesses about the state of the economy and probably introducing completely inappropriate policy changes.

We conclude this chapter with some remarks on the implementation of foreign trade plans (see Wiles, 1968, and Kaser, 1967, for fuller discussion). Clearly trade offers markets for products of the domestic economy and sources of supply for goods and services it does not or cannot produce; this includes possibilities for the import and export of technical knowledge and capital goods embodying innovations. As far as is practicable, all such possibilities should be taken into account at the time of plan formulation, so that part of any plan is a *trade* plan. For centrally planned economies like the Soviet Union these plans are almost wholly administered by the ministry of foreign trade, though not without some pressure and initiative from enterprise level. Consequently the plans are rather detailed for that country, since specific amounts of each commodity are built into the various material balances. In addition, especially in its trade within Comecon, individual product prices are rarely considered particularly important; what matters is the over-all cost of imports in relation to exports. Comecon trade is treated very much as a package deal. In Hungary and France foreign trade is much more decentralised, with plans being expressed in a more aggregated form, leaving enterprises to take decisions about individual exports and imports. In the Hungarian case enterprises do still face a number of restrictions, since a fairly wide range of import controls is still maintained there, and trade within Comecon continues to be subject to more detailed control and regulation from the centre.

Since enterprises are the main agents concerned with foreign trade, it would appear that in France and Hungary the prices payable or obtainable for the various products would exert a greater influence on the course of trade than is likely in the Soviet Union. This is undoubtedly right, though one should not forget the numerous means available to governments for distorting prices to favour some particular types of transaction. Despite this qualification, the importance of prices justifies our concentration now on the relations between domestic and foreign prices, and their effects on trade flows.

Even in a very centralised economy the implementation of a trade plan is not so 'straightforward' as that of a production plan for a domestic enterprise, for the planners can no longer determine both prices and quantities. Thus, if they insist on exporting so much of a particular good, they might, if market conditions are unfavourable, have to accept an uneconomically low price for it. Similarly, if they insist on a price based on, say, an average of recent prices, actual sales could turn out much lower than expected. On the other hand, in favourable market conditions results could be far better than anticipated at the time of plan formulation. In general, foreign trade is often subject to greater uncertainty and far weaker possibilities for central control than the bulk of domestic production. Central planners can certainly restrict trade, but they have very limited powers to enforce an expansion, especially in Western markets. Such considerations make it easier to understand why many Eastern European countries saw attempts to develop in an excessively autarkic manner in the 1950s, striving to avoid the uncertainties of trade and international competition. And given the importance of trade for the smaller countries, it is not at all surprising that they were among the first to develop reasonably sensible criteria for trade — export efficiency indexes, and so on — as the failure and futility of autarky was increasingly recognised. The question then arises: how should these indexes be calculated? In practice, this reduces to a question about the prices which should be employed in the calculations.

There are several ways of treating trade flows in an input—output framework, and the following is a convenient and fairly simple version (for a fuller account, see Barker, 1972). Imports are classified as 'competitive' or 'non-competitive', the latter being mainly raw materials and other goods which cannot be produced in the country being analysed; imports are used either directly in final demand or as intermediate inputs in production. As a result, the product balances introduced in Chapter 2 now take the more complicated form:

$$x + m = Ax + c + g + e$$
$$m^0 = A^0 x + c^0 + g^0 \tag{8.3}$$

where the first equation represents competitive balances, the vector of imports being m (all exports are assumed to be competitive, the vector of exports being e), and the second equation represents the non-competitive balances, the vector of imports being m^0. A^0 is a matrix of input coefficients giving the non-competitive import requirements of domestic production, and c^0, g^0 are the corresponding vectors of consumption and government demand met by non-competitive imports. Notice that (8.3) neglects substitution possibilities between competitive and non-competitive inputs, a convenient but not always valid simplification.

Let $\bar{f} = (f, f^0)$ be a vector of trade prices, f applying to competitive and f^0 to non-competitive transactions, ignoring any differences between import and export prices. Let $\bar{m} = (m, m^0)$ and $\bar{e} = (e, 0)$ be the over-all import and export vectors, respectively. Then, in terms of foreign prices, the requirement of foreign-exchange balance takes the form:

$$\bar{f}(\bar{m} - \bar{e}) \leqslant b \tag{8.4}$$

where b is the maximum acceptable deficit for the period of interest.

In a centralised economy like the Soviet Union trade plans are likely to be expressed in terms of a detailed commodity breakdown, so that $\bar{m}$ and $\bar{e}$ would be specified component by component. In contrast, relatively decentralised economies like Hungary (possibly) and France (certainly) would only indicate broad aggregates at the initial planning stage; thus total imports, $(\bar{f}\bar{m})$, and total exports, $(\bar{f}\bar{e})$, might be specified. Naturally numerous uncertainties lie between the plan and its implementation, however the plan is expressed. But at least in the socialist countries it is an equation such as (8.4) which is employed to guide decisions about the exchange rate, as can be seen from an examination of the relationships between foreign and domestic prices.

The equations concerned with price formation have to allow for imported materials, which gives the following form:

$$p = pA + (zf^0 + t^0)A^0 + wa_0 + s \tag{8.5}$$

where z is the foreign-exchange rate, and t^0 is the vector of import duties imposed on non-competitive imports. Prices of competitive imports do not enter into this equation, but if such imports are not subject to quantitative restrictions their equilibrium prices must be related to domestic production costs, for the desirability of domestic production from the point of view of domestic producers depends on the availability of imports (given quantitative restrictions), or on the tariff-adjusted world price in relation to domestic costs.

Given the exchange rate z and domestic prices from the above relations, the vector $u = (zf - p)$ measures the unit profitability of exporting the various competitive goods over and above the surplus s realised on domestic sales. Enough has to be exported to satisfy the balance (8.4), which means that whatever u indicates about profitability exports have to be found from somewhere. For example, suppose that the domestic currency is over-valued (z is too low); then (8.5) implies that export profitability, as measured by u, will be low or negative. Thus if enterprises have some freedom in deciding whether to supply domestic or foreign buyers, they will prefer the former unless their exports are subsidised. Alternatively, if trade is conducted by special foreign-trade enterprises, they will pay for exports at domestic producer prices and absorb a loss on final sales. Conversely, if the exchange rate makes exports appear to be too profitable, the planners may wish to impose export taxes to protect market balance domestically. In general, when the exchange rate is set correctly the planners should not need to impose very high tariffs to protect domestic production, nor offer high subsidies to stimulate exports. It is hard to be more precise than this for a planned economy, since there is no free market in foreign exchange which is equilibrated by the choice of z; and quantitative restrictions on trade are quite widespread, even in Hungary.

It is worth noting that some of the most commonly used export efficiency indexes can be expressed in terms of the above notation (see Boltho, 1971). Exportables are often ranked according to the ratios (f_i/p_i), expressing foreign-exchange earnings per unit of domestic outlays. Obviously products with the highest ratios appear to be the most attractive exports. In addition, the crude ratios are sometimes adjusted to allow for the import content of domestic production, which raises severe practical difficulties, for it presupposes a value for the foreign-exchange rate which the crude ratios do not, and it is often impossible to compute the complete import content of each product; in practice, the calculations tend to allow for only one or two rounds of import content. These problems mean that even a rank ordering of preferred exports cannot be calculated reliably, given the complex and often high tariffs which many planned economies operate. Nevertheless, it is probably true to say that some improvements in the efficiency of foreign trade have been achieved by consideration of these indicators, not least by the elimination from international trade of totally unprofitable products.

9 THE INCENTIVE PROBLEM

Incentives play a central role in the operation of any planning system, both at the stage of constructing the plan and at the stage of implementation. If an efficient plan is to be compiled, agents must impart truthful information at the stage of plan construction, and then at the implementation stage they must act as required.

In Chapters 2 and 3 we considered the impact of the incentive systems operating in centrally planned economies both before and after the reforms. An incentive system was defined there as a set of values specifying how the rewards received by certain economic agents are to be related to certain measures of performance. The incentive system must determine who gets the rewards and how large they are, what performance indicators are used, and how the rewards are related to them.

In this chapter we analyse in a fairly formal way the likely consequences of alternative ways of relating managerial bonuses to indicators used in plan construction and implementation. Managerial bonuses are emphasised because of the important role of enterprise directors in the economy. We devote little attention to the absolute size of bonuses, assuming merely that they are sufficiently large to influence managerial behaviour. Moreover, we concentrate on the role of incentives in achieving an efficient allocation of resources. Other possible objectives of an incentive system are ignored.

A planning system embodying a system of incentives which elicits truthful information at the stage of plan construction and which encourages agents to execute the plan as required is said to be incentive-compatible. (The discussion in this chapter is mainly limited to so-called 'individual' incentive-compatibility: i.e. by assumption agents are precluded from forming coalitions and co-ordinating their strategies. This assumption is restricting but not too unrealistic in cases where agents have difficulty in communicating with one another. Enterprise managers in centrally planned economies are probably fairly isolated in this sense.) The classic example of an incentive-compatible system is that assumed in the Walrasian model of general equilibrium under perfect competition. Agents are led by the invisible hand to divulge information which establishes an equilibrium vector of prices. Then consumers by maximising utility and producers by maximising profits at those prices achieve a Pareto-optimal allocation. As is well known, the incentive-compatibility of perfect competition breaks down in the presence of public goods, as agents have an incentive to represent their preferences untruthfully. Some solutions of this problem are now available, and the principle behind them is used in a scheme discussed below to make enterprises in a planned economy reveal their production possibilities truthfully.

The perfect-competition framework is also open to the objection that there is no agent in the system to adjust prices to the equilibrium set, unless the existence of an auctioneer is posited. The simplest models of indicative planning overcome this objection by assigning the role of price adjuster to a planning board. The incentive-compatibility of the model of perfect competition then carries over to a simple system of indicative planning under competition, though within oligopolistic industries the information exchanges involved in indicative planning may foster collusive behaviour by firms and discourage competition (Meade, 1970, pp. 51–6).

Thus, unfortunately, the assumption of perfect competition is required to maintain incentive-compatibility. In the case of a small number of agents in a market each agent will be able to improve his position by acting as a monopolist or monopsonist, though if other agents do likewise all may end up worse off. (The optimum tariff argument in international trade theory illustrates this proposition.) The outcome will clearly not be Pareto-optimal. This is scarcely surprising. What is less obvious is a proposition, shown by Hurwicz (1972, pp. 320–34), that in cases where the economy is not atomistic (i.e. whenever all traders are not infinitesimal – which is, of course, the normal case, especially for producers), then if all other agents act competitively a remaining agent can improve his position by behaving monopolistically while at the same time appearing to behave competitively with respect to a plausible but false set of preferences or production possibilities. Thus the property of incentive-compatibility depends crucially upon the existence of atomistic competition, though the gains from cheating shrink as the number of agents increases.

The above observation is of relevance both to capitalist economies using systems of indicative planning and models of centrally planned economies based on decentralised market-type procedures, such as the Lange process. But the problem of incentives also looms very large in traditional centrally planned economies, where incentive payments are based not on absolute levels of performance, but on performance relative to a plan. The sections below deal first with the incentive system operating under traditional (unreformed) central planning, and then with the adaptations of the traditional incentive system which have been proposed in recent years.

9.1 Managerial incentives and the traditional planning system

If a planning system is to work efficiently, agents must have an incentive to make it do so. Such incentives may be negative (for example, dismissal for failure to implement plan targets) or positive (for example, the offer of promotion or increased earnings to those achieving their targets). Both the above examples fall into the category of material incentives – or incentives which reward an individual or protect him from harm. Moral incentives, which motivate an individual to act in the interests of the collective without offering a specific individual reward, also play a role in influencing behaviour. (An example of a moral incentive operating is the *subbotnik* or free day of work provided by workers in some centrally planned economies.) At certain periods the role of moral incentives has been substantial. In recent times, however, incentives in the Soviet Union and Eastern Europe have been chiefly material in character. Of course, some agents in these economies may have been motivated by idealistic considerations to fulfil or overfulfil plan targets, but these wishes have been reinforced (and in some cases dominated) by a system of material incentives, and we shall concentrate on the latter.

In a traditional centrally planned economy the incomes of the director and of a small number of senior managers in an enterprise consist of basic salary and a bonus, of which the chief part is received for fulfilment. (We consider below the nature of the plan indicators to which bonuses are attached.) Bonuses made up about 35 per cent of the director's income in the Soviet Union in 1970, though this proportion has varied substantially over the years (Berliner, 1976, pp. 478–84). As a reasonable first approximation the director can be assumed to be a bonus maximiser. However, this hypothesis is both ambiguous and arguable. It is arguable because although a director's bonus income may be slightly increased by overfulfilment of targets, his standing in the organisation and chances of promotion are likely to be affected primarily by whether he achieves his target or not, with little extra credit available for overfulfilment. For this reason several models of enterprise behaviour have ignored overfulfilment bonuses and concentrated attention solely on the basic bonus for plan fulfilment (Keren, 1979). This leads to patterns of behaviour similar to those implied by 'satisficing' theories of the firm.

An ambiguity in the assumption that managers maximise their bonuses furnishes an additional argument for the procedure, for the bonus may be maximised either over the short run or over the long run. If next year's plan is based on this year's output level (the so-called 'planning from the achieved level'), then substantial overfulfilment this year will jeopardise attainment of the basic plan targets and reduce bonuses next year. The same problem of defining the time period also arises with the assumption of profit maximisation made for firms in capitalist economies. However, just as profit maximisation is useful as a first approximation in capitalist economies, so is bonus maximisation in centrally planned economies.

Let us now consider the behaviour of the enterprise director in more detail. The main outlines of the traditional system of planning were described in Chapter 2; we observed there that the enterprise's activity is directed towards fulfilment of a very detailed annual plan covering all aspects of enterprise performance; in particular, targets are set for gross output, main assortment (output of particular products), inputs, costs, profits, and so on. We also saw that plan construction is a hurried and imperfect process, and that the resulting plan contains inconsistencies.

How do directors behave in the face of these inconsistencies? To begin with they protect themselves against them by building slack into the plans; in particular, they minimise their production possibilities and exaggerate their input requirements, accumulating large stocks of raw materials and other inputs. The point is that such behaviour has no harmful consequences for the director, as bonuses are calculated on the basis of enterprise performance relative to the plan, not on the basis of absolute performance; hence efforts directed towards reducing the level of the plan can yield as large a return to the director as efforts to fulfil the plan when it has been adopted.

Second, because of the inconsistencies in the plan, directors have to decide which targets to meet and which to neglect. Under the traditional system of central planning the gross output target predominates in practice, and other targets take a secondary place. The crucial point here is that the director's superiors in the ministry have discretion to waive fulfilment of some plan targets and may permit the payment of the major bonus for plan fulfilment even if some targets are not fulfilled. One target which often falls into abeyance is the assortment plan (see Keren, 1979, p. 8; Berliner, 1976, pp. 408–13); cost and profit targets are also subordinated to fulfilment of the gross output target, provided that the violation is not excessive. Of course, if a campaign is raging to economise on some input (energy or steel, for example) or to achieve a particular target (for technological change, for example), a director will make sure that he fulfils his plan in this regard, possibly even at the cost of falling short of the gross output target. Doubts as to which subsidiary targets will be insisted on in any given year introduce uncertainty in the director's position, in addition to the uncertainty created by the ministry's propensity to revise the plan in the course of implementation.

We can now set out the director's problem more formally for the simple two-period case. The director maximises his utility over the two periods (W), where W is the discounted sum of his utility level in each period:

$$W = U_1 + \frac{1}{(1+r)} U_2 \tag{9.1}$$

and r is the director's rate of time preference. Utility in any period is itself a simple additive function in two arguments: the money bonus for plan fulfilment and overfulfilment (B_t), and the effort expended on production,

$$U_t = B_t - c(y_t) \tag{9.2}$$

where $B_t = A + b(y_t - \bar{y}_t)$ for $y_t \geqslant \bar{y}_t$; otherwise $B_t = 0$.

Here $\bar{y}_t$ is planned output at time t; $t = 1, 2$

y_t is actual output at time t; $\quad t = 1, 2$

A is the basic bonus for plan fulfilment

b is the bonus coefficient for overfulfilment

$c(y_t)$ is the disutility associated with the effort required to produce y_t; $c'(y_t) > 0$; $c''(y_t) > 0$.

We assume that the director knows — or at least believes, since it is his perception of the solution which is important — that next year's plan is based on this year's output:

$$\bar{y}_2 = \begin{cases} \bar{y}_1 + d(y_1 - \bar{y}_1) & \text{for } y_1 \geqslant \bar{y}_1 \\ \bar{y}_1 & \text{otherwise} \end{cases} \tag{9.3}$$

(Here we use the simplest linear formulation of the ratchet. The more realistic non-linear formulation makes little essential difference.)

Substituting this expression into the maximand we derive the following first-order condition for y_1 (for simplicity we assume that the director maximises his utility by at least fulfilling the plan in each period; this overcomes problems associated with discontinuity of the bonus function):

$$\frac{\partial W}{\partial y_1} = b - c'(y_1) - bd/(1 + r) = 0 \tag{9.4}$$

If the second-order conditions are satisfied, the utility-maximising output level in period 1 is found by solving the equation

$$c'(y_1) = b - bd/(1 + r) \tag{9.5}$$

The 'ratchet' equation has introduced the second term on the right-hand side of the expression, which, since $c''(y_1) > 0$, reduces y_1. Evidently the level of overfulfillment in the first period will be the greater, the greater the value of b, the overfulfilment bonus coefficient, and the lesser the value of d, the 'ratchet' coefficient. Output will also be greater in year 1 the greater is r, the director's rate of time preference. A director expecting to be transferrred to another enterprise will place a lower value on bonus income to be derived in the future from his present position. Hence a fast turnover of management personnel may encourage enterprises to operate closer to capacity. On the other hand, if over-fulfilment, as opposed to bare fulfilment of the gross output target, benefits the long-term career prospects of the director by only a small amount, then the coefficient b will be relatively very small compared with A, the bonus for basic plan fulfilment, and overfulfilment will be lower. This can be demonstrated rigorously by introducing a stochastic element in plan fulfilment.

The system we have described is one in which there is a clear conflict of interest between the enterprise director and his superior in the ministry. The former both distorts the information sent to the ministry and maintains surplus capacity in implementing the plan. The system fails to meet the requirement of incentive-compatibility either in plan formation or in plan implementation. At the same time, the superior is constantly seeking to raise the targets of enterprises, and constantly trying to maintain the tautness of the planning system. Within limits, raising output targets will call forth greater efforts from those executing plans, except that if plan targets are excessive directors may despair of achieving them and maximise utility by applying themselves to the minimum possible extent.

Several writers have constructed more complex models of enterprise behaviour under the traditional planning system and drawn the following conclusions within the framework of their specific models. Portes (1969) has shown that the tauter the plan as specified in quantitative targets, the more responsive enterprises are to changes in the plan, and that the fewer above-plan inputs enterprises are able to obtain, the smaller adjustments they can make to the (probably irrational) price incentives in a centrally planned economy. Keren (1979), within the framework of a different model, shows that increasing the tautness of the plan may increase the gross value of output, but at the cost of increasing violations of other plan indicators. This occurs because enterprise directors faced with high plan targets are forced to take increasing chances with other indicators, hoping that their superiors will not enforce them rigidly. Higher targets, Keren shows, may increase output, but at the cost of production efficiency, technical progress, assortment of output and product quality. The sacrifice of these other plan indicators to gross output becomes less and less acceptable as the economy develops. Increasing pressure builds up for reforms of the incentive system as part of an over-all economic reform.

9.2 The reform of incentives: elicitation schemes

The traditional incentive system in centrally planned economies geared managerial bonuses principally to the fulfilment of the gross output target; as a result, all other indicators were subordinated to the objective of meeting that target. The economic reforms of the 1960s introduced substantial changes in incentive systems. In Hungary managerial bonuses ceased to be based on performance relative to the plan (which in any case came to be formed by the enterprise itself rather than being imposed from above); this change eliminated the incentives for reporting false information and for avoiding substantial overfulfilment of the plan (see Chapter 3).

In the Soviet Union changes in the incentive system were made in 1965 (as part of the economic reform) and in 1971. The latter change is more interesting from a theoretical point of view but there are doubts about how widely it has been implemented. We consider both changes in turn.

The 1965 economic reform in the Soviet Union set managerial incentives on a new footing by instituting three incentive funds – the material incentive fund (for payment of bonuses to managers), a social and cultural fund (which provides such services as housing for workers), and a production development fund (to finance decentralised investment).

The construction of the material incentive fund (with which we are chiefly concerned here) and the derivation of managerial bonuses from it are complicated processes, but their essentials can be presented simply (see Ellman, 1971, ch. 7, for details). In the interests of persuading enterprise directors to adopt taut plans the material incentive fund was established in such a way that a planned increase in sales and other bonus-forming indicators would increase the fund by at least 30 per cent more than an unplanned increase. The aim of this was obviously to discourage firms from concealing production reserves. However, the reform contained a second provision which denied all bonuses to enterprises which failed to fulfil the plan. The very sharp discontinuity in the bonus formula at 100 per cent fulfilment was thus retained, and this provision clearly negated the encouragement offered to enterprises to adopt a taut plan present in other parts of the scheme. Enterprise directors, faced with supply failures, frequent plan changes and other uncertainties, would hardly be tempted to adopt taut plans by the very modest additional reward offered for adopting a higher plan rather than overfulfilling a lower one. The risk of underfulfilment was too large, and more-over the ratchet effect still operated.

The reform also substituted sales for gross output as the major bonus-forming indicator. This change was intended to prevent production of unwanted goods, but in the prevailing sellers' market (certainly for producer goods and for some consumer goods) it may have had little effect. In addition, the reform linked bonuses to a profitability measure. Domar (1974) has argued that a bonus based jointly on sales and profits gives planners the opportunity, by altering the relative importance of the two indicators, of moving the enterprise to any desired output level; he asserts that it can thus be used to discourage enterprises from curtailing production for monopolistic reasons. This model assumes that enterprises are price-setters, but in the Soviet Union enterprises have no power over prices, except in the case of a few new or exceptional products. It is thus unlikely that the incorporation of profitability as a bonus-forming indicator made an essential difference. In its effect on incentives, as in other respects, the Soviet economic reform of 1965 had little impact.

The drawback of the 1965 changes in incentives is the draconian penalty they imposed for non-fulfilment — loss of all bonuses. In 1971 further revisions were made to incentive schemes in the Soviet Union, and these have provoked a sub-stantial literature on their optimality properties. We describe first the changes themselves, and then certain elaborations based upon them.

The central idea in the 1971 change was the development of a system of counter-planning, or planning from below, and the changes were related to the greater prominence given to five-year planning at enterprise level. When annual plans are compiled enterprises are asked to submit counter-plans, imposing higher targets upon themselves.

Enterprises receive additional bonuses for accepting such higher targets, as in the 1965 system; the crucial differences are (i) that basic bonuses are received even if the counter-plan is not achieved, provided only that the original plan targets are met, and (ii) that initial plans are in principle fixed for a five-year period rather than revised every year — this should prevent the ratchet system from operating. Thus the new procedure is designed to elicit truthful information from enterprises.

Before considering the practical impact of these changes we examine the resulting system for incentive-compatibility. For this purpose we adopt a simpli-fied but elegant formalisation of the scheme proposed by Weitzman (1976).

The procedure begins with the planners proposing an initial plan, expressed by the single indicator $\bar{y}$, and the associated managerial bonus $\bar{B}$. The planners also establish the value of certain coefficients.

The first of these coefficients, a, tells enterprise directors by how much their bonuses will be increased if they accepted a higher target $\hat{y}$ in the counter-planning stage:

$$\hat{B} = \bar{B} + a(\hat{y} - \bar{y}) \tag{9.6}$$

The enterprise prepares its counter-plan $\hat{y}$ in the light of this formula.

Subsequently actual bonuses B are paid on the basis of actual performance y in relation to counter-plan $\hat{y}$ as follows:

$$B = \begin{cases} \hat{B} + b(y - \hat{y}) & \text{for } y \geqslant \hat{y} \\ \hat{B} + c(y - \hat{y}) & \text{for } \bar{y} \leqslant y \leqslant \hat{y} \\ 0 & \text{for } y < \bar{y} \end{cases} \tag{9.7}$$

(To simplify matters, we ignore the final provision in the analysis below.) To encourage enterprises to accept taut but not unrealistic plans it is necessary that all coefficients should be positive and that a should lie between b and c, i.e. $c > a > b > 0$.

It is easily seen that in conditions of perfect certainty enterprise directors will maximise their bonuses by adopting a plan equal to the actual outcome (which is assumed to be forecast accurately and independent of the exertions of the director). The incentive scheme does therefore elicit accurate information. However, this is a simple and unrealistic case. We must check the scheme for incentive-compatibility under each of the following circumstances: (i) uncertainty; (ii) managerial effort as an input; (iii) multiple success indicators; (iv) the multi-period case; and (v) the case where input allocations depend on the targets adopted in the counter-plan.

(i) *Uncertainty*. Let us suppose that plan fulfilment is subject to some uncertainty, arising (for example) from random failures of the supply system, against which the enterprise cannot protect itself by its own efforts. The effect of this is to make output y a random variable with a known probability distribution.

How will the enterprise behave in these circumstances? The simplest assumption is that the enterprise director chooses a plan which maximises the expected value of his bonus. In this case Weitzman has shown that the output target will be chosen so that the probability of achieving it is given by the following expression:

$$P(y \geqslant \hat{y}) = \frac{c - a}{c - b} \tag{9.8}$$

where $P(y \geqslant \hat{y})$ is the probability of fulfilment or overfulfilment, and coefficients a, b and c are defined as above.

This formula makes intuitive sense. Increasing c (the penalty for underfulfilment) raises the probability of fulfilment or overfulfilment by discouraging enterprises from submitting ambitious counter-plans. Similarly, the plan adopted by the enterprise will be lower, the higher is b (the bonus for overfulfilment) or the lower is a (the bonus for adopting a tauter plan). Weitzman has pointed out that the planners can set different coefficients for different branches. For an industry where a shortfall in plan fulfilment has serious consequences, c would be high; where above-plan output is of little value b would be low. On this basis c would be high for intermediate goods or primary products, shortfalls in the production of which have secondary consequences throughout the whole economy. In a similar way a should reflect the social benefit of an extra unit promised at the planning stage. However, no such differentiation between sectors seems to operate in practice in the Soviet Union.

This simple result follows from our assumption that directors maximise their expected bonus. More generally, they maximise their expected utility from bonuses. Directors will exhibit risk-aversion if the marginal utility of bonuses declines.

If managers are risk-averse, the first-order condition given above for the risk-neutral case (expected bonus maximisation) is replaced by an inequality:

$$P(y \geqslant \hat{y}) \geqslant \frac{c - a}{c - b} \tag{9.9}$$

The more pronounced the risk-aversion, the less ambitious the targets adopted by the enterprise. For a given degree of risk-aversion changes in coefficients b and c have the same effect as before. However, the effect of an increase in a is ambiguous. The properties of the incentive scheme imply that planners can, by a suitable choice of coefficients, counter private risk-averse behaviour by enterprise directors.

(ii) *Managerial effort.* Hitherto the output of the enterprise has been assumed to be a random variable independent of the enterprise director's efforts. Yet the director can clearly influence output by galvanising production workers, ensuring the supply of inputs, and so on. We first incorporate this possibility into the analysis for the case of certainty.

In Figure 9.1 point A indicates the planners' initial bonus $\bar{B}$ and the implied managerial effort level $\bar{e}$. The enterprise director can adopt higher targets, and the corresponding input of effort is shown by the curve AC (here we assume a diminishing marginal return to effort). The director chooses a point D which sets him on the highest attainable indifference curve $I_1 I_1$. Once the counter-plan has been submitted the relationship between bonus and effort is given by the curve EDF, which has a discontinuity at D; underfulfilment of the counter-plan is more heavily penalised than overfulfilment is rewarded $(c > a > b)$. Under conditions of certainty, then, the counter-plan is exactly fulfilled.

Uncertainty can be introduced in the following way. The director chooses a counter-plan y which maximises the expected utility derived from bonuses, and the associated expected value of effort; assume that these expected utility-

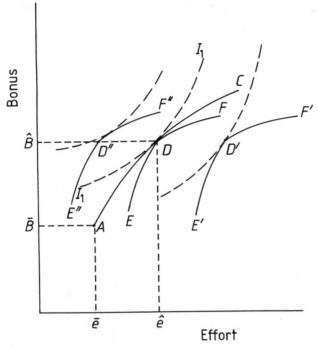

Figure 9.1

maximising levels of bonus and effort are B and e in Figure 9.1. The director chooses this counter-plan in conditions of uncertainty. Subsequently, however, before he implements the plan the director observes the value of the random variable which affects his ability to do so. This alters the relationship he perceives between bonus and effort. For example, unexpectedly severe supply difficulties may displace the *ex post* bonus—effort relationship to the right $(E'D'F')$; or favourable circumstances may shift it to the left $(E''D''F'')$. The director then chooses the utility-maximising levels of bonus and effort. The discontinuity in the *ex post* bonus—effort relationship tends to keep fulfilment at or close to the plan. (With the indifference curves in Figure 9.1, for example, the counter-plan is exactly fulfilled even in the adverse case $(E'D'F')$, while the favourable circumstances $(E''D''F'')$ lead to only a modest overfulfilment). The main point, however, is that the enterprise director has no incentive to disguise his production capacities at the counter-planning stage.

Changes in the bonus coefficients have a complicated impact on output levels. They not only influence the counter-plan chosen by altering the slope of line AC in Figure 9.1 and the penalties and rewards for under- and overfulfilment (as in (i) above), they also affect the amount of effort put into achieving a given plan with a known value for the random variable; this arises because coefficients b and c determine the slope of lines $E''D''F''$, etc. In particular, it can be shown that simultaneous increases in a, the reward for adopting a tauter plan (i.e. an increase in the slope of line AC in Figure 9.1) and in c, the penalty for failing to fulfil it (i.e. an increase in the slope of ED), can both increase the expected level of output and reduce the probability of underfulfilment (Miller and Thornton, 1978, p. 441). This advantage is gained, however, at the cost of larger bonus payments.

(iii) *Multiple indicators*. So far we have assumed a single performance indicator for the enterprise. Yet the Soviet enterprise is faced with several indicators, with complicated relationships between them. In the 1976–80 plan the major indicators fixing the size of the bonus fund in any enterprise are three chosen by the ministry from the following list: labour productivity; percentage of output classified as being of the highest quality; level of output or profit; rate of profit; or some other indicator. The functional relationships between these indicators are obviously highly complex, and enterprise directors at the stage of submitting counter-plans would, if the incentive system were operating as assumed here, be faced with the task of equating ratios of marginal benefits from indicators (which will depend on the bonus coefficients set by the planners), and marginal rates of transformation between them (as determined by the technological possibilities of the enterprise). Directors may choose at the implementation stage to ignore some indicators and concentrate on others, but such behaviour is less likely, the greater the difference in absolute value between bonuses for overfulfilment and penalties for underfulfilment (see Snowberger, 1977, pp. 596–7). However, multiple indicators do not alter the general principles of the incentive scheme under consideration, which so far has been shown to have desirable elicitation properties.

(iv) *The multi-period case*. The classical incentive system for an enterprise not only discouraged truthful revelation of production possibilities, it also discouraged overfulfilment because of the operation of the ratchet principle. Is this system we are discussing now open to the same objection?

The simplest case is that of certainty, where, as we have seen, the enterprise director maximises the bonus by exactly fulfilling the counter-plan. As before, we can formulate the operation of the ratchet as follows:

$$\bar{y}_2 = \bar{y}_1 + d(y_1 - \bar{y}_1)$$

The bonus-adjustment function facing the enterprise at the counter-planning stage in the second period becomes:

$$\hat{B}_2 = \bar{B}_2 + a(\hat{y}_2 - \bar{y}_2)$$
$$= \bar{B}_2 + a\{\hat{y}_2 - [\bar{y}_1 + d(y_1 - \bar{y}_1)]\} \tag{9.10}$$

The director's bonus opportunities in the second period would thus be reduced by a high level of fulfilment in the first period. This would reduce the output of the enterprise, though the director would continue to fulfil exactly his (now reduced) counter-plan.

Under uncertainty the ratchet can operate in terms of either or both of two variables, the difference between the original plan and plan fulfilment in the previous year, or the difference between the original plan and the counter-plan in the previous year. In the first case

$$\bar{y}_2 = \bar{y}_1 + d(y_1 - \bar{y}_1)$$

as above. In the second case

$$\bar{y}_2 = \bar{y}_1 + e(\hat{y}_1 - \bar{y}_1) \qquad (9.11)$$

The second formulation is more logical, as actual fulfilment, y_1, depends upon the particular value of the random variable observed in period 1, while the counter-plan, $\hat{y}_1$, is chosen by the director to maximise the expected bonus, on the basis of some average value for the random variable. However, the second formulation may lead to a situation in which the original plan in period 2 is increased even when fulfilment in period 1 is below the original plan for that period (if $y_1 < \bar{y}_1 < \hat{y}_1$).

Whichever formulation is adopted the effect is the same: the ratchet principle discourages directors from operating their enterprises at full capacity. It reduces the benefit, as perceived by the manager, of adopting higher targets by an amount which increases with the size of the ratchet coefficients d and e. And it reduces still further the benefits of overfulfilling a given counter-plan. In particular, if $b < ad/(1 + r)$ (where r is the rate of time preference), the return to overfulfilment becomes negative.

(v) *The case where input allocations depend on the counter-plan.* This case introduces a new consideration. Suppose that enterprises which adopt large counter-plans receive additional allocations of scarce resources for which they are not charged yet which allow them to increase their output beyond the original plan level. (Not surprisingly, Soviet official procedures do provide for such increased allocations.) The director will then have to consider the following strategy. He adopts an ambitious counter-plan, which may in fact be infeasible. This not only increases his planned bonus $\hat{B}$ but also entitles him to an additional allocation of resources. With the increased input he produces perhaps not as much as his counter-plan but more than he could have produced with a lower counter-plan and fewer inputs. His actual bonus is given by

$$B = \bar{B} + a(\hat{y} - \bar{y}) + c(y - \hat{y})$$
$$= \bar{B} - a\bar{y} + (a - c)\hat{y} + cy \text{ (where } c > a) \qquad (9.12)$$

Previously this expression has been maximised by setting $y = \hat{y}$. Now, however, y is itself an increasing function of $\hat{y}$, as a higher counter-plan earns more inputs and hence yields more output. Directors no longer have an incentive to reveal their production possibilities truthfully.

This completes our taxonomy of cases. As we have seen, the 1971 incentive system introduced in the Soviet Union has certain desirable static properties, in that it elicits truthful revelation of production possibilities from enterprises in a one-period model, provided that input allocations are not related too closely to counter-plans. In a multi-period model it is less satisfactory, with production being held back in earlier years to reduce output targets later on.

The Soviet authorities have tried to overcome this problem by establishing initial plan targets which are independent of performance over a five-year period, though they may alter from year to year. This should, in principle at least, give enterprises confidence to produce at or close to maximum capacity – allowing of course for risk-aversion – at least in the earlier part of the plan, when the later penalties for overfulfilment are heavily discounted.

However, there is some evidence that the new system has had little impact. In 1978, for example, the counter-plans submitted by enterprises seem to have amounted to only 0.25 per cent of those enterprises' total output (this figure has been calculated by Dr P. Hanson of Birmingham University, using data in Bachurin, 1979). The reasons for this are not hard to seek. The ratchet continues to operate, not on a five-yearly basis, but far more frequently. Ministries retain their right to alter plans in the course of implementation. As a Soviet writer notes, 'the ministry does not respect the counter-plan; the habitual procedure was followed: reduce the plan for the laggards, increase it for the successful. After these arithmetic procedures, not a single enterprise failed to fulfil the plan' (quoted in Nove, 1977, p. 106). Other authors writing since the 1971 reform note that underfulfilment still carries a stigma; in other words, the penalty for underfulfilment, the coefficient c, is large, and (as we have seen) this discourages the adoption of taut plans in the presence of uncertainty, and doubly so when managers are risk-averse. In short, the legacy of the traditional regime has prevented the 1971 amendments from creating a truly incentive-compatible system.

9.3 Is there an incentive-compatible mechanism?

We conclude this chapter by discussing an incentive scheme which overcomes one of the major difficulties in the elicitation schemes discussed in the previous section: namely, that when input allocations depend on the counter-plan, enterprises may gain higher bonuses by adopting unrealistic counter-plans.

The procedure to be discussed is analogous to one proposed to elicit truthful preferences for the provision of public goods. The difficulty here is that any individual has an incentive to exaggerate the value he places on the provision of the public good in order to ensure that it is provided. The problem is that of achieving a coincidence of interests between society as a whole and the individual.

In the public-good case this is achieved by a system of side-payments which ensures that if the project is accepted agent i receives not only his actual benefit from the project but also an additional payment equal to the *reported* benefits of all other agents (minus, where necessary, a constant amount to limit the cost of the elicitation scheme). If the project is not accepted, the agent receives nothing. This scheme works for the following reason. Suppose that all other agents report in aggregate a negative value for the project; agent i will only want it to be undertaken if his positive return outweighs the negative return of the other agents — otherwise, agent i will have to make a side-payment in excess of his private benefit. Equally, agent i has no incentive to exaggerate or understate his benefit from the scheme when the over-all return is positive, as he receives a side-payment equal to the reported benefit of all other agents *except himself*. Each agent finds it advantageous to report truthfully, regardless of what other agents do.

There is a precise analogy between the public-good case and the case of finding optimal output targets for enterprises when those targets influence input allocations. Incentive-compatibility can be achieved by ensuring that each enterprise director faces what is essentially the social decision problem. This is done by making each director's bonus depend on his enterprise's actual performance and also on the *forecast* performance of all other enterprises (minus, where necessary, an amount which is independent of that enterprise's forecast or actual output level). This procedure was originally discovered by Groves (1973).

Our account is based on a simple model in which the centre has a single input to allocate among n enterprises, each of which produces the same output according to an actual production function:

$$y_i = f_i^A(k_i, l_i) \qquad i = 1, 2, \ldots, n \tag{9.13}$$

where y_i is output of enterprise i, l_i is the transferable resource and k_i is a non-shiftable factor of production at each enterprise.

The centre's aim is to maximise output from all enterprises:

$$Y = \sum_{i=1}^{n} f_i^A(k_i, l_i) \tag{9.14}$$

The optimal allocation is characterised by the condition that $\partial y_i/\partial l_i = \partial y_j/\partial l_j$ (all i, j). However, the centre allocates resources on the basis of the production function reported to it by each enterprise: $y_i = f_i^R(k_i, l_i)$. In the simple case where the director's bonus is based on his output (or on his performance *vis-à-vis* some plan target) the director has an incentive to report a production function which differs from his actual one in order to secure a larger input allocation. Elicitation schemes of the type discussed above are not therefore incentive-compatible in this case.

Now consider the following bonus formula:

$$B_i = a \left\{ f_i^A(k_i, l_i^*) + \sum_{\substack{j=1 \\ j \neq i}}^{n} f_j^R(k_j, l_j^*) - A_i \right\} \tag{9.15}$$

Here l_i^*, l_j^* are the optimal allocations of l made by the centre on the basis of the production functions reported to it by the enterprises, and A_i is a constant (discussed below). This incentive scheme has two desirable properties. First, once an allocation has been made directors have an incentive to maximise output. Second, the system encourages directors to report their production functions accurately, so that $f_i^R(k_i, l_i) = f_i^A(k_i, l_i)$. Suppose the director of enterprise i exaggerates his production possibilities in order to receive a larger allocation l_i^*. His enterprise will produce more output, but the director's bonus will suffer because, as a result of the misallocation, the output of all other enterprises will go down by an amount which exceeds the increase in enterprise i's output. The term within the braces will thus be less than it would be with a truthful statement of production possibilities, and the director's bonus will be reduced. Being truthful carries its own reward as the scheme generates a coincidence of interests between each enterprise and the economy as a whole.

At first sight the scheme looks expensive in bonus payments. However, we can subtract any amount from the bonus paid to the director of enterprise i, provided that that amount does not depend on the director's output, y_i, or on the information he reports, $f_i^R(k_i, l_i)$. One possibility which has been discussed is to choose A_i to be equal to the total output forecast for the economy if zero resources were allocated to enterprise i, and the constant is thus the total output achievable in the economy without enterprise i. With this specification for A_i the director of enterprise i receives a bonus which is a proportion of the contribution made by his enterprise to the total output of the economy.

We have demonstrated the incentive-compatibility of this scheme in the simplest case of certainty. The results also carry over to the case where a random element enters in the enterprise's production function, provided that the director maximises his expected bonus. For this case it has been shown that the incentive system above (or some linear tranformation of it) is uniquely optimal in the strong sense that each enterprise finds it advantageous to report truthfully whatever strategy is adopted by other enterprises. This is proved in Conn (1979). Conn also reports results found by others suggesting that the system works under risk-aversion, but notes that inclusion of effort in the director's utility function raises serious difficulties (Conn, 1979, p. 273; see also Bonin and Marcus, 1979).

It is interesting to know that an incentive-compatible mechanism exists, and particularly interesting to have its uniqueness demonstrated. The uniqueness result may seem rather discouraging, however, as the informational properties of the mechanism as described are not favourable. Enterprises have to communicate what may be a complicated function to the centre; the incentive system only ensures that they find it to their advantage to communicate truthfully. On the other hand, an informationally decentralised version of the mechanism can be worked out, based on the Lange process described in Chapter 6 above, and Groves (1973) has shown that this has very desirable informational properties.

The discussion in this chapter has shown that incentives still pose a number of serious problems for centrally planned economies. A solution exists at a theoretical level; but it is subject to many practical difficulties and is hardly likely to be adopted in practice. On the other hand, elicitation schemes like that embodied in the 1971 Soviet incentive scheme, though imperfect theoretically, have the potential to make substantial improvements to enterprise behaviour. They remove what Kornai has called the fetish of 100 per cent fulfilment, by permitting bonuses to be paid even if the counter-plan is not achieved. Variations in the coefficients give the planners the ability to influence the probability of fulfilment of the plan. The most serious defect of the scheme is its vulnerability to the ratchet principle. This is a problem which can only be overcome by implementing the much-discussed precept of establishing stable long-term norms or targets for enterprises. It is noticeable that changes in the Soviet economic arrangements decided in July 1979 (see p. 45 above) contain provisions to strengthen the importance of five-year plans for enterprises, and some commentaries on them have acknowledged that stability in norms had not been achieved. In fact, ministry officials, trained under the old regime of unremitting interference in enterprise affairs, have until now continued to see counter-plans as evidence of concealed reserves and to adjust plan targets accordingly. It is probably this factor rather than the more sophisticated theoretical objection which has limited the impact of the incentive reforms.

Part III Applications and Prospects

10 MATHEMATICAL METHODS AND PLANNING

In this chapter we are no longer concerned to employ mathematical techniques merely to illuminate certain aspects of the theory of planning; instead, we shall be discussing those techniques and models which have actually been used in planning practice in one or other of the countries examined in this book. Accordingly the first three sections of the chapter are each devoted to the models applied in a single country; section 10.1 covers the Soviet Union, section 10.2 Hungary, and section 10.3 France. In each case one can enquire how far the introduction of mathematical methods into the planning process can actually lead to real improvements in the quality of planning and economic management. This is the subject of section 10.4, which concludes the chapter.

10.1 The Soviet Union

In the 1920s Soviet economists were path-breakers in developing mathematical models with the potential for application in economic planning. Some Soviet work in the early 1920s on balances of intersectoral flows within the economy was an important influence on Wassily Leontief's subsequent development of input–output methods. (Leontief left the Soviet Union in 1925; his review of the balance of the economy in 1923–4, prepared by the Soviet statistical agency, appeared in a Soviet journal in 1925 (Leontief, 1977, pp. 3–9).) Moreover, the Soviet economist Fel'dman developed in the mid-1920s a remarkable two-sector model of economic growth which is a precursor of much of the more recent mathematical growth theory (see Jones, 1975, pp. 113–22). These are merely the most distinguished examples of a large body of similar work.

However, the mathematical formulations did not find practical application during the Soviet industrialisation drive of the first five-year plans. Instead, they were rejected as empty formalisms which imposed a straitjacket on the virtually unlimited potential of the economy under socialism; as a result, mathematical studies in economics went into abeyance. The period saw instead the development of the material-balance system, described in Chapter 2, which still plays an important role in planning practice in the Soviet Union.

In the mid-1950s, however, mathematical economics revived in the Soviet Union, the revival being led by economists active in the 1920s (see Ellman, 1973). The growing complexity of the economy and the increase in information flows imposed a greater strain on the existing management system, and developments in computer technology throughout the 1950s and 1960s made it conceivable that mathematical planning models could be developed and actually used in planning practice. Experience has shown that the formal development of models is a relatively easy part of the process of getting mathematical models into use. Collecting the data, programming the computer, and above all integrating the model into the routine of planning officials, have all presented serious problems. As a result, practical implementation of many models has lagged disappointingly behind their original development and some of the more ambitious models seem incapable of implementation at present or in the foreseeable future.

In institutional terms the application of mathematical methods for planning in the Soviet Union has, since 1971, been part of an ambitious scheme for applying computers and automation at all levels in the administrative hierarchy and for all management functions — including planning, operational control of production and accounting. (Cave, 1980, gives a full account of these developments.) The aim is to equip all organisations, individually or jointly, with compatible computer centres which will channel information and instructions up and down the hierarchy and perform calculations. There is no intention, of course, of installing a completely automated or pre-programmed system. Officials and managers would still take major decisions, and the computational and data-exchange equipment is intended merely to perform certain calculations, many of them routine, and to effect the transfer of data.

Building up such a system has presented many serious technical and administrative problems and it is fair to say that at present the individual computer-based systems installed in different organisations (in Soviet terminology they are called 'automated management systems') operate largely independently of one another, rather than as an integrated whole. However, systems at every level — state planning commission, supply organisation, ministry and enterprise — have sub-systems for economic planning as well as for other management functions, and in the present section we shall briefly describe the type of mathematical model used at each level and its apparent impact on planning practice.

The organisation principally concerned with economic planning in the Soviet Union is Gosplan, the State Planning Commission. As noted in Chapter 2, Gosplan prepares plans for fifteen years (soon to be raised to twenty years), and five years ahead, as well as more detailed annual plans. It is noticeable that mathematical models have found greatest application in longer-term planning. There are a number of reasons for this, of which the most important is probably that the size of the models used for long-term planning is much smaller than the size of model which would be required for annual planning. A typical fifteen-year plan might distinguish eighteen sectors and a model used for five-year planning about 250. Yet for annual planning Gosplan currently compiles 2,000 material balances; moreover, every plan target in the annual plan must ultimately be assigned to a specified executant, so the process as a whole ultimately requires a very fine disaggregation which places a heavy informational burden on all participants, including Gosplan.

For long-term planning at Gosplan level several groups of Soviet economists have proposed models based on elaborate techniques for decomposing global models into sets of sub-models which are then solved iteratively. [The section below on Hungary outlines a simple version of such a procedure (two-level planning) which has in fact been applied.] However, none of these has gone beyond the stage of experimental calculation, and we confine ourselves here to outlining the model most generally applied in practice, a dynamic input—output model. In the static version:

$$\text{Gross output} = \text{Intermediate inputs} + \text{Final demand}$$
$$X \quad = \quad AX \quad + \quad Y$$

where X is a vector of gross outputs, Y is a vector of net outputs, and A is a matrix of direct input coefficients.

The model is solved for the gross outputs, X, given the desired net outputs:

$$X = [I - A]^{-1} Y$$

In the dynamic version final demand is divided into investment and consumption. Investment requirements for any increases in gross output are then determined using a matrix B of capital input coefficients, whose elements b_{ij} express the quantity of capital of goods of type i which must be accumulated to produce one extra unit of output of j. (Most elements of the matrix are zero, of course, because only a few sectors produce capital goods.) The model is thus written:

$$\text{Gross output} = \text{Intermediate} + \text{Investment} + \text{Consumption}$$
$$\text{demand} \quad \text{requirement}$$
$$X_t \quad = \quad AX_t \quad + \quad B\Delta X_t \quad + \quad C_t$$

where $\Delta X_t = X_{t+1} - X_t$, the vector of increments to gross output in year t, and all other variables are as before (except that they are now dated).

Models of this kind are used in the Soviet Union to explore possible paths of development for the economy. One version in current use is an eighteen-sector dynamic input—output model which optimises the level of consumption in the final year of the plan, while ensuring proportionate rates of growth throughout the plan. Only two sectors produce investment goods, in the forms of machinery and structures. A labour constraint is also imposed in each year of the plan to close the model (Birger *et al.*, 1979).

The advantage of such models is that they allow numerous alternative growth paths to be computed and presented to the political leadership for a final decision. We must, however, be aware of their drawbacks. The assumption of linearity — constant returns to scale and a single technique for each sector — is a restrictive one. Moreover, forecasting technological coefficients (the matrices A and B) five or twenty years ahead presents serious problems. At the present state of knowledge in the Soviet Union such models also present problems of computation, and until recently only semi-dynamic versions have been used. These focus only on the last year of the plan and largely ignore the path by which the economy reaches that final state. They are simpler but of less potential value.

Medium-term (five-year) plans are currently compiled in the Soviet Union with the assistance of a more disaggregated input—output model with something of the order of 250 sectors. Development paths for the economy are broken down by year, and these plans are one of the starting-points for annual planning. The five-year plan, however, goes beyond the simple setting of targets in quantity terms. Many value indicators have to be calculated as well, in planning the balance of income and expenditure of the population, for example (the relation between demand for and supply of consumer goods), or the financial plan. Special mathematical models could be used to compile these aspects of the plan, but Soviet work in these areas — in the analysis and forecasting of consumer demand, for example — lags behind the West, and applications are scarce (McAuley, 1979).

We come finally to the use of mathematical models by Gosplan for the purposes of annual planning. Applications here are few and far between. In particular, for reasons discussed in Chapter 2, input—output methods have made little or no progress in superseding the traditional material-balance methods. Where input—output techniques are used — as they were to estimate the impact of shortfalls in output of iron and energy on the rest of the economy in 1973 — they are used as a preliminary to, rather than a replacement for, traditional methods.

Gosplan's function in economic planning in the Soviet Union is to set out the over-all framework for the plan, which subordinate organisations later articulate at a more detailed level. Ministries play a central role here as the link between Gosplan and the basic production units — enterprises or production associations. However, before discussing the use which ministries make of sectoral planning models, we briefly turn our attention to the use of a rather specialised mathematical model by the supply organisations. We do so because the use of this model illustrates a general problem in a particularly clear form.

One of the principal aims of the supply organisation in the Soviet Union (Gossnab) is to compile the so-called 'attachment plan'. This plan is the culminating stage of the administrative planning of inputs, and it assigns each customer to a specified supplier for each of its inputs. Gossnab knows the entitlement of each customer to supplies, and the output targets for each producing firm. It also knows the costs (or the distance) of shipment from each possible supplier to each customer. With this knowledge Gossnab can formulate and solve a so-called 'transportation problem', a simple and widely used type of linear programming model which minimises the total costs or distance of shipments (see Dorfman *et al.*, 1958, ch. 5). Such problems have been formulated in the Soviet Union since the early 1960s.

The interesting thing, however, is that when specialist bodies within the supply system have compiled optimal attachment plans in this way, the supply organisations have by and large declined to implement them. The reason for this reluctance is not hard to seek. Supply organisations themselves receive quantitative output targets in terms of tonne-kilometres (the size of shipments multiplied by the distance). An optimal attachment plan minimises the very variable which supply organisations seek to maximise to earn their bonuses. This illogical system evidently still operates (Kantorovich *et al.*, 1979). Similar conflicts between the incentive system and optimal allocations of resources computed by mathematical methods are found elsewhere in the economy, and are one of the factors limiting the impact of mathematical methods.

We now turn briefly to sectoral planning models used in ministries. Almost all ministries in the Soviet Union, and certainly all centralised or All-Union ministries have their own computer centres and automated management systems which are used in the preparation of both annual and longer-term plans. The use of formal models is more common in compiling plans of the latter type, particularly investment plans over a time horizon of five to twenty years. (Similar models are used in Hungary (see Kornai, 1975, chs 5 and 6) and indeed by large firms in the West.)

The formulation of such models is quite straightforward. The ministry is given output targets for five, ten and fifteen years hence (often found from the solution of a dynamic input—output model of the type described above). It also receives a figure for the cost of capital, equivalent to an interest rate. It prepares development alternatives for its existing enterprises and for possible new factories (these can be discrete or continuous variables) and calculates the current and capital costs of each. It then solves a mathematical programme to minimise the total cost, including capital charge, of meeting the output target. The plan thus selects an activity level for each existing or potential enterprise (which may in some cases involve closing down the enterprise) and thus establishes an investment plan for the sector. By 1978 models of this type were employed in numerous ministries, and standard procedures had been laid down ('Standard methodology', 1978). Such models are often employed in parallel with traditional investment planning methods, and considerable cost savings are claimed for the new methods.

According to one interesting proposal, sectoral models of this kind could be solved in conjunction with an economy-wide dynamic input—output model. The role of the sectoral models would be to choose the optimal techniques (i.e. the elements of matrices A and B) for inclusion in the economy-wide model, which would then be recomputed to yield different levels for sectoral output requirements. (Such a procedure was also envisaged in Hungary in the late 1960s, but little has been heard about it more recently.) This might in turn necessitate an alteration to the 'cost of capital' element in the sectoral objective function; a new investment plan would be computed, yielding new coefficients for the economy-wide model (Kossov and Pugachev, 1974). This model offers an opportunity for combining the two most successful and general mathematical models currently in use in the Soviet Union, but it is still at an experimental stage.

Mathematical models are also used to a limited extent for current planning in the Soviet Union at both ministry and enterprise level. The most general form is a standard linear programming model which allocates ministry targets among enterprises, or enterprise targets among individual shops. Production scheduling models are also widely used for short-term planning, but we do not describe them here (see Cave, 1980).

Over-all, then, the use of mathematical models for planning in the Soviet Union is rather limited and patchy. The most interesting applications are in long-term planning, which is freer from the pressures of a rigid planning time-table than short-term planning, and where, because of the high degree of aggregation, data problems are less acute. However, such models supplement rather than replace traditional procedures. In the standard phrase in Soviet literature, the results of the models are 'taken into account' in the final decision.

A notable absentee from this catalogue is any model for *price formation*. Indeed, in the models described above, prices play no important role (with the exception of the proposed scheme limiting sectoral and economy-wide models, where the capital charge or interest rate is varied to influence choice of technique – but this model is only experimental). None of the models contains procedures for revising prices in the light of the solution for quantities, or for allowing such revised prices to influence quantity decisions. Nor is any serious use made of the dual variables or shadow prices associated with the primal solutions of optimising models. This is a reflection of the continued use in the Soviet Union of administrative rather than market methods, and of the limited autonomy of lower-level units, especially in investment decisions. In Hungary, as we shall see, changed institutional relationships offer different opportunities for, and place different constraints on, the use of mathematical models.

10.2 Hungary

The most interesting planning models in Hungary have been developed to assist in the process of formulating medium-term (i.e. five-year) plans, or to facilitate comparisons between alternative growth paths over a longer period (i.e. fifteen to twenty years). In addition, mainly since the economic reform, some price planning models have appeared for use in computing price revisions and estimating the likely effects of changes in foreign-trade prices. Other types of model – for example, concerned with demand planning, some aspects of regional planning, and the planning of individual sectors – have also been proposed, but we lack the space to discuss these. Indeed, even for the types of model we do discuss, we have had to be extremely selective, and only outline one or two examples of each type. The following specific models are discussed in this section:

(1) The model of plan sounding (Dániel *et al.*, 1971).
(2) Aggregate planning model (Dániel, 1971; Ujlaki, 1970).
(3) Two-level planning (Kornai and Liptak, 1965; Kornai, 1975).
(4) Model used for the fourth five-year plan (1971–5) (Ganczer, 1973).
(5) Price planning model (Glattfelder and Mátéffy, 1971).

There is a fairly detailed analysis of models (2), (3) and (4) in Hare (1973), which also contains an outline of model (5).

Since three of the models ((2), (3) and (4)) have a number of common features, as well as having definite relationships to the traditional plan-formulation process, some general remarks on these points may provide a useful introduction to the individual models. In Hungarian planning practice the process of constructing a medium-term plan comprises two principal stages. The first explores the alternative development paths in rather aggregated terms, to identify the main constraints, bottlenecks and opportunities, while the second seeks to determine a more detailed breakdown of the aggregated plan conception agreed in the first stage. The models correspond closely to these stages, with model (2) being designed for the first, and models (3) and (4) for the second. All three models were proposed at a time when mathematical techniques met with a certain amount of suspicion from the traditional planners — as in fact they still do. Partly because of this, but also because of genuine difficulties of formulating agreed economy-wide objective functions, the models accepted quite limited goals. Typically they took as constraints some indicators from a preliminary plan formulated in the traditional manner, and merely sought to find some feasible plan which could improve on some or all of these indicators, without attempting to propose more radical changes in economic structure or to subject the traditional plan to fundamental criticism. This cautious approach is discussed further in section 10.4 below.

Models (2), (3) and (4) are all based on a framework of input—output relationships of the kind that we introduced in chapter 2 when discussing material balances. In the Hungarian case such models are more easily constructed than in other countries, since Hungary has produced a large number of input—output tables since the late 1950s — with an aggregated table nearly every year (less than twenty sectors distinguished), tables with just over sixty branches every four years or so, and a few tables distinguishing just over 200 product groups. This represents an impressive data base for modelling work, though as we shall see the models are still not without their technical difficulties.

The philosophy of model-building changed in an important way between models (3) and (4), reflecting to some extent the reform in the economic management system; this is why we have chosen to present these particular models in this chapter. Kornai's model of two-level planning was developed partly for its theoretical interest and partly as an attempt to model the processes of communication between the central agencies involved in plan formulation — that is, primarily the ministries and the national planning office. The model has nothing to say about enterprise behaviour, which is not surprising given that it was prepared before the economic reforms of 1968. In contrast, the model developed for the fourth five-year plan was much less concerned about the communication between the central agencies, but it contained a number of constraints describing enterprise responses to the economic regulators. Thus the planners accepted that under the conditions of the economic reform certain technically feasible allocations might still not be attainable because of such responses. Let us now turn to the models themselves.

(1) *The model of plan sounding*

This is the only Hungarian model to be examined which is not explicitly based on an input—output structure. It distinguishes twelve sectors, of which two produce investment goods, but most equations are just as they would be in a one-good model. GNP in year t, Y^t, is related to gross outputs in individual sectors by the single equation:

$$Y^t = \sum_j a_j^t x_j^t \tag{10.1}$$

Consumption is a fixed fraction of GNP, and investment in fixed capital is allocated between sectors as given proportions of total fixed investment, I^t, the latter being determined from the income—expenditure balance. This procedure does not guarantee that the demand and supply of investment goods is in balance, but subsequent versions of the model have avoided such disequilibria. The model has been employed to study alternative investment policies, including the effects of changes in the over-all investment ratio and changes in the ratio of infrastructural investment. Partly because of this concentration, it neglects any consideration of labour-force constraints or foreign trade; it seems, however, that its conclusions are not out of line with those obtained in more complex models. The model was solved in forty variants for the eighteen-year period 1968—85.

From these calculations it transpired that the growth rate of consumption over a period of interest was hardly affected at all by variations in the investment ratio, with capital coefficients and the general efficiency of resource utilisation being much more important. On the other hand, the growth rates of production and consumption were much more sensitive to the division of investment between infrastructural branches and the directly productive branches. But infrastructure has been neglected for a long time in Hungary, so that the model implies that catching up requires the acceptance of some slow-down in over-all growth. Finally, the model suggests that the low proportion of total investment currently allocated to the investment-goods and construction sectors inevitably leads to persistent shortages; a shift in the allocation in favour of these sectors could allow the whole economy to grow more quickly.

(2) *Aggregate planning model*

Models in this category were first developed in connection with work on the third five-year plan (1966—70), and were improved in time for the fourth plan, as reported in Ujlaki (1970). Since then the main extension has been in the direction of constructing longer-term models covering several five-year plan periods, using a variant of the original model as a building-block. This makes it convenient to outline the model of Ujlaki (1970), as an introduction to Dániel (1971).

Mathematically Mrs Ujlaki's model has very much the same structure as the larger models which follow. However, it is much more aggregated, distinguishing less than twenty sectors, and contains no relationships representing enterprise behaviour. Moreover, it was intended for application in the first stage of plan formulation, when rather broad policy alternatives would still be under consideration. By the time it becomes appropriate to use the more detailed models, however, many features of the development path will already have been decided, including some of the major regulators and the large investments; consequently it is both possible and necessary to predict enterprise incomes, the resulting flows of taxation and fund formation, and the expenditures which these generate, as is done in model (4).

The aggregate planning model contains all the constraints one would expect, and explores the feasible region using a range of objective functions. The treatment of investment deserves separate mention, since it is quite different from the more detailed models. In each sector of the model output produced in the final year of the plan period is the sum of output from existing capacity (x_i^I) and that from new capacity created during the plan period (x_i^{II}). Such new capacity is assumed, curiously, to have the same technical coefficients – describing its domestic and imported material requirements, and labour requirements – as the old capacity. But the output available from the latter is obviously limited, and investment funds are required to create the former. The model actually provided two constraints on investment resources, one a financial limit, and the other (in view of the shortage of hard currency) a limit on machinery imported from capitalist countries. In both this and the previous model some allowance had to be made in the investment equations for investments already under way at the start of the plan period and projects which would only be completed after the plan period in question. This was done in a fairly *ad hoc* fashion by appropriate adjustments to the financial resources available for investment, and the investment component of final demand in the input–output balances.

The model proposed in Dániel (1971) was intended as a contribution to long-term planning exercises covering the period 1971–90. A substantial amount of work was done by various institutes in the early 1970s on long-term planning, though many of the results were soon left behind by the energy crisis and the fundamental change in the world economic situation to which this gave rise. However, the model is not without interest. It breaks the economy down into twenty-seven sectors in each of four five-year periods, and within each period production is represented in a similar manner as in the last model, except that new technologies have input coefficients different from the old. As one would expect, the capacity constraints in each period depend on investment in the previous ones. Also, to avoid solutions in which the patterns of output and investment change drastically from period to period, the model includes a number of so-called 'smoothness' constraints to restrict rates of change. Constraints of this type are frequently introduced into linear models to avoid instability, though their economic rationale is often not very clear. A large number of solutions to this model have been computed with alternative objective functions, different investment structures, and different assumptions about the labour force and balance of payments, in order to explore the implications of alternative growth strategies.

(3) *Two-level planning*

This model was developed to provide a detailed representation of Hungarian economic structure and possibilities to aid in the formulation of the third five-year plan (1966–70). In fact, various difficulties with the computations meant that the full results were available too late to be used directly as a basis for the plan; however, some of the sectoral calculations which formed partial solutions of the over-all model were used. The model envisages the central planners allocating labour and materials to individual branches, which then respond by advising the centre of the marginal productivities of the resources they have been allocated; this leads the centre to revise its initial allocation, and the process continues, in principle, until it converges to the optimal plan. In practice, only a few iterations might be feasible; also, of course, the actual communication which took place among the agencies involved in plan formulation was considerably more complex than that represented in the model. The model itself is an example of a planning algorithm, of the kind we discussed more fully in Chapter 6.

The economy is described by a series of branch models covering production, investment and trade possibilities in each branch, linked by centrally controlled resource allocations and requirements. It was not specified in advance whether the output required of each branch should be produced by the branch itself, or imported. In line with the usual practice of Hungarian plan formulation the model concentrated on describing production possibilities in the last year of the five-year plan period in most detail. Expressing it as a linear programme the economy-wide problem may be written in the following form:

$$\text{Maximise } (c_1 x_1 + c_2 x_2 + \ldots + c_m x_m) \tag{10.2}$$

subject to the constraints:

$$A_{01} x_1 + A_{02} x_2 + \ldots + A_{0m} x_m \leqslant b_0 \tag{10.3}$$

$$\left.\begin{array}{l} A_1 x_1 \leqslant b_1 \\ \qquad A_2 x_2 \leqslant b_2 \\ \qquad\qquad \vdots \qquad \vdots \\ \qquad\qquad A_m x_m \leqslant b_m \end{array}\right\} \tag{10.4}$$

where (10.2) is the economy-wide objective function, (10.3) are the over-all constraints, essentially input–output balances and a few other balances (e.g. the balance of payments), (10.4) are the sets of constraints referring to individual branches, and the variables x_i are vectors of branch activity levels giving output, investment and trade flows for branch i. In section 10.4 we comment on some of the less satisfactory assumptions entailed by this particular formulation of the problem.

In the two-level planning conception this programme is not solved directly but by a sequence of iterations between two levels. This is done by breaking down the over-all problem into a number of sub-problems, one for each branch; the centre provisionally allocates the resources and requirements represented in the constraints (10.3), giving targets z_i to branch i (obviously the sum of the z_is must equal b_0). The sub-problem for branch i then takes the following form:

$$\left. \begin{array}{l} \text{Maximise } (c_i x_i) \\[12pt] \text{subject to } A_{0i} x_i \leqslant z_i, \text{ and } A_i x_i \leqslant b_i \end{array} \right\} \tag{10.5}$$

Thus the over-all problem is decomposed into $m + 1$ smaller problems, one for each branch, and the central allocation problem. Now we can explain how the algorithm was intended to work.

Given a central allocation (the z_is), the branches solve the sub-problems (10.5), obtaining as part of the solutions shadow prices on the centrally allocated resources – which are reported to the centre. This price information then leads to a revised central allocation, with resources being directed towards areas where they are most productive. It can be proved that provided that revisions to allocations are appropriately calculated the procedure converges to the optimal plan. Unfortunately, however, it does not possess all the other properties which Malinvaud (1967) considered desirable, and which we discussed in Chapter 6. Although the procedure is feasible – all intermediate plan proposals generated by the procedure are consistent with the economy's production possibilities – it is not monotonic, so the objective function may be worse after a few iterations than it was at the beginning! This rather serious drawback of the procedure is one reason why it met with computational problems, and eventually a variant of the Dantzig–Wolfe procedure was employed to obtain solutions (Dantzig, 1963, ch. 23).

(4) *Model used for the fourth five-year plan*

Just as the previous model this one was formulated as a large linear programme, again describing the final year of the plan period (1975) in most detail; it differs from Kornai's model in that it was not designed to be solved by some form of decomposition procedure. To a large extent this reflects improvements in computing capacity between the two periods, though in spite of these improvements there were still delays in producing solutions with the new model. Given the strict time schedule to which plan formulation must adhere, it was again only possible to use partial solutions to assist the process.

The model contains eighteen sectors, sixty-three branches and 207 product groups. Output of each product group is a real variable, but since the product groups within any branch do not exhaust the total production of that branch they are supplemented by a category, 'other production', measured in value terms to account for the remainder. As a result, the model contains two sets of product balances, one in value terms for sectors, and another in real terms for product groups. This complexity, and the problem of basing the relationships in the model on estimated 1975 prices, was undoubtedly a source of error, though the product-group structure facilitated the description of investment alternatives and enterprise behaviour.

Many of the constraints in the model require no special comment and it is sufficient merely to list them. Such relationships include the following:

(a) *Branch production*, as a sum of outputs of product groups within each branch, produced by existing capacity, and new capacities created during the plan period.

(b) *Sector production*, as a sum of production in the branches within each sector.

(c) *Production balances*, based on input—output relationships.

(d) *Import constraints for socialist trade*, based on long-term agreements.

(e) *Export constraints on capitalist markets*, based on 'expert' estimates of demand and the need to supply domestic markets.

(f) *Foreign exchange balances* for socialist and capitalist markets.

(g) *Labour balances* for several types of labour.

(h) *The balance between income and expenditure of the population*, in which consumption above certain basic levels is assumed to have a fixed commodity structure.

(i) *Constraints relating to investment*; there are three groups of these: (i) material requirements for investment in 1975 — the total volume of such investment is not a choice variable, though its composition can be varied; (ii) constraints on resources required for investment in the period 1971–4; (iii) constraints relating financial sources of investment — mainly bank credits and sectoral development funds — to the executed investments.

In addition to the above, production cost estimates are needed for working out the distribution of profits into enterprise development and distribution funds. The model distinguishes between three categories of costs: namely, those proportional to production variables, those depending on other variables, and some fixed costs. In general the enterprise profits are not simply proportional to production, but the model employs linear approximations to give each branch a profit constraint for 1975. As noted earlier, this model contains some equations representing the regulators in force during the plan period. (The main components of these economic regulators were discussed fully in Chapter 3 above.) Some of these concern profit distribution within branches, which is important because it affects population incomes via the distribution funds, and also affects credit requirements via the development funds. The most serious simplifications of the model occur here because the model is relatively aggregated and linear. Profit is enterprise-based, while the model is branch (or product group) based, and the profit distribution and taxation rules are highly non-linear at enterprise level. However, some experimental calculations suggested that the linear approximations used for these rules were still satisfactory after small plausible changes in the size distribution of firms within a branch. For each branch the model has constraints representing the distribution of profits, fund formation, and the maintenance of the branch credit position.

This rather complicated model actually works in quite a simple way. Thus investment and consumption are both constrained from below sector by sector, while investment during the plan period is limited above by various resource constraints. Production levels, which include some choices about the techniques of production to be employed, must be determined together with trade patterns in order to satisfy balance-of-payments and other restrictions of the model. Since many of the constant terms in the constraints derive from a preliminary plan based on traditional techniques of formulation, any solution of the model would represent an improvement on that plan. Particular solutions were obtained using a number of different objective functions, most notably the maximisation of consumption in excess of the minimum specified in the preliminary plan, and the maximisation of one or other trade balance; as we emphasise later, it is not easy to provide a rationale in strict welfare terms for such objectives, though they may be defended as means of exploring the feasible region. The model constructed to aid in the formulation of the fifth five-year plan (1976–80) had a structure very similar to the model just examined, so that it does not merit a separate discussion.

(5) *Price planning model*

The basic idea of all such models is to employ equations like those set out at the end of Chapter 8 to estimate producer prices as a function of technical parameters, foreign prices, tax rates, and so on. Price models have been constructed both for the study of price types and price distortions (as, for example, in Bródy, 1970, and Glattfelder and Mátéffy, 1971, in Hungary, and Brown and Walker, 1973, in the West, using Hungarian data), and in the prediction of prices needed for planning purposes. The latter kind of application is the more demanding technically, as it is not satisfactory to base the analysis on the usual *ex post* input–output tables. As a result, much of the Hungarian work on price models has concentrated on the question of revising input–output coefficients; for example Szakolczai (1974) used variants of the well-known RAS method, which is analysed in detail in Bacharach (1970). In addition, Szakolczai has attempted to identify branch production functions rather than using constant coefficients, though without great success.

10.3 France

The French planning models are rather more interesting from a theoretical point of view than either the Hungarian or Soviet ones, in that they devote less attention to the description of production possibilities *per se*, and concentrate more on the explanation of behaviour. This corresponds of course to the much greater degree of decentralisation within the French economy than in the other two countries studied here. In order to illustrate the French approach we concentrate on just two models: the first, referred to as Fifi, was built to guide the preparation of the sixth plan (1971–5), and was subsequently used for the seventh plan as well, while the second, referred to as DMS, has been developed to overcome some of the limitations of Fifi. It is intended that an updated version of DMS will be employed in studying the alternative development paths for the French economy over the period of the eighth plan (1981–5).

Fifi (physical and financial model)

This is a model with several features in common with some of the models we have discussed in the two sections above. Like the Hungarian models it provides a detailed account of the economic situation in the final year of the period being planned, without at the same time explaining the path from the present to that expected future state. In addition, it contains a core of input–output relationships, though in extremely aggregated form, with only seven branches being distinguished. In all the model has around 2,000 equations.

Theoretically the most interesting aspect of the model is its treatment of the French economy's response to international competition, following arguments set out in Courbis (1972a). The sectors in the model are classified into 'sheltered' and 'exposed' ones, the former having the power to raise prices in response to cost increases, the latter taking international prices as given. More recent models have treated international aspects of French economic policy in greater detail and have not simply taken certain prices as exogenous. However, in Fifi itself, even the recognition that different sectors of the economy would respond in different ways to any disturbances and fluctuations on world markets represented a considerable advance over the cruder approaches followed in the earlier plans. As one might guess, in Fifi manufacturing was the major sector assumed to be exposed.

The model included a Phillips curve type of relationship between wages and the level of unemployment. Since this is normally supposed to be a short-run function, it was necessary to amend the initially estimated form by assuming – probably not very plausibly – that progress to the final state described by Fifi would be regular, as Liggins (1975) explains. Given the nature of the approximations employed here, it is not surprising that subsequent study revealed that the area of price and wage determination accounted for about 80 per cent of the forecasting error involved in the model (Deleau and Malgrange, 1977, p. 443). Another key assumption was that firms tended to set prices on the basis of a fairly stable desired rate of self-financing. In sheltered sectors this generated a sequence of determination which went from demand to desired investment to price, while in the exposed part of the economy the sequence was reversed; there it would go from price (set by international competition) to investment, with the resulting levels of domestic production then determining how much of demand would be met from imports.

Given this structure of causality within the model, it follows that its policy implications are not the conventional Keynesian ones. Indeed, the standard policies which Keynesian macroeconomics would suggest are likely to be highly inefficient, often doing little more than shifting employment between sheltered and exposed sectors with almost no impact on the over-all level of employment.

What the model tends to favour most strongly is those policies which increase price competitiveness especially in industry, as Siebel (1975, p. 161) observes. Such policies could include both various forms of subsidy or tax credit to the firms in the exposed sector, as well as efforts to raise productivity in those firms. That Fifi should lead on to structurally differentiated policies of this kind was to be expected, of course, given the structure of the model itself. After all, the simple Keynesian models with which Fifi has sometimes been favourably compared only contain a single good, so can hardly be expected to propose different policies for different sectors.

Let us now consider how Fifi was used in plan formulation, taking the preparation of the sixth plan as an example (Deleau and Malgrange, 1977, p. 438). Three stages of preparation can be distinguished: namely, a preliminary phase in which the main medium-term problems facing the economy are defined and clarified; an options phase in which the feasible states of the economy in the terminal year of the plan period are explored; and a terminal phase in which the plan is finally agreed, together with the measures required to implement it. These phases are somewhat similar to the two-stage procedure followed in Hungary, but whereas the latter employs different models in each stage the French planners were able to make use of Fifi in all three phases of their own procedure. The first phase involves projecting forward existing policies to examine their implications, while the second considers alternative combinations of instruments in order to study the set of feasible outcomes; it also considered alternative values for some exogenous variables to yield basic projects with different rates of growth, 5.5, 6.0 and 6.5 per cent being the main variants. The third phase took the 6 per cent growth-rate path and examined alternative means of reaching it to arrive at the final plan.

Experience with Fifi in connection with the sixth plan made clear a number of its limitations. First, it was unable by itself to provide a sufficiently detailed account of the French economic situation, and it was soon supplemented by a series of additional models – often referred to in the French literature as 'peripheral' models – covering aspects of the economy not adequately treated in Fifi itself. For example, regional aspects of the plan came to be represented in a separate model called *Regina* (Liggins, 1975; Courbis, 1972b, 1978). In addition, international aspects of French economic policy and activity benefited from a world model, *Moise*, in which the main trade flows were endogenous, at the time the seventh plan was being formulated. Other problems could not be handled merely by building more models to be linked into the central model, but led to important changes in the structure of the central model itself. We have already referred to analysis of the forecasting errors associated with Fifi, and it is obviously necessary to study these in order to learn how the model might be improved. But the recognition that much of the economic environment is uncertain also gave rise to demands for a more 'strategic' approach to planning, whereby a number of different solutions would be calculated, each conditional on different assumptions about the exogenous variables. Such variant calculations occurred to some extent with Fifi, as noted above, but the range of variations allowed for was extremely narrow and probably gave an unrealistically favourable impression of the accuracy of forecasting models. One difficulty, of course, is that much of the deviation between forecast and actual outcome must be attributed not to incorrect judgements about the exogenous variables of the model but rather to incorrect specification of certain parts of the model. This eventually creates pressures to change the model, but given the present state of economic theory there is no guarantee that the resulting modifications would actually improve planning very much.

The final problem with Fifi is one which could be eliminated given a new type of model which would improve the quality of economic forecasts. It is a feature of Fifi that is also a characteristic of the Hungarian models: namely, that it describes the economic situation in the final year of the planning period without explaining how the economy would move from the initial to the final state. In the Hungarian case, where economic growth has been fairly steady in recent years, the errors involved in basing plan calculations on projections of the final year may not be great, though there are certainly some difficulties when structural changes are being planned for; but for France the errors are likely to be considerably greater. Consequently it is the French who first developed a dynamic model for use in plan-formulation exercises, to which we now turn.

DMS (dynamic multi-sectoral model)

A dynamic multi-sectoral model, referred to simply as DMS, was developed in 1976 as a successor to Fifi for use in the eighth plan (Fouquet *et al.*, 1976). The new model is smaller than Fifi, comprising about 1,000 equations, of which only around 300 are behavioural. Nevertheless, it distinguishes eleven sectors as compared with Fifi's seven, and is dynamic in the sense that it traces development paths year by year for up to eight years. While the structure of the model within each period is quite similar to Fifi's, including the retention of Phillips curve relationships to explain wage and price movements, DMS is able to give a much more satisfactory formulation of investment decisions. Investment is treated as a function of both real and financial factors; the principal real factor is the degree of capacity utilisation, while the rate of return on capital picks up the financial aspect of investment decisions. The latter is in turn influenced by the pricing policy pursued in the different branches of the economy which are affected by government policies and the competitive situation (as explained above for the Fifi model).

However, while the competitive position in various branches was the key element of Fifi, it has been overtaken in DMS by the detailed analysis of the development path. This partly reflects the experience of recent years that external events and shocks have made it increasingly difficult to plan for five years at a time, whereas a model like DMS can be used in a system of rolling plans which can be revised and updated annually or as circumstances dictate. It also reflects a view that events along the development path will affect government policies, and as far as possible this should be allowed for at the time of plan formulation. Finally, it has become clear that the feasible terminal states are not independent of the type of path which is chosen. For all these reasons it is important to examine the course of development more fully than was possible with earlier models. Of course, this new orientation has not meant the abandonment of all the earlier models, and DMS will continue to be one of a family of interconnected models, just as Fifi used to be.

10.4 Can mathematical methods improve planning?

In earlier sections of this chapter we concentrated on outlining a number of models used in the formulation of medium-term plans in the Soviet Union, Hungary and France; except for France these models were completely, or almost completely, linear, being based on a framework of input—output relationships. In terms of the mathematical techniques involved this is a very narrow class of models, but is is the class which has proved most fruitful in practical applications. It is therefore important to consider how far and in what respects such models might lead to improvements in economic planning.

In arriving at any assessment we must begin by dispelling any illusions which the reader might have about the possibilities for computing optimal plans, and then instructing that they be fulfilled. This book has already provided many reasons for scepticism about any such possibility, and the present section provides some more. Essentially it is just not technically feasible to assemble all the data required for a complete model of even a small national economy, and then optimise it. All the relevant data can never be brought together at the same time, the computational demands are unimaginably huge, even with the most modern computers, and so far there is little sign of agreement on the 'correct' objective function. Consequently the question of improvements in planning must be approached with more modest expectations about what models can do; we must also take into account the way in which modelling work fits into the more traditional forms of planning activity.

The ways in which models may be integrated into the traditional planning process are discussed fully in Augustinovics (1975). Although written with Hungary in mind, this study is applicable to all three countries considered in this book. It distinguishes between three stages in the application of modelling techniques, referred to as 'experimental', 'parallel' and 'integrated'; all countries which began their planning before the 1960s need to pass through these stages, since computers were simply not capable of solving large models before then. Moreover, civil servants and economists concerned with planning need to be convinced that formal models — in which they may have little training or understanding — can really help in their day-to-day work.

The experimental stage begins the learning process by using mathematical methods to examine certain problems not solved satisfactorily by traditional methods. The work may be initiated by research institutes and supported by some of the planners; it often calls for new sources of data, or demands greater consistency in the treatment of different branches, and gives rise to serious mathematical, theoretical and computational difficulties. As a result, such exercises are frequently completed far too late to have any influence on planning, though the experience gained no doubt wins over some planners — convincing them that models do have something to offer — and paves the way for more successful applications.

In the second, parallel stage of application it is no longer a question of winning over the planners. Mathematical methods are accepted as one of the tools for solving a particular problem, for example the formulation of a medium-term plan (as in most of the models considered in this chapter). But they are not the only tool, and typically the familiar procedures continue to be used at the same time; the models may reveal some possibilities for improving on the traditional plan but they cannot do more than that. Finally, when models are fully integrated into the planning process, they completely take over certain phases of it, displacing traditional methods. In practice, there are few examples of this stage, and most models discussed above fall into the first and second stages described above, but mainly the latter. It is not hard to see why this is the case.

Models are much more rigid than traditional methods, there is lack of agreement on objective functions, the linear models we have been discussing have some technical drawbacks, and the planners are quite rightly unwilling to rely entirely on a single source of solutions to their planning problems. As far as rigidity and flexibility are concerned, we need to consider in what respects models are rigid — and what might be done about it — and the nature of the flexibility claimed for traditional techniques of planning. Let us imagine the set of balances and constraints which have to be taken into account in a plan-formulation exercise. The number of such relationships is large, the quality of data on them is very variable and some are only imperfectly understood, a situation which leads, according to Kornai (1975, ch. 2), to the development of a hierarchy among the equations; the planners seek to satisfy the most important ones, and make some allowance for the others, but are unable to check everything in detail. In a model, however, it is normally the case that a relationship is either present or not; and if it is present, the data required for it must be complete. Given the time constraints on most planning exercises, this can be a serious drawback, since results have to be ready by a definite date whether all the data which might be helpful are available or not. Even if models can offer gains in precision, and the ability to examine alternatives, they must meet the time schedule already laid down if they are to be useful; difficulties in this area explain why it is often partial models which find applications rather than the much more demanding economy-wide models. On the positive side, however, we may note that the data requirements of models often provide a stimulus to the general improvement of economic statistics, both in quality and scope, which improves traditional methods even if the models themselves are not used very much.

Some models are deterministic, but many of the ones discussed earlier were optimising models based on an input—output framework. Much of the theoretical literature on planning, for example most of Heal (1973), casually assumes that an agreed objective function is readily available for insertion into any model which happens to need it. Unfortunately, this is far from the truth, and the lack of agreement on such a function severely limits the role of optimising models. The planners are frequently able to list a number of indicators of the economic situation, usually expressed in very aggregated from, in which they would like to see improvements: for example, the level of national income, the volume of consumption, the balance of payments, and so on. But there appears to be no way of arriving at agreed weights which would allow these desiderata to be combined into some over-all objective. Consequently the role of optimisation is not to locate the unique optimal plan but to facilitate exploration of the feasible set. Moreover, even this is frequently restricted further than purely technical considerations would entail — because of the well-known instability of linear models.

Linear models often contain constraints which prevent the solutions from departing too far from either the initial allocation of resources, or some expected future allocation. For example, the Hungarian and Soviet models, as noted earlier, tend to constrain solutions to do at least as well as some preliminary plan worked out using traditional techniques; similarly, the French models restrict some rates of change depending on what the economy is believed capable of sustaining, though market forces themselves also limit change to some extent. The reasons for such conservative model formulation are partly political — the need to get the models accepted, which means that they should not propose anything too drastic and implausible — and partly the result of aggregation and stability problems. Figure 10.1 illustrates the situation for a typical Hungarian model. For simplicity the economy is restricted to two outputs, y_1 and y_2. P is a plan formulated using traditional techniques, OAB is the feasible region defined by purely technical considerations — production possibilities, and so one — while PCD is the feasible region which improves on the original plan. There are good reasons for the planners to restrict the region of interest in this way, and to use alternative objective functions to explore PCD rather than OAB.

First, medium-term planning models are always fairly aggregated and they usually consider no more than a single five-year plan period. Both these points make them extremely unsuitable models within which to take investment decisions, either about individual sectors or even projects. Alternative objective functions are likely to generate large changes in the proposed structure of investment which bear little relation to real relative efficiencies of different structures. Second, linear models make very peculiar assumptions about substitutability, namely that it is either perfect or impossible, and this, too, should make planners wary about accepting recommendations about major structural change from them. Admittedly some of the French models are more satisfactory in that relative prices do have some effect on input coefficients and relative costs, and some of the Hungarian and Soviet models are beginning to move in this

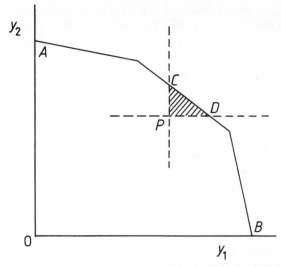

Figure 10.1   Feasible region in linear planning models

direction. However, the fact remains that all these models contain a large number of fixed coefficients — which means that their solutions should be treated with some caution. Of course, the traditional approach also tends to assume a large number of constant coefficients in the form of input norms, and so on, but the planners would probably argue, not without justification, that they can allow for some structural change using their informal procedures rather more satisfactorily than is possible in large-scale models.

Having commented on some of the limitations of linear planning models, we can now attempt to answer the question which heads this section. Probably most important of all, the development of models tends to stimulate orderly thinking about economic alternatives for the future in ways which lead both to better and more systematic data collection and to the serious consideration of plan variants. The latter is at least a step in the direction of recognising some of the important uncertainties which all planners have to face, though no one would wish to claim that an ideal solution has yet been devised. The above point suggests that it is not models themselves but the discipline they impose on the plan-formulation process which yields the greatest benefits. One should not of course deduce from this that we consider all traditional planners to be rather sloppy and disorganised in their approach to planning; indeed, we would hope that much of this book proves just the contrary, while making clear the very real difficulties to be overcome. In this connection models can be helpful, but rarely decisive.

Models based on input—output relationships typically satisfy the main accounting identities in the economy of interest; accordingly solutions from such models will provide consistent plans. Thus the models may be used to check on the consistency of plans formulated using traditional procedures, and to propose alternative consistent plans. At first sight this would appear to be an important advantage of models, and to some extent it is. But the property of consistency should not be overrated, because in the present context it is a property of a model, and the models themselves are always incomplete and approximate representations of the real economy. However, in practice one cannot do any better than this, and consistency at least provides a criterion for distinguishing between acceptable and unacceptable solutions. As we have already observed, optimality criteria are less helpful in this respect, though they still have a role to play in the generation of plan variants. Over-all, then, the models we have been discussing can make an important contribution to the process of plan formulation, but we are very clearly far from a situation where models can more or less take over from traditional methods of planning. Ideas about such an elevated status for economic models are mere fairly tales, as Kornai (1975, ch. 30) emphasises.

So far, this section has concentrated on models based on an input–output structure. But many countries, include France, have developed economy-wide econometric models since the Second World War, for use in forecasting exercises, policy simulations, and so on. These models are usually rather more aggregative than those of the input–output type but make a more systematic effort to model some of the economy's behavioural relationships. It is appropriate to conclude this chapter with a few remarks on econometric models both in the West and in the East, the main features of which have been summarised in two very useful articles by Shapiro and Halabuk (1976), and Shapiro (1977).

Unlike input–output models, much of whose structure is estimated from data of a single period, econometric models used for planning purposes are estimated from time-series data. Such models comprise identities, technical relationships (e.g. production functions) and behavioural equations like investment functions and consumption functions. These variables had to be determined in the earlier models, of course, but at least for Hungary or the Soviet Union the planners retain sufficient control over the economy to regulate them fairly closely; this leaves a rather limited sphere for behavioural relationships. In the French models, Fifi in particular, several behavioural constraints were already incorporated, notably the Phillips curve and relationships representing the effects of foreign competition, reflecting the much smaller independent role of centrally deter-mined policies as compared with private decisions.

The effects of central policies are often better reflected in econometric models than in input–output ones. This is not surprising since the former provide a good description of agents' responses to the policy environment, while the latter concentrate on describing production possibilities. Perhaps for this reason there have been some attempts in recent years to integrate the two types of model to gain the advantages of both. Indeed, some of the French models are clear examples of this tendency.

In terms of general approach there is an important difference between the econometric models produced in the East and in the West. Almost all Western models are demand-orientated in the sense that exogenous components of demand, together with Keynesian multiplier effects via the consumption function, determine the equilibrium levels of output and hence employment. Then the pressure of demand in relation to either the total labour force or total capacity affects price and wage movements, and so on. Moreover, these models are increasingly estimated using quarterly data, in order to pick up and predict short-term fluctuations in activity levels. In contrast, Eastern models are still almost all based on annual data and are expected to aid plan formulation, though they have not been applied as widely as input—output models. Their emphasis is on five-year planning, and relatively little interest is shown in short-run fluctuations.

The structure of the Eastern models is very different from the standard Western ones since they take employment as exogenous; full employment is assumed, and one group of equations determines the composition and level of supply that would be forthcoming in the period of interest. Thus the models are supply-determined, and the various components of demand somehow have to accommodate to this supply; models differ considerably in their manner of achieving the accommodation, but space prevents us from going into the details here.

We may conclude our discussion of econometric models by noting that all three countries studied in this book have shown an interest in their development; in Hungary and the Soviet Union they are only just beginning to move beyond the experimental stage to serious applications, while in France they have already achieved somewhat greater importance.

11 CONCLUSIONS AND PROSPECTS

In the earlier chapters of the book we have examined several aspects of economic planning, sometimes in a fairly general and abstract setting, sometimes with reference to the concrete experience of the Soviet Union, Hungary and France. No doubt enough has been said both to convince the reader that planning is an extremely complex activity and also to make clear that many of the more naive views of it which may be found in the literature are not really justified. In addition, while we cannot pretend to have complete solutions to all the issues which have been raised, we hope that our approach to various problems has been of sufficient interest to stimulate further thought and wider reading; there is certainly no shortage of problems in need of additional study.

This concluding chapter falls into three sections. Section 11.1 offers some general remarks and suggestions on the question of constructing a general theory of economic planning, while section 11.2 is concerned with some of the social and political aspects of planning which earlier chapters have neglected. The object of that section is to provide a link between the rather technical character of much of the abstract theory of planning and the more concrete issues which arise in, and the constraints imposed by, a specific social environment. Our comments on this difficult topic will inevitably be somewhat sketchy, to say the least. Finally, section 11.3 outlines our views about the likely development of planning in the East and in West in the next few years.

11.1 On constructing a theory of planning

Some ideas from general-equilibrium theory formed the basis for some of our earlier theoretical discussions, particularly in Chapters 1, 5, 6, 8, and to a lesser extent in Chapters 7, 9 and 10. In addition, it proved helpful in several chapters to organise the discussion around the idea of agents maximising some objective function subject to constraints, even when the full general-equilibrium apparatus could not readily be applied. It seems important to devote some space to an examination of this procedure, and to explain why we consider it to represent a useful approach to the analysis of economic planning. In order to make any progress, of course, it is essential to begin by explaining why it is important to have a theory of planning at all.

Now in considering any particular planned economy, whether it be the Soviet Union, Hungary, France, or some abstract model, there is an immense number of questions which it would be interesting or useful to be able to answer.

The bulk of such questions may be grouped together into the following major categories:

(1) *Descriptive.* Here we merely enquire about the main features of the system under examination; interest centres on the behaviour of enterprises, households and other agents under various conditions. It may prove possible to characterise certain states as representing some form of equilibrium, and to study the allocations which result.

(2) *Predictive.* The emphasis is now on explaining how changes in the economic environment, either of individual agents, groups of agents (e.g. an industry) or the economy as a whole, affect those aspects of economic behaviour which happen to be of immediate interest. In a planned economy, for example, the government might wish to know how enterprise investment will respond to some change in credit regulations, an important matter since it could affect the investment balance.

(3) *Prescriptive.* It is often the case that instead of being primarily concerned with the effects of existing policies we wish to propose better policies or, more ambitiously, policies which are optimal in some sense. Thus the planners, or the economists advising them, wish to make economic-policy prescriptions.

While questions of type (1) may be answered without the assistance of any formally specified theory, it is obvious that little could be said about (2) or (3) in the absence of theoretical guidance. Even for (1) few people are likely to find either interesting or illuminating an exhaustive description of the given economic system, preferring instead an account organised around a few basic principles which facilitate understanding of the system. But this amounts to a demand for a theoretical framework.

This book is certainly not the place for an extended examination of the nature and role of theories in economics, but a few remarks are in order. In the context of economic planning, which is our prime concern, theories fulfil a number of different functions: they provide a means of discriminating between interesting and uninteresting hypotheses; they organise the mass of data about any given system into a manageable and coherent set of categories; and they focus attention on a limited number of concepts, relationships and techniques of analysis. By doing all this they also, as Loasby (1976) and others have observed, entail some degree of abstraction, simplification and selection. Consequently the adoption of a particular theory not only makes possible the formulation of replies to certain types of question but also tends to exclude certain other types of question altogether. No doubt such exclusions partly explain why many people working on the planned economies, particularly those in Eastern Europe, often appear to be suspicious of any theory. In our view, however, this kind of theoretical nihilism is not particularly fruitful, for it leads either to lengthy descriptive tracts lacking a clear structure, or if some structure is imposed then the approach is already theoretical without admitting the fact. We prefer to be more open about our theoretical standpoint, and infer from the limitations of any particular theory not that all theory is useless but rather that it is important to delineate in advance the types of question to which answers are being sought. That is what we were attempting to do in Chapter 1.

It might be expected that given our concern with the Soviet Union and Hungary a Marxist theoretical approach would be the most appropriate, though it would obviously be rather less so in the case of France. Now it is certainly the case that many policies pursued in Hungary and the Soviet Union are justified by reference to their Marxist character, but the justification is frequently disturbingly vague, and rarely seems to help in understanding the nature of the policies in question. There are two reasons why this state of affairs is not especially surprising. First, neither Marx nor Engels (nor even Lenin) has much of interest to say about economic planning other than a few broad generalisations; subsequently Stalin's dogmatic approach to economics inhibited development of a Marxist theory of planning until well into the 1950s, and such a theory is still distinctly fragmentary. Second, it may be argued that Marxist theory is best adapted for tackling broad questions of socio-historical change and development and is not very successful at the resolution of questions about the behaviour of specific economic agents under given conditions in the immediate future. Both Marx and Lenin were undoubtedly concerned about the former type of question, as indeed were many Soviet writers in the years immediately following the 1917 revolution, for example Preobrazhensky (1965). Similarly, recent Western Marxists have tended to devote their attention to such questions as whether the Eastern European societies should be regarded as a form of 'state capitalism', and whether they should be seen as societies in transition between capitalism and socialism; Bettelheim and Sweezy (1971) and Ticktin (1976, 1978) are examples of works in this genre. While these writers are tackling important questions, they are not the questions we have been most concerned to answer in this book; this is why we have not employed a Marxist theoretical framework. (Ellman (1979) examines some issues of planning of a more historical character, and consequently finds a Marxist approach more helpful.)

Instead, as noted earlier, much of our approach is based on the conceptual framework of general-equilibrium theory, not because we consider it to be descriptively 'correct', but because its structure allows the issues we wished to examine to be formulated fairly naturally. Essentially the framework involves (i) a number of agents – usually households or firms, though the list can readily be extended – each seeking to maximise some objective function subject to a number of constraints, and (ii) a notion of equilibrium; equilibrium is said to obtain when the decisions of the various agents distinguished in the model are mutually compatible. The familiar Walrasian model of competitive equilibrium fits into this framework, and it is prices which bring about the co-ordination of decisions of the individual agents in that model. But that is far from being the only interesting case, and the framework also includes models with quantity constraints on individual supplies and demands, as well as signals other than prices for achieving co-ordination. Thus Kornai (1971, 1980) is wrong to claim that general-equilibrium theory is unhelpful for the analysis of planning problems,

a conclusion he is only able to reach by adopting an excessively narrow interpretation of the theory. In fact, his own approach itself falls within the class of
theories which we refer to as 'general equilibrium', though it is substantially
more sophisticated than most work in the area. Surprisingly, Kornai frequently
asserts that he is developing what he calls a 'descriptive theory' of the shortage
economy and stresses the need for descriptive adequacy in formulating economic
models; but at the same time he never shrinks from simplification or generalisa-
tion when it seems fruitful. And he, too, eventually finds in a form of general-
equilibrium theory a powerful tool for studying the properties of the phenomena
he wishes to explain.

It is quite incorrect to dismiss general-equilibrium theory as completely
unsuitable for the discussion of planning problems on the grounds that it is a
theory of markets and prices while in practice planned economies are striving to
abolish markets. In the first place we have already argued that only the most
restricted interpretation of general-equilibrium theory insists that it is simply a
theory of markets; it is more appropriately regarded as a theory of economic
co-ordination, in which case it is clearly of relevance to planning problems. In
the second place the economies we have characterised as planned are certainly
not striving to do without markets. In the French case there is no doubt about
this, as we have made clear in Chapter 4 as well as in our discussion of the
theoretical basis of indicative planning (Chapter 7). But even in the Soviet Union
and Hungary markets have never been totally irrelevant; they were always used
to allocate the bulk of the labour force to the available jobs, and to allocate
most consumer goods. Nowadays their use is more widely advocated in the
Soviet Union, and more widely practised in Hungary. Accordingly it makes sense
to discuss planning problems with models which can incorporate certain market
elements but which are not restricted to that form of resource allocation. Our
approach set out to do just this.

11.2 Social and political aspects of planning

As a consequence of our theoretical approach we have tended to treat many
issues which arise in economic planning as if they were predominantly technical
in character, neglecting their associated social and political aspects. The present
section points out some of the implications of this neglect, and discusses what
might be involved in remedying it; but space considerations prevent us from
going very far in that direction.

In several recent articles Hurwicz (e.g. 1971, 1973) has set out a general
model of resource-allocation procedures which offers a useful introduction to
our discussion. In this model there is a set of agents who exchange messages in
order to arrive at a satisfactory allocation of resources, these messages depending
on observations of the environment, production possibilities, etc., according to
definite rules. In addition, the model provides an outcome function to determine
the allocation which results after the exchange of messages is complete and a
welfare function to evaluate these outcomes. The model is very abstract and

general, but it leads to some interesting questions about allocation mechanisms, as we explained more fully in Chapter 5. At the same time, it suffers from precisely the neglect of social and political issues – which is our concern in this section.

Specifically, by setting out with the assumption of a given set of economic agents sending messages according to specified rules, the model is unable to contribute much to discussions of institutional change. In addition, it is not easy for Hurwicz's framework to account for power relations between agents which are likely to impose quite strict constraints on the allocations which would be acceptable as outcomes from any particular allocation mechanism. It does not seem to be satisfactory merely to incorporate such constraints into the outcome function itself, for reasons which will become clear later on. Let us begin, however, by suggesting a few examples to show why institutional change and power relationships pose problems for theories of planning.

The examples we consider concern the position of trade unions in a centrally planned economy, constraints on central agencies, relationships between the central agencies, and preferences for particular forms of allocation. Trade unions exist in all three of the countries we have been studying, though their official roles are viewed somewhat differently. In France they are expected to further the workers' interests, both in terms of working conditions and in terms of earnings, and play an important political role. In the Soviet Union the authorities are reluctant to concede that the workers might have interests different from those of 'society as a whole', so that at least officially their role is confined to the promotion of plan fulfilment and matters of social welfare and safety at work. The Hungarian position lies between these extremes, though remains closer to the Soviet end of the spectrum. Despite these differences in all cases the trade unions can exert a significant effect on the planning process by constraining management choices. This happens not only within individual enterprises, in connection with employment protection, but also at national level when the trade unions participate in negotiations on economic policy, for example on incomes policy, and policies for the development of personal and social consumption. Their influence in such fields implies that it is not quite legitimate to treat enterprises or the central government as agents seeking to maximise some well-defined objective subject to certain constraints. In principle, one might try to rescue the standard models by taking as the basic unit of analysis something smaller than the enterprise, and by modelling the centre as a group of agents with partially conflicting interests, but so far little progress has been made in that direction.

Constraints on central agencies and relationships between them also pose problems. Much planning theory, including the major part of that discussed in this book, takes a very simple-minded view of the centre, paying almost no attention to the interactions which political scientists would consider important. We have already mentioned the trade unions in this connection, but there are also the political parties to consider, as well as the individual branch ministries and functional bodies which all acquire their own separate interests. Aside from the difficulties this can cause for the definition of a social objective (or welfare) function, the various interests have to be taken into account when considering the possibilities of economic reform and the implications of any particular reform, for any reform, other than the most trivial kind which only proposes slight amendments to the *status quo*, necessarily poses a threat to the existing configuration of interests between the bodies dealing with economic management. Thus reforms which fail to recognise this, like some of the proposals in Eastern Europe, are soon reversed, while the more successful reforms have taken account of the relevant institutional obstacles to their implementation. This suggests that the success or failure of any particular reform depends not only on the formal properties of the resulting allocation procedure, which we can certainly try to analyse by means of standard models, but also on historical, social and political factors.

In the course of operating a particular economic mechanism the agents involved frequently develop preferences for certain allocation mechanisms, usually those with which they happen to be familiar, against others. Such preferences gain weight from the political positions of the agents holding them, and can severely limit the possibilities for economic change, at least in the short run. The experience of a given system also leads to various forms of habitual behaviour, or what Kornai (1976) calls behaviour in accordance with norms; these tend to facilitate the operation of the given system, but inhibit fundamental change. Thus in Hungary, even after the 1968 reforms, when managers were granted a great deal of formal autonomy, they generally reacted to the new conditions with considerable caution and, as Bauer (1976) observes, continued to consult the ministerial authorities in cases where there was no requirement to do so. Institutions and practices established before 1968 continued to function despite the attempt to inaugurate a fundamental change in the management mechanism. Similarly, the organisations concerned with planning in France have had little success in convincing private-sector employers and investors that co-ordination through the plan might be more effective than that provided by the already operating market institutions; partly for this reason the framework of plans has had limited impact on private-sector decisions, and only a slightly greater impact on decisions concerning the public sector. One must conclude that whatever the theoretical advantages and disadvantages of alternative approaches to economic planning familiarity with and preferences for certain aspects of the system which is currently in force will always be important considerations when change is on the agenda.

This point may be clearer if we illustrate it with reference to a simple model which we introduced in Chapter 8: namely, the model developed by Weitzman (1974) for examining the question of regulating the production of a single commodity by means of price (market) or quantity (administrative-control) signals. In the theoretical model the solution turns on the shapes of the cost curves and demand curves involved, but in practice it would also depend on the institutional arrangements entailed by each alternative. The market solution requires someone to fix the price – who should certainly not be (one of) the producer(s) – while the administrative one needs some agency to work out appropriate output targets. These different arrangements involve collecting very different information from market participants, and would not have the same incentive properties. In these circumstances a comparative evaluation of the two schemes is rather more complex than Weitzman suggests. And once a particular allocation procedure is established, agents get used to its mode of operation, so that questions of change or reform are also more complex than he suggests. Substituting market-type allocation for administrative allocation in some field, for example, is not only a technical matter of implementing the conclusions of some piece of economic analysis but involves acceptance of changes in the roles and relative positions of a number of social organisations.

These are just the kinds of change which are not at all easy to incorporate into standard theories of planning, though they are nevertheless extremely important. The difficulty is somewhat similar to that which arises when we move from first-best to second-best welfare economics: while the former maximises welfare subject to the 'objective' constraints of preferences and production possibilities, the latter incorporates additional constraints which somehow prevent the first best from being achieved. But these additional constraints are almost always introduced in an extremely *ad hoc* fashion – which may lead to interesting economic analysis, but without providing a satisfactory institutional or political justification for their precise form (Sen (1972) has criticised welfare economics along these lines.) Exactly the same arguments apply to the kind of planning theory employed in this book, though, as Frisch (1976) has argued, the *ad hoc* approach suggested above can at least indicate the 'costs' of various institutional constraints.

This means that the usefulness and power of our theoretical tools in tackling the questions explored in earlier chapters should not blind us to the limitations of the approach. It may be possible to allow for some of the problems alluded to in this section by modifying Hurwicz's model in some way, for example by amending the outcome rule – which we suggested earlier as a potential way ahead. However, although in a formal sense that might offer some scope, its principal defect is just that which we have outlined in relation to welfare economics. The social and political aspects of planning should certainly not be ignored in any work which claims to be comprehensive, but it seems to us that the theory of planning, as currently developed, can only make limited use of such considerations. This is because the theory of social and political change is not yet sufficiently advanced to permit the theory of planning to arise as a branch of some more general social theory; there is simply too much that we do not understand. It is equally easy to argue that a purely technical approach to planning which totally ignores institutional, political issues, etc., is quite unacceptable, while the compromise whereby some institutional considerations are allowed for by means of *ad hoc* constraints in a general model only represents a small step forward. Instead of accepting such a negative appraisal of existing planning theory, we would prefer to emphasise that, with all its imperfections, the theory has increased our understanding of a wide range of planning problems and will undoubtedly be developed further in the coming years. We would hope that such developments will be accompanied by a much better understanding of the social and political issues related to economic planning.

11.3 Planning in East and West – the prospects

Having studied many features of the planning systems functioning in the Soviet Union, Hungary, and France, we take the opportunity provided by this conclud-ing section to stand back from the details of the systems in order to ask more general questions about their prospects. For example, can planning in France continue in its present form, and how might it change? Will the Hungarian system retain the main features of the so-called 'New Economic Mechanism', or will it slowly revert back towards something like the traditional Soviet model? As for the Soviet system itself, can we expect to see further piecemeal reforms and minor adjustments in its economic arrangements, or are more fundamental changes at all likely? After outlining answers to these questions, we shall also comment on the *convergence* debate, which has generated an extremely confused literature.

Let us begin with the Soviet Union, the country with the longest experience of economic planning. In this case there is no doubt that the traditional central-ised system works reasonably successfully, a basic fact which outweighs all the inefficiencies, poor incentives, imperfect organisation, etc., that attract the attention of most Western writings on the Soviet economy. While the economy does not grow nowadays as quickly as the leadership might desire, it is not subject to the alternation of boom and depression, nor to the periodic and, more recently, persistent unemployment which afflict Western countries. Moreover, it has largely avoided the inflation which has plagued the non-socialist world since the early 1970s. It is true that performance in certain sectors of the economy, notably agriculture and infrastructure, has been particularly poor; on the other hand, however, it is not clear that these failures can be wholly attributed to shortcomings of the economic mechanism itself, since other explanations are available. In the case of agriculture the obvious problem facing the Soviet Union is one over which it has only limited control: namely, its high proportion of inferior land, coupled with an appalling climate. In both agriculture and infra-structure low rates of investment for many years have resulted from the priority attached to industrialisation, and only in the last decade has there been a serious effort to remedy the neglect. Over-all, then, economic performance as a whole does not provide much reason for expecting major changes in economic arrange-ments in the Soviet Union.

It is sometimes suggested that the increasing complexity of economic develop-ment as incomes increase and consumer demands become increasingly diversified, associated with the complexity of and rapid changes in modern technology, will eventually force the system to accept some fundamental reforms. This seems very doubtful, for several reasons. First, it is quite possible for the traditional system to become more flexible in a few sectors, such as those concerned with consumer goods, while leaving much of the system almost unchanged; indeed, this adoption of different approaches to planning in different sectors is a change which would be supported by some of the more formal planning theory, as we pointed out in Chapter 1. Second, the notion of complexity is a relative one, closely connected with the way in which the economy is partitioned for planning purposes. Thus many recently developed products seem to involve greater complexity than the more traditional ones; but if the problem is one of technical complexity, then it should be tackled within an individual enterprise established just for that purpose, while if the difficulties arise from an inappropriate organisational structure, then that structure should be changed. A good illustration of these problems in the Soviet Union is provided by the manufacture and development of computer technology which cuts across ministerial boundaries in a way which made the assignment of responsibility extremely contentious. It is surely wrong, however, to deduce from such examples that the Soviet system is reaching the limit of its capacities, for eventually we would expect the kinds of problem which arise to be solved moderately well by means of organisational adjustments – the formation of new enterprises, and even the creation of entirely new ministries – within the framework of the traditional model. It is not yet clear how well the innovation process can be handled through such adjustments, and recent work has expressed some scepticism about the possibilities available within the centralised framework (see Hanson, 1980, ch. 4).

A third reason for doubting arguments about complexity is the obvious one that the technical developments taking place nowadays affect both the pattern of consumption and the possibilities for organising the required supplies, for many recent inventions have their most important impact on the technology of communication and computation, including data-processing. In principle, therefore, it should be feasible to take advantage of the new technology by improving some of the traditional means of assembling and handling the data required for plan formulation and for monitoring plan implementation. As we indicated in the last chapter, progress is already being made in this direction, but there should be scope for a great deal more. Accordingly, without making absurd claims about the approach of 'computopia' (Kornai, 1975), we would anticipate that the Soviet Union will continue along the path of incorporating more and more elements of modern techniques into the traditional planning process.

One may wonder whether there might be any social or political factors or pressures conducive to reform. If anything, however, the reverse is the case, with the interest groups favouring more or less the present system well entrenched and secure in their positions, and opposition weak or suppressed without great difficulty. The press frequently carries criticisms of individual enterprise managers, or conducts vigorous campaigns against some or other undesirable practice; but these are not attacks on the system itself, only attempts to make it behave more closely in accordance with the officially laid-down rules. More radical proposals, often from the mathematically minded economists, are less influential since most of their proponents are safely housed in various research institutes where they can do no 'harm'. Since the trade unions, emasculated in the 1920s, are the sole permitted form of worker organisation (aside from the Communist Party itself) and are subject to strict regulation by the central authorities, one should not expect to find fundamental reform being proposed in that quarter – nor does one do so. The discussion could be extended by considering other social groups, but the conclusion is already apparent; there would appear to be very little reason to expect the Soviet Union to pursue economic policies substantially different from those it has followed in recent years. There will be fairly frequent small modifications to the traditional central-ised model, including changes in organisation, planning techniques, the pattern of priorities between sectors, and so on, but without substantially amending the essential features of the system which we discussed in earlier chapters.

Turning next to Hungary, the issues are somewhat different, but our con-clusion is broadly the same: namely, that only quite minor changes can be expected in the near future. The economic mechanism appears to have stabilised in a form which is certainly distinctive in Eastern Europe, with its abandonment of short-run administrative allocation of resources and the introduction of predominantly financial regulators. Aside from the points made about the Soviet Union, some of which also apply to Hungary, the main reasons for expecting rather limited changes have to do with the problems currently being faced by the country. These include the need to improve the balance of trade with the West, and the maintenance of economic growth in the face of serious labour shortages. Any solution to the former problem depends partly on factors beyond Hungary's control, like the volume of world trade, its rate of growth, and the extent of trade restrictions imposed against Hungary's exports. But it also depends on the development of new exportable products, as well as on an improvement in the range and quality of domestic production, in order to bring about some import substitution. Immediately after the 1968 reforms it was expected that the relatively free competition, both between domestic producers and between their products and imports, would stimulate rapid improvements in economic effic-iency. But too many special taxes and subsidies were imposed to allow this effect to operate properly, and in any case the trade balance was not strong enough for unlimited import competiton to be permitted. Consequently, although firms were supposed to respond to market influences to a much greater extent than had been possible before, they still faced inappropriate prices and had the protection of import restrictions. In such circumstances firms could hardly be relied on to promote the exports required by the plans without further central interventions. These took the form of central investment decisions to expand the production of certain exportables, the (largely formal) requirement that all major investment projects be evaluated at world market prices, and more recently preferential credit for enterprise investment which would lead to higher exports in Western markets. The important point here is that the promotion of exports is regarded as a central responsibility, to which enterprises may be induced to contribute if appropriate incentives are offered. Other than a small number of economists who are strongly inclined towards greater use of the free market, few people believe that market forces alone could help to improve trade perform-ance in the absence of central interventions. Consequently there is virtually no pressure to widen the sphere of influence of market forces on foreign-trade grounds.

A similar situation obtains regarding the labour market. When the reforms were first introduced there were fears that some enterprises would reduce their work-forces, possibly leading to unemployment if other firms failed to take on the displaced workers. Since unemployment was considered politically unaccept-able in a society like Hungary, the government took steps to avoid such an outcome, partly by arranging for some workers to go to East Germany for a time to work on projects there, and partly by introducing generous allowances to encourage mothers to stay out of the labour force for up to three years follow-ing the birth of a child. In the event demand for labour was stronger than expected, and by the early 1970s it was labour shortage rather than surplus that was the major problem. The system of wage regulation encouraged firms to retain more unskilled workers than they really needed, and it was increasingly suspected that the price system did not encourage sufficiently capital-intensive investment variants to be chosen. In a market economy such problems might have been tackled by allowing wages to rise quite sharply; with price competition from imports holding down the prive level, profits would be squeezed and the prices of capital goods would fall relative to the price of wages. However, this mode of adjustment would prove to be more inflationary than Hungary has been willing to tolerate in recent years, and would require a much more flexible price system than the reforms in fact introduced. Just as we observed for the trade problems mentioned above, the solution to tension in the labour market is not seen to lie within the sphere of enterprise adaptation unaided by further central interventions; indeed, the proposed 1980 price revision is designed precisely to bring about the kind of structural change in the price system which seems to be necessary, and this revision is a central measure.

Thus the major problems in the Hungarian economy are not expected to be solved by extending market relations and increasing enterprise autonomy; rather, we can expect to see more central measures. Does this mean that the reform will gradually be undermined, with the eventual restoration of something very like the traditional Soviet model? It is most unlikely that central allocation of materials will be restored, partly because the forms of allocation developed since the reform — a mixture of market allocation and informal rationing by producers of products in short supply — have functioned well, and partly because there is virtually no pressure from central agencies to restore the old system. In addition, the climate of opinion among economists in Hungary is substantially more hostile to the pre-reform system than one might expect in the Soviet Union if a

similar reform took place there, with many economists favouring major developments to extend the original reform concepts even further. While advice from
economists is rarely decisive, it appears reasonable to suggest that the prevailing
climate of opinion would at least suffice to inhibit any recentralising moves
which may emanate from the central authorities.

We next examine France. It is convenient to recall the discussion of Chapter 4,
where it was observed that French plans had changed from being plans of the
nation to being the more modest plans of the government. In Chapter 7 we
discussed some of the theory which helps to explain such a shift by revealing
some of the contradictions and limitations in the concept of 'indicative' planning.
Given these theoretical problems, and the already declining role of planning in
the practice of economic management, can it be said that French planning has a
future? Since this is a complex and general question, we only make a few
observations on it. First, it does seem clear that the plan can no longer be regarded
as a definitive statement about the economy's development path, to be enforced
by means of appropriate instruments. In this strong sense planning in France has
been dead for some time. Second, it is doubtful whether even the government
now takes the plan especially seriously in relation to the demands for intervention
imposed by short-term problems of the economy. Consequently the plan and its
supporting institutions are left with a very restricted role as compared with the
original aspirations of the French planners. The process of preparing the plans
involves systematic study of many sectors and aspects of the economy, and this
provides an important source of information for policy-making. In addition, the
communication between private and public sectors entailed by various planning
exercises may well improve mutual understanding to the benefit of both. It is
hard to make this rather vague point more precise, since we cannot claim that
the plan itself is agreed or accepted by all the parties who have contributed to
it. But the government should be able to learn about the needs and expectations
of private producers and consumers, while the private sector can be informed
about government intentions and the scope for policy changes.

There are several reasons for expecting planning in France to play no more
than the limited role we have just set out. Planning is becoming more difficult
because of the uncertainties of the international environment and which appear
to be becoming more severe. Also, while the private sector is always willing to
accept government grants and subsidies of various kinds, it is not willing to accept
the constraints entailed by genuine efforts to implement a national plan, for
markets are constantly providing new signals to which it prefers to adjust.
Moreover, it is probable that many forms of intervention which might result
from more comprehensive planning would be contrary to France's obligations to
the EEC, so that the domestic advantages of such interventions would have to be
extremely clear cut. At present, neither the theory nor the practice of planning
has attained such a state of development for this to be the case in the majority
of cases.

Finally, we comment briefly on the debate about *convergence* between alternative economic systems (see Tinbergen, 1961; Ward, 1971, pp. 126, 131; Wilczynski, 1977, ch. 15; Galbraith, 1967). In the 1960s, while the scope of government intervention in many Western countries gradually widened, it appeared that the centrally planned economies were moving in the reverse direction, with proposals for economic reforms involving greater reliance on market signals and incentives and correspondingly less on detailed central plans. In the event such reforms did not get as far as many observers expected, except in Hungary (discussed in some detail earlier in this book). Elsewhere early attempts at reform were soon reversed, or turned out to be much less far reaching than had been supposed, with the traditional Soviet model of the planned economy remaining more or less intact. Similarly, far from continuing to expand, the public sector in many Western countries is now under attack; the view that the government's role both in the production of goods and services and in the regulation of private-sector activities should be much more limited than used to be accepted is becoming increasingly widespread. (This is not to say that we agree with such views. For expositions relating to the United Kingdom, see Bacon and Eltis (1976) and Littlechild (1978).) As a result of these more recent tendencies the fashion of the 1960s for convergence is no longer so tenable as it then was; accordingly we no longer observe a great outpouring of literature either explaining, regretting, or welcoming the convergence of economic systems.

Convergence can be understood in at least two senses, of course: these are convergence in terms of *outcomes*, and convergence in terms of *institutions*. By outcomes, we mean the patterns of output, consumption and employment generated by the system in question; convergence in outcomes thus means that these tend to become more similar over time between countries with different types of economic system. This is not an implausible hypothesis, given that the Eastern European countries are gradually catching up with Western Europe and the USA in terms of *per capita* income. Even with different institutional structures, with such differences as remain owing more to historical than to institutional convergence itself would require that the ways in which resources come to be allocated and distributed should themselves come to be similar, irrespective of any agreement over outcomes. However, we have already pointed out that this idea arose at a time when it could claim some empirical support but that recent developments make it appear much less plausible. Consequently we expect the systems studied in this book to continue to exhibit important institutional differences, as a result of which they will provide fascinating objects of study for many years to come.

BIBLIOGRAPHY

ABOUCHAR, A. (1973) 'The New Soviet Methodology for Investment Allocation', *Soviet Studies*, vol. 24, pp. 402–10.

AMANN, R. *et al.* (eds) (1977) *The Technological Level of Soviet Industry*, Yale University Press.

AMES, E. (1965) *Soviet Economic Processes*, Homewood, Ill., Irwin.

ANDO, A. and MODIGLIANI, F. (1963) 'The "Life Cycle" Hypothesis of Saving: Aggregate Implications and Tests', *American Economic Review*, vol. 53, pp. 55–84.

ANDRLE, V. (1976) *Managerial Power in the Soviet Union*, Farnborough, Saxon House.

ARROW, K. J. (1959) 'Towards a Theory of Price Adjustment', in *The Allocation of Economic Resources*, ed. M. Abromovitz *et al.*, Stanford University Press.

ARROW, K. J. (1963) *Social Choice and Individual Values* (2nd edn) New York, Wiley.

ARROW, K. J. (1970) *Essays in the Theory of Risk Bearing*, Amsterdam, North-Holland.

ARROW, K. J. (1974) *The Limits of Organization*, New York, Norton.

ARROW, K. J. and HURWICZ, L. (1977) *Studies in Resource Allocation Processes*, Cambridge University Press.

ATREIZE (pseudonym) (1971) *La planification française en pratique*, Paris, Editions Ouvrières.

AUGUSTINOVICS, M. (1975) 'Integration of Mathematical and Traditional Methods of Planning', in Bornstein (1975).

BACHARACH, M. (1970) *Biproportional Matrices and Input–Output Change*, Cambridge University Press.

BACHURIN, A. V. (1979) 'Sorevnovanie i pyatiletki' ('Competition and Five-year Plans'), *Ekonomicheskaya Gazeta*, no. 19, p. 9.

BACON, R. and ELTIS, W. (1976) *Britain's Economic Problem: Too Few Producers*, London, Macmillan.

BAJT, A. (1971) 'Investment Cycles in European Socialist Economies: a Review Article', *Journal of Economic Literature*, vol. 9, pp. 53–63.

BALASSA, R. (1959) *The Hungarian Experience in Economic Planning*, Yale University Press.

BARKER, T. S. (1972) 'Foreign Trade in Multisectoral Models', in *Input–Output Techniques*, ed. A. Bródy and A. Carter, Amsterdam, North-Holland.

BARRO, R. and GROSSMAN, H. (1974) 'Suppressed Inflation and the Supply Multiplier', *Review of Economic Studies*, vol. 41, pp. 87–104.

BARRO, R. and GROSSMAN, H. (1976) *Money, Employment and Inflation*, Cambridge University Press.

BAUER, T. (1976) 'The Contradictory Position of the Enterprise under the New Hungarian Economic Mechanism', *Eastern European Economics*, vol. 15, pp. 3–23 (translated from Hungarian original).

BAUMOL, W. J. (1962) *Business Behavior, Value and Growth*, New York, Harcourt & Brace.

BECKERMAN, W. *et al.* (1965) *The British Economy in 1975*, Cambridge University Press.

BERLINER, J. S. (1957) *Factory and Manager in the USSR*, Harvard University Press.

BERLINER, J. S. (1976) *The Innovation Decision in Soviet Industry*, MIT Press.

BETTELHEIM, C. and SWEEZY, P. (1971) *On the Transition to Socialism*, New York, Monthly Review Press.

BIRGER, E. S. *et al.* (1979) 'Experimental Construction of a Dynamic Input—Output Model', *Matekon*, vol. 15, no. 3, pp. 59—82 (translated from Russian original).

BIRMAN, I. (1978) 'From the Achieved Level', *Soviet Studies*, vol. 30, pp. 153—72.

BLISS, C. J. (1975) *Capital Theory and the Distribution of Income*, Amsterdam, North-Holland.

BOLTHO, A. (1971) *Foreign Trade Criteria in Socialist Economies*, Cambridge University Press.

BONIN, J. P. and MARCUS, A. J. (1979) 'Information, Motivation and Control in Decentralised Planning: the Case of Discretionary Managerial Behaviour', *Journal of Comparative Economics*, vol. 3, pp. 235—53.

BONNAUD, J.-J. (1975) 'Planning and Industry in France', in Hayward and Watson (1975).

BORNSTEIN, M. (1974) 'Soviet Price Theory and Policy', in *The Soviet Economy: A Book of Readings*, ed. M. Bornstein and D. Fusfeld (4th edn), Homewood, Ill., Irwin.

BORNSTEIN, M. (ed.) (1975) *Economic Planning, East and West*, Cambridge, Mass., Ballinger.

BORNSTEIN, M. (1976) 'Soviet Price Policy in the 1970s', in *The Soviet Economy in a New Perspective*, US Congress Joint Economic Committee, Washington, D.C., US Government Printing Office.

BORNSTEIN, M. (1977) 'Economic Reform in Eastern Europe', in *Compendium on East European Economies*, US Congress Joint Economic Committee, Washington, D.C., US Government Printing Office.

BRANSON, W. H. (1979) *Macroeconomic Theory and Policy* (2nd edn), New York, Harper & Row.

BRÓDY, A. (1970) *Proportions, Prices and Planning*, Amsterdam, North-Holland.

BROWN, A. and NEUBERGER, E. (eds) (1968) *International Trade and Central Planning*, University of California Press.

BROWN, A. and WALKER, D. (1973) 'Hungarian Input—Output Tables: Description, Reconstruction and Price Adjustment', *International Development Research Center Working Papers* (Indiana University), no. 20, March 1973.

CALSAMIGLIA, X. (1977) 'Decentralised Resource Allocation and Increasing Returns', *Journal of Economic Theory*, vol. 14, pp. 263—83.

CARASSUS, J. (1978) 'The Budget and the Plan in France', in Hayward and Narkiewicz (1978).

CARRÉ, J.-J. *et al.* (1972) *La Croissance française*, Paris, Editions du Seuil.

CAVE, M. (1980) *Computers and Economic Planning — The Soviet Experience*, Cambridge University Press.

CAZES, B. (1969) 'French Planning', in *Planning and Markets*, ed. J. T. Dunlop and N. P. Fedorenko, New York, McGraw-Hill.

CHRYSTAL, K. A. (1979) *Controversies in British Macroeconomics*, Deddington, Philip Allan.

CONN, D. (1978) 'Economic Theory and Comparative Economic Systems: a Partial Literature Survey', *Journal of Comparative Economics*, vol. 2, pp. 355–81.

CONN, D. (1979) 'A Comparison of Alternative Incentive Structures for Centrally-planned Economic Systems', *Journal of Comparative Economics*, vol. 3, pp. 261–76.

COURBIS, R. (1972a) 'The Fifi Model used in the Preparation of the French Plan', *Economics of Planning*, vol. 12, pp. 37–78.

COURBIS, R. (1972b) 'The Regina Model: a Regional–National Model of the French Economy', *Economics of Planning*, vol. 12, pp. 133–52.

COURBIS, R. (1978) 'The Regina Model: Presentation and First Contributions to Economic Policy', in *Econometric Contributions to Public Policy*, ed. R. Stone and W. Peterson, London, Macmillan.

CREMER, J. (1977) 'A Quantity–Quantity Algorithm for Planning under Increasing Returns to Scale', *Econometrica*, vol. 45, pp. 1339–48.

CREMER, J. (1978) 'A Comment on "Decentralised Planning and Increasing Returns" ', *Journal of Economic Theory*, vol. 19, pp. 217–21.

DÁNIEL, Zs. (1971) 'Planning and Exploration: a Dynamic Multisectoral Model of Hungary', *Economics of Planning*, vol. 11, pp. 120–46.

DÁNIEL, Zs. *et al.* (1971) 'Plan Sounding', *Economics of Planning*, vol. 11, pp. 31–58.

DANTZIG, G. B. (1963) *Linear Programming and Extensions*, Princeton University Press.

DELEAU, M. and MALGRANGE, P. (1977) 'Recent Trends in French Planning', in *Frontiers of Quantitative Economics*, ed. M. D. Intrilligator, Amsterdam, North-Holland, vol. III B.

DIXIT, A. K. (1976) *Optimisation in Economic Theory*, Oxford University Press.

DOBB, M. (1960) *An Essay on Economic Growth and Planning*, London, Routledge & Kegan Paul.

DOBB, M. (1969) *Welfare Economics and the Economics of Socialism*, Cambridge University Press.

DOMAR, E. D. (1974) 'On the Optimal Compensation of a Socialist Manager', *Quarterly Journal of Economics*, vol. 88, pp. 1–18.

DORFMAN, R. *et al.* (1958) *Linear Programming and Economic Analysis*, New York, McGraw-Hill.

DREWNOWSKI, J. (1961) 'The Economic Theory of Socialism: a Suggestion for Reconsideration', *Journal of Political Economy*, vol. 69, pp. 341–54.

ECKSTEIN, A. (ed.) (1971) *Comparison of Economic Systems*, University of California Press.

VIIIe Plan (1979) *Rapport sur les principales options du VIIIe plan*, Paris, La Documentation Française.

ELLMAN, M. (1971) *Soviet Planning Today*, Cambridge University Press.

ELLMAN, M. (1973) *Planning Problems in the USSR*, Cambridge University Press.

ELLMAN, M. (1979) *Socialist Planning*, Cambridge University Press.

EÖRSI, Gy. and HARMATHY, A. (1971) *Law and Economic Reform in Socialist Countries*, Budapest, Akademiai Kiado.

FEARN, R. M. (1965) 'Control over Wage Funds and Inflationary Pressure in the USSR', *Industrial Labour Relations Review*, vol. 18, pp. 186–95.

216   *Bibliography*

FOUQUET, D. *et al.* (1976) 'DMS, modèle de prévision à moyen terme', *Economie et statistique*, part 79, pp. 33—48.

FRISCH, R. (1976) *Economic Planning Studies*, Dordrecht, Holland, Reidel.

FRISS, I. (ed.) (1969) *Reform of the Economic Mechanism in Hungary*, Budapest, Akademiai Kiado.

FURUBOTN, E. G. and PEJOVICH, S. (1972) 'Property Rights and Economic Theory: a Survey of the Literature', *Journal of Economic Literature*, vol. 10, pp. 1137—62.

GÁCS, J. and LACKO, M. (1973) 'A Study of Planning Behaviour on the National—Economic Level', *Economics of Planning*, vol. 13, pp. 91—119.

GADO, O. (ed.) (1972) *Reform of the Economic Mechanism in Hungary, Development 1968—71*, Budapest, Akademiai Kiado.

GADO, O. (1976) *The Economic Mechanism in Hungary — How it Works in 1976*, Budapest, Akademiai Kiado.

GALBRAITH, J. K. (1967) *The New Industrial State*, Boston, Houghton Mifflin.

GANCZER, S. (ed.) (1973) *Népgazdasagi tervezés és programozás*, (*National economic planning and programming*), Budapest, Közgazdosági es Jogi Konyvkiado (Economic and Legal Publishers).

GARVY, G. (1977) *Money, Financial Flows and Credit in the Soviet Union*, Cambridge, Mass., Ballinger.

GILLULA, J. (1977) 'Industrial Interdependence and Production Planning', in *Studies in Soviet Input—Output Analysis*, ed. V. G. Treml, New York, Praeger.

GLATTFELDER, P. and MÁTÉFFY, P. (1971) 'Price Type Calculations in Hungary: Experience and New Directions', *Acta Oeconomica*, vol. 7, no. 1, pp. 97—108.

GORLIN, A. (1974) 'The Soviet Economic Associations', *Soviet Studies*, vol. 26, pp. 3—27.

GORLIN, A. (1976) 'Industrial Reorganization: the Associations', in *The Soviet Economy in a New Perspective*, ed. US Congress Joint Economic Committee, Washington, D.C., US Government Printing Office.

GRANICK, D. (1975) *Enterprise Guidance in Eastern Europe*, Princeton University Press.

GREEN, D. and HIGGINS, C. (1977) *SOVMOD 1: a Macroeconometric Model of the Soviet Union*, New York, Academic Press.

GREGORY, P. R. and STUART, R. C. (1974) *Soviet Economic Structure and Performance*, New York, Harper & Row.

GROVES, T. (1973) 'Incentives in Teams', *Econometrica*, vol. 41, pp. 617—63.

GUESNERIE, R. and MALGRANGE, P. (1972) 'Formalisation des objectifs à moyen terme: application au VIème plan, *Revue Economique*, vol. 23, pp. 442—92.

HANSON, P. (1980) *Trade and Technology in Soviet—Western Relations*, London, Macmillan (forthcoming).

HARDT, J. P. *et al.* (eds) (1967) *Mathematics and Computers in Soviet Economic Planning*, Yale University Press.

HARE, P. G. (1973) 'Hungarian Planning Models Based on Input—Output', D. Phil. thesis, Oxford University.

HARE, P. G. (1976) 'Industrial Prices in Hungary', *Soviet Studies*, vol. 28, pp. 189—206 and 362—90.

HARE, P. G. (1977) 'Economic Reform in Hungary: Problems and Prospects', *Cambridge Journal of Economics*, vol. 1, pp. 317—33.

HARE, P. G. (1978) 'Aggregate Planning by Means of Input–Output and Material Balance Systems', Stirling University Discussion Paper.

HARE, P. G. (1979) 'The Investment System in Hungary', Paper presented at Stirling Colloquium on Economic Trends and Economic Management in Hungary.

HAYEK, F. (ed.) (1935) *Collective Economic Planning*, London, Routledge & Kegan Paul.

HAYEK, F. (1945) 'The Use of Knowledge in Society', *American Economic Review*, vol. 35, pp. 519–30.

HAYWARD, J. and NARKIEWICZ, O. (eds) (1978) *Planning in Europe*, London, Croom Helm.

HAYWARD, J. and WATSON, M. (eds) (1975) *Planning Policies and Public Policy*, Cambridge University Press.

HEAL, G. M. (1971) 'Planning, Prices and Increasing Returns', *Review of Economic Studies*, vol. 38, pp. 281–94.

HEAL, G. M. (1973) *The Theory of Economic Planning*, Amsterdam, North-Holland.

HENRY, C. and ZYLBERBERG, A. (1978) 'Planning Algorithms to deal with Increasing Returns', *Review of Economic Studies*, vol. 45, pp. 67–75.

HIRSHLEIFER, J. (1970) *Investment, Interest and Capital*, Englewood Cliffs, N.J., Prentice-Hall.

HÖHMANN, H.-H. *et al.* (1975) *The New Economic Systems of Eastern Europe*, London, C. Hurst & Co.

HOWARD, D. (1965) 'The Disequilibrium Model in a Controlled Economy', *American Economic Review*, vol. 66, pp. 871–9.

HOWARD, D. (1979) 'Reply and Further Results', *American Economic Review*, vol. 69, pp. 733–8.

HUNTER, H. (1961) 'Optimal Tautness in Development Planning', *Economic Development and Cultural Change*, vol. 9, pp. 561–72.

HURWICZ, L. (1971) 'Centralization and Decentralization in Economic Processes', in Eckstein.

HURWICZ, L. (1972) 'On Informationally Decentralized Systems', in McGuire and Radner.

HURWICZ, L. (1973) 'The Design of Resource Allocation Mechanisms', *American Economic Review*, Papers and Proceedings, vol. 63, pp. 1–30.

JACKSON, M. R. (1971) 'Information and Incentives in Planning Soviet Investment Projects', *Soviet Studies*, vol. 23, pp. 3–25.

JOHANSEN, L. (1977) *Lectures on Macroeconomic Planning*, vol. 1: *General Aspects*, Amsterdam, North-Holland.

JOHANSEN, L. (1978) *Lectures on Macroeconomic Planning*, vol. 2: *Centralisation, Decentralisation, Planning Under Uncertainty*, Amsterdam, North-Holland.

JONES, H. G. (1975) *An Introduction to Modern Theories of Economic Growth*, London, Nelson.

KANTOROVICH, L. V. *et al.* (1979) 'On the Use of Optimisation Models in Automated Management Systems for Economic Ministries', *Matekon*, vol. 15, no. 4, pp. 42–66 (translated from Russian original).

KASER, M. (1967) *Comecon: Integration Problems of the Planned Economies* (2nd edn), Oxford University Press.

KASER, M. and ZIELINSKI, J. (1970) *Planning in Eastern Europe*, London, The Bodley Head.

KEREN, M. (1964) 'Industrial vs. Regional Partitioning of Soviet Planning Organisation: a Comparison', *Economics of Planning*, vol. 4, pp. 143—60.

KEREN, M. (1972) 'On the Tautness of Plans', *Review of Economic Studies*, vol. 39, pp. 469—86.

KEREN, M. (1979) 'The Incentive Effects of Plan Targets and Priorities in a Disaggregated Model', *Journal of Comparative Economics*, vol. 3, pp. 1—26.

KOOPMANS, T. C. (1957) *Three Essays on the State of Economic Science*, New York, McGraw-Hill.

KORNAI, J. (1959) *Overcentralisation in Economic Administration*, Oxford University Press.

KORNAI, J. (1971) *Anti-equilibrium*, Amsterdam, North-Holland.

KORNAI, J. (1975) *The Mathematical Planning of Structural Decisions* (2nd edn), Amsterdam, North-Holland.

KORNAI, J. (1976) 'A gazdasagi viselkedes normai es a norma szerinti szabaly-ozas' ('Norms of Economic Behaviour and Control by Norms'), *Kozgazdasayi Szemle*, vol. 9, pp. 1—14.

KORNAI, J. (1979) 'Resource-constrained versus Demand-constrained Systems', *Econometrica*, vol. 47, pp. 801—19.

KORNAI, J. (1980) *Economics of Shortage*, Amsterdam, North-Holland (forthcoming).

KORNAI, J. and MARTOS, B. (1973) 'Autonomous Control of the Economic System', *Econometrica*, vol. 41, pp. 509—28.

KORNAI, J. and LIPTAK, T. (1975) 'Two-level Planning', *Econometrica*, vol. 33, pp. 141—69.

KOSSOV, V. and PUGACHEV, V. (1974) 'A Multi-stage System for Computing Optimal Long-term National Economic Plans' (A translation of the Russian title), *Planovoe khozyaistvo*, no. 10, pp. 12—20.

KOUTSOYIANNIS, A. (1975) *Modern Microeconomics*, London, Macmillan.

LANCASTER, K. (1968) *Mathematical Economics*, London, Macmillan.

LANGE, O. (1938) 'On the Economic Theory of Socialism', in Lippincott.

LANGE, O. (1967) 'The Computer and the Market', in *Socialism, Capitalism and Economic Growth*, ed. C. Feinstein, Cambridge University Press.

LAVIGNE, M. (1974) *The Socialist Economies of the Soviet Union and Eastern Europe*, London, Martin Robertson.

LEIBENSTEIN, H. (1978) *General X-efficiency Theory and Economic Development*, Oxford University Press.

LEONTIEF, W. (1951) *The Structure of the American Economy*, Oxford University Press.

LEONTIEF, W. (1977) *Essays in Economics II*, Oxford, Blackwell.

LERUEZ, J. (1978) 'Macroeconomic Planning in Mixed Economies: the French and British Experience', in Hayward and Narkiewicz.

LEVINE, H. (1966) 'Pressure and Planning in the Soviet Economy', in *Industrialisation in Two Systems*, ed. H. Rosovsky, New York, Wiley.

LEVY-LAMBERT, H. (1977) 'Investment and Pricing Policy in the French Public Sector', *American Economic Review*, Papers and Proceedings, vol. 67, pp. 302—13.

LIGGINS, D. (1972a) 'The Models used in French Short-term Macroeconomic Forecasting', *Economics of Planning*, vol. 12, pp. 3—36.

LIGGINS, D. (1972b) 'Monitoring the Medium-term French Plan', *Economics of Planning*, vol. 12, pp. 153—73.

LIGGINS, D. (1975) *National Economic Planning in France*, Farnborough, Saxon House.

LIGGINS, P. (1976) 'What can we Learn from French Planning?', *Lloyds Bank Review*, no. 120, April 1976, pp. 1–12.

LIPPINCOTT, B. (ed.) (1938) *On the Economy Theory of Socialism*, University of Minnesota Press.

LITTLECHILD, S. C. (1978) *The Fallacy of the Mixed Economy*, Hobart Paper 80, London, Institute of Economic Affairs.

LOASBY, B. J. (1976) *Choice, Complexity and Ignorance*, Cambridge University Press.

LOASBY, B. J. (1977) 'On Imperfections and Adjustments', Stirling University Discussion Paper No. 50.

LOEB, M. and MAGAT, A. (1978) 'Success Indicators in the Soviet Union: the Problem of Incentives and Efficient Allocations', *American Economic Review*, vol. 68, pp. 173–81.

LUTZ, V. (1969) *Central Planning for the Market Economy*, London, Longman.

McARTHUR, J. and SCOTT, B. (1969) *Industrial Planning in France*, Harvard University Press.

McAULEY, A. (1979) 'The Empirical Study of Demand in the Soviet Union', *Jahrbuch der Wirtschaft Osteuropas*, vol. 10.

McGUIRE, C. B. and RADNER, R. (eds) (1972) *Decision and Organisation*, Amsterdam, North-Holland.

MAKAROV, V. L. and PERMINOV, S. B. (1979) 'On Some Aspects of Modelling the process of Plan Fulfilment', *Matekon*, vol. 16, no. 1 (translated from Russian original).

MALINVAUD, E. (1967) 'Decentralised Procedures for Planning', in *Activity Analysis in the Theory of Growth and Planning*, ed. E. Malinvaud and M. Bacharach, London, Macmillan.

MANOVE, M. (1973) 'Non-price Rationing of Intermediate Goods in a Centrally-planned Economy', *Econometrica*, vol. 41, pp. 829–52.

MARGLIN, S. A. (1963) 'The Opportunity Costs of Public Investment', *Quarterly Journal of Economics*, vol. 77, pp. 75–111.

MARRIS, R. and WOOD, A. (eds) (1971) *The Corporate Economy*, London, Macmillan.

MARSCHAK, T. (1959) 'Centralization and Decentralization in Economic Organizations', *Econometrica*, vol. 27, pp. 399–430.

MARSCHAK, T. (1972) 'Computation in Organisations: the Comparison of Price Mechanisms and other Adjustment Processes', in McGuire and Radner (1972).

MARSCHAK, J. and RADNER, R. (1972) *The Economic Theory of Teams*, Yale University Press.

MASSÉ, P. (1965) 'The French Plan and Economic Theory', *Econometrica*, vol. 33, pp. 265–76.

MEADE, J. E. (1951) *The Theory of International Economic Policy*, vol. 1: *The Balance of Payments*, Oxford University Press.

MEADE, J. E. (1970) *The Theory of Indicative Planning*, Manchester University Press.

MEADE, J. E. (1971) *The Controlled Economy*, London, Allen & Unwin.

MILLER, J. B. (1979) 'Meade on Indicative Planning: a Review of Informational Problems', *Journal of Comparative Economics*, vol. 3, pp. 27–40.

MILLER, J. B. and THORNTON, J. R. (1978) 'Effort, Uncertainty and the New Soviet Incentive System', *Southern Economic Journal*, vol. 45, pp. 432–46.

MIRRLEES, J. A. (1969) 'The Price Mechanism in a Planned Economy', in

Planning and Markets, ed. J. T. Dunlop and N. P. Fedorenko, New York, McGraw-Hill.

MONTIAS, J. M. (1962) *Central Planning in Poland*, Yale University Press.

MONTIAS, J. M. (1963) 'On the Consistency and Efficiency of Central Plans', *Review of Economic Studies*, vol. 30, pp. 283–90.

MONTIAS, J. M. (1976) *The Structure of Economic Systems*, Yale University Press.

MONTIAS, J. M. (1977) 'The Aggregation of Controls and the Autonomy of Subordinates', *Journal of Economic Theory*, vol. 15, pp. 123–34.

MUELLBAUER, J. and PORTES, R. (1978) 'Macroeconomic Models with Quantity Rationing', *Economic Journal*, vol. 88, pp. 788–821.

MUNDELL, R. A. (1962) 'The Appropriate Use of Monetary and Fiscal Policy for Internal and External Stability', *IMF Staff Papers*, vol. 9, pp. 70–79.

NICKELL, S. J. (1974) 'On Expectations, Government Policy and the Rate of Investment', *Economica*, vol. 41, pp. 241–55.

NICKELL, S. J. (1977) 'The Influence of Uncertainty on Investment', *Economic Journal*, vol. 87, pp. 47–70.

NICKELL, S. J. (1978) *The Investment Decisions of Firms*, Welwyn, James Nisbet & Co.

NISSANKE, M. (1979) 'Comment', *American Economic Review*, vol. 69, pp. 726–32.

NOVE, A. (1968) *The Soviet Economy* (3rd edn), London, Allen & Unwin.

NOVE, A. (1977) *The Soviet Economic System*, London, Allen & Unwin.

NOVOZHILOV, V. (1970) *Problems of Cost–Benefit Analysis in Optimal Planning*, New York, International Arts and Sciences Press.

OB ULUSHCHENII (1979) 'Ob ulushchenii planirovaniya i usilenii vozdeistviya khozyaistvennogo mekhanizma na povyshenie effektivnosti proizvodstva i kachestva raboty' ('On Improving Planning and Strengthening the impact of the Economic Mechanism to Increase Efficiency in Production and the Quality of Work'), *Planovoe Khozyaistvo*, no. 9, pp. 4–36.

PICKERSGILL, J. (1976) 'Soviet Household Savings Behaviour', *Review of Economics and Statistics*, vol. 58, pp. 139–47.

PLANIFICATION (1976) 'Planification francaise et redeploiement industriel', *Economie et Humanisme*, no. 231, September–October 1976.

PORTES, R. D. (1969) 'The Enterprise under Central Planning', *Review of Economic Studies*, vol. 36, pp. 197–212.

PORTES, R. D. (1971) 'Decentralized Planning Procedures and Centrally-planned Economies', *American Economic Review*, Papers and Procedings, vol. 61, pp. 422–9.

PORTES, R. D. (1972) 'The Strategy and Tactics of Economic Decentralization', *Soviet Studies*, vol. 23, pp. 629–58.

PORTES, R. D. (1978a) 'Macroeconomic Modelling of Centrally-planned Economies: Thoughts on SOVMOD I', Harvard University Discussion Paper No. 621, May 1978. (A shortened version appears in *Economic Journal*, vol. 89, 1979, pp. 669–72.)

PORTES, R. D. (1978b) 'Macroeconomic Equilibrium and Disequilibrium in Centrally-planned Economies', Harvard University Discussion Paper No. 638, July 1978.

PORTES, R. and WINTER, D. (1977) 'The Supply of Consumption Goods in Centrally-planned Economies', *Journal of Comparative Economics*, vol. 1, pp. 351–65.

PORTES, R. and WINTER, D. (1978) 'The Demand for Money and for Consumption Goods in Centrally-planned Economies', *Review of Economics and Statistics*, vol. 60, pp. 8–18.

PORTES, R. and WINTER, D. (1980) 'Disequilibrium Estimates for Consumption Goods Markets in Centrally-planned Economies', *Review of Economic Studies*, vol. 47, pp. 137–59.

POWELL, D. (1977) 'Labour Turnover in the USSR', *Slavic Review*, vol. 36, pp. 268–75.

POWELL, R. (1977) 'Plan Execution and the Workability of Soviet Planning', *Journal of Comparative Economics*, vol. 1, pp. 51–76.

PREOBRAZHENSKY, E. (1965) *The New Economics*, Oxford University Press (original Russian edition 1926).

PRYOR, E. (1977) 'Some Costs and Benefits of Markets – an Empirical Study', *Quarterly Journal of Economics*, vol. 91, pp. 81–102.

RADICE, H. K. (1978) 'On the Scottish Development Agency and the Contradictions of State Entrepreneurship', Stirling University Discussion Paper No. 59, May 1978.

RADNER, R. (1975) 'Satisficing', *Journal of Mathematical Economics*, vol. 2, pp. 253–62.

RAU, N. (1974) *Trade Cycles: Theory and Evidence*, London, Macmillan.

REES, R. (1976) *Public Enterprise Economics*, London, Weidenfeld & Nicolson.

RICHARDSON, G. B. (1960) *Information and Investment*, Oxford University Press.

RICHARDSON, G. B. (1971) 'Planning versus Competition', *Soviet Studies*, vol. 22, pp. 433–47.

SCARF, H. (1973) *The Computation of Economic Equilibria*, Yale University Press.

SEN, A. K. (1972) 'Control Areas and Accounting Prices: an Approach to Economic Evaluation', *Economic Journal*, vol. 82, pp. 486–501.

SEN, A. K. (1973) *On Economic Inequality*, Oxford University Press.

VIIe Plan (1976) *VIIe plan de développement économique et sociale*, Paris, Union Générale d'Editions.

SHAPIRO, H. T. (1977) 'Macroeconomic models of the Soviet Union and Eastern Europe Economies: a Tabular Survey', *Econometrica*, vol. 45, pp. 1747–66.

SHAPIRO, H. T. and HALABUK, L. (1976) 'Macro-econometric Model Building in Socialist and Non-socialist Countries: a Comparative Study', *International Economic Review*, vol. 17, pp. 529–65.

SHARPE, M. E. (ed.) (1966) *Planning, Profit and Incentives in the USSR*, vol. I: *The Liberman Discussion*; Vol. II: *Reform of Soviet Economic Management*, New York, International Arts and Sciences Press.

SIEBEL, C. (1975) 'Planning in France', in Bornstein (1975).

SIMON, H. (1972) 'Theories of Bounded Rationality', in McGuire and Radner (1972).

SIMON, H. and ANDO, A. (1961) 'Aggregation of Variables in Dynamic Systems', *Econometrica*, vol. 29, pp. 111–38.

VIe Plan (1973) *VIe Economic and Social Development Plan: General Report*, Paris, La Documentation Française.

SNOWBERGER, V. (1977) 'The New Soviet Incentive Model: Comment', *Bell Journal of Economics*, vol. 8, pp. 591–600.

SÓOS, K. A. (1975–6) 'Causes of Investment Fluctuations in the Hungarian Economy', *Eastern European Economics*, vol. 14, pp. 25–36 (translated from Hungarian original).

SPRAOS, J. (1977) 'New Cambridge Macroeconomics, Assignment Rules and Interdependence', in *The Political Economy of Monetary Reform*, ed. R. Z. Aliber, London, Macmillan.

STANDARD METHODOLOGY (1978) 'Standard Methodology for Calculations to Optimise the Development and Location of Production over the Long-term', *Matekon*, vol. 15, no. 1, pp. 75–96.

SZAKOLCZAI, G. (1974) 'The Valuation of Resources', *Eastern European Economics*, vol. 12, pp. 75–100 (translated from Hungarian original).

SZAKOLCZAI, G. and BARANY, B. (1978) 'Real Costs of Production and Pricing Problems', *Eastern European Economics*, vol. 16, pp. 25–96 (translated from Hungarian original).

TARDOS, M. (1976) 'Enterprise Independence and Central Control', *Eastern European Economics*, vol. 15, pp. 24–44 (translated from Hungarian original).

TARDOS, M. (1979) 'L'adaptation de la Hongrie à l'évolution du marché mondial', in *Régulation et Division Internationales du Travail*, ed. F. Renversez and M. Lavigne, Paris, Economica.

TAYLOR, F. M. (1938) 'The Guidance of Production in a Socialist State', in Lippincott.

TICKTIN, H. (1976) 'The Contradictions of Soviet Society and Professor Bettleheim', *Critique*, no. 6, pp. 17–44.

TICKTIN, H. (1978) 'The Class Structure of the USSR and the Elite', *Critique*, no. 9, pp. 37–62.

TINBERGEN, J. (1952) *On the Theory of Economic Policy*, Amsterdam, North-Holland.

TINBERGEN, J. (1961) 'Do Communist and Free Economies show a Converging Pattern?', *Soviet Studies*, vol. 12, pp. 333–41.

TRETYAKOVA, A. and BIRMAN, I. (1976) 'Input–Output Analysis in the USSR', *Soviet Studies*, vol. 28, pp. 157–86.

UJLAKI, Zs. (1970) 'Application of an Aggregate Programming Model in Preparing the Fourth Five-year Plan', *Acta Oeconomica*, vol. 6, pp. 55–72.

ULLMO, Y. (1974) *La planification en France*, Paris, Dalloz.

ULLMO, Y. (1975) 'France', in Hayward and Watson (1975).

WARD, B. (1971) 'Organization and Comparative Economics: Some Approaches', in Eckstein (1971).

WEITZMAN, M. (1970) 'Iterative Multi-level Planning with Production Targets', *Econometrica*, vol. 38, pp. 50–65.

WEITZMAN, M. (1974) 'Prices versus Quantities', *Review of Economic Studies*, vol. 41, pp. 477–91.

WEITZMAN, M. (1976) 'The New Soviet Incentive Model', *Bell Journal of Economics*, vol. 7, pp. 251–57.

WILCZYNSKI, J. (1977) *The Economics of Socialism* (3rd edn), London, Allen & Unwin.

WILES, P. J. (1968) *Communist International Economics*, Oxford, Blackwell.

WINCH, D. (1971) *Analytical Welfare Economics*, Harmondsworth, Penguin.

YANOV, A. (1977) *Détente after Brezhnev: the Domestic Roots of Soviet Foreign Policy*, Institute of International Studies, University of California Press.

ZIELINSKI, J. G. (1973) *Economic Reforms in Polish Industry*, Oxford University Press.

ZWASS, A. (1978) *Money, Banking and Credit in the Soviet Union and Eastern Europe*, New York, M. E. Sharpe Inc.

INDEX